# Treasures
## *of the*
# Italian Table

# Treasures
## of the
# Italian Table

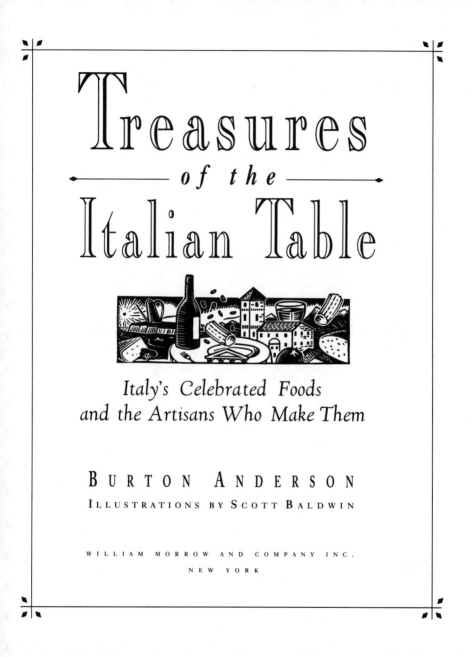

## Italy's Celebrated Foods
## and the Artisans Who Make Them

### BURTON ANDERSON
ILLUSTRATIONS BY SCOTT BALDWIN

WILLIAM MORROW AND COMPANY INC.

NEW YORK

Library of Congress Cataloging-in-Publication Data

Anderson, Burton.
Treasures of the Italian table / Burton Anderson.
p.      cm.
ISBN 0-688-11557-8
1. Gastronomy.   2. Food habits—Italy.   3. Cookery—Italy.
I. Title.
TX641.A53  1994
641'.01'030945—dc20                                          93–14272
CIP

Printed in the United States of America

First Edition

1   2   3   4   5   6   7   8   9   10

BOOK DESIGN BY JOEL AVIROM

*For Gaia and Benjamin
and the Italy of their childhood*

◆

# CONTENTS

◆

# ACKNOWLEDGMENTS

◆

*A*mong the many persons who have helped me with this book, some who have participated directly are described in the text. Others who deserve more than just a mention include Corrado Barberis, Primetto Barelli, Gabriele Bazzini, Vittorio Bellon, Anna Bologna and family, Federico Carletti, Gaddo Castelli, Franco Colombani, Carlo Cortesi, Maddalena De Bartoli, Rudi Eberspacher, Angelo and Lucia Gaja, Nancy Harmon Jenkins, Loren Jenkins, James Johnson, Emilio Lancellotti and family, Valentino Migliorini, Giovanna Moretti, Giovanna Morganti, Gilberto Nardi, Giancarlo Notari, Gilberto Paghi, Riccardo Riccardi, and PierLuigi and Chama Rogate.

Special thanks are due to Harriet Bell, my editor at Morrow, whose love of Italian food made this book possible, and Doe Coover, my agent, who helped me forget how far Oliveto is from the hubs of the publishing world. My wife, Nancy, daughter, Gaia, and son, Benjamin, accompanied me on some of the trips and, as always, provided inspiration for my work.

# INTRODUCTION

♦

## *The makings of a feast*

*T*he subject is gastronomy, though this is not a recipe book or, strictly speaking, a reference or guide, but a series of investigative reports on the making of some of Italy's most treasured foods. I might have picked more than a dozen topics from the national archives of good things to eat and drink. But I preferred to concentrate on an eclectic array of foods and their sources in profiles that reflect back upon highlights of the past yet keep the focus on the present, on artisans who continue to dignify their ancestral heritage of taste.

Italy's vast and varied inventory of dishes illustrates that *la cucina italiana* isn't really a national cuisine but a miscellany of local modes of cooking. True, certain comestibles are encountered everywhere: bread, cheese, salami, pasta, and wine, among the evident. Yet Italians from the Mediterranean isles to the Alps interpret popular themes in personal ways. Each province, each town, each family boasts its own recipes, not necessarily written down but relayed intuitively from one generation to the next.

Beyond its legendary versatility, Italian cooking evokes freshness and spontaneity. But kitchen flair sometimes looks more casual than it really is, for behind the scenes stand hidden providers, masters of the arts of elaborating raw materials to enhance their innate virtues. Every worthy artisan covets trade secrets to create specialties that are singularly local, though Italy's food crafts share a legacy in the wisdom of the ages.

Early Mediterranean peoples pioneered methods of milling grains and leavening flour for bread, crushing olives for oil, transforming milk to cheese and grapes to wine or vinegar. The ancient Romans, influenced by Greeks and Etruscans, knew nearly every means of refining and conserving vegetables, fruit, meat, fish, and cheese used until the industrial age. Their methods included salt curing, smoking, and heating or drying in ovens or by exposure to the sun. Preserves were pickled in vinegar with herbs or spices; immersed in olive oil, lard, honey, wine, or alcohol; sheathed in membrane, cloth, or leaves; coated with pepper, mold, ash, wax, or clay.

Most such practices are still in use, though techniques were revised over time as the fund of flavors grew with the arrival of edibles from other places. The Americas contributed the potato, beans, corn for polenta, the tomato as the essence of the most Italian of sauces, and chili peppers to enliven it. Pasta probably was made first in China, though invention has been contended in several parts of Italy. Pizza was almost certainly conceived somewhere away from its now indisputable capital of Naples.

Coffee, epitomized in espresso, has always been imported from the tropics. The first rice for what became risotto arrived from Asia Minor, where wine and olive oil were produced long before Roman times. But whether the elements were native or naturalized, Italian climate and ingenuity raised them to new heights.

Italy has shared its culinary arts with due generosity, starting with the Romans, who brought western civilization its first sophisticated form of cookery, and resuming in the Middle Ages with Venetian merchants, who disseminated Mediterranean flavors through Europe. Caterina de' Medici, summoned from Renaissance Florence to wed King Henri II, brought along the cooks and methods that revolutionized French cuisine. History's most prodigious gastronomic spread may have come with the exodus of Italians, mainly from the south, who brought the world pasta, pizza, and other delights in places with checkered tablecloths, Chianti flasks, and pictures of Vesuvius and the Colosseum on the walls.

Stereotypes persist, but the popularity of Italian cooking abroad is no longer always a tribute to being zesty, filling, and cheap. Some *ristoranti* have moved upscale with refined dishes that satisfy modern ideals of diet while gratifying gourmet tastes. Yet menus, adjusted to foreign attitudes and conditions, often confuse notions about ''Mediterranean'' and ''northern Italian'' cooking, to take the themes that most inspire chefs and writers.

The Mediterranean diet is international, of course, though many of its liberally interpreted ideas originated in Italy's maritime south and center. Traditional cooking there advocated the basics of olive oil, dried pasta, bread, fresh vegetables, fruit, herbs, fish, sheep's cheese, and wine from the nearest hillsides.

Northern cooking often relied on butter or lard and ranged over richer fare: egg pasta, risotto, polenta, pâtés, elaborate meat dishes, ripe cheeses, and vintage wines, for instance. But the "northern Italian cuisine" proposed in restaurants abroad presumes to mix in a mythical pot the cooking of eight proudly diverse regions—eleven if you count all those north of Rome. Such propaganda was no doubt contrived to distinguish menus composed of select northern dishes from the specter of spaghetti and meatballs with garlicky tomato sauce and other leftovers from southern immigrant days. But in snubbing the Mezzogiorno, it ignores the flavors, aromas, colors, and textures of foods that glow with Mediterranean vitality.

No, Italy's idiosyncratic ways of cooking shouldn't be muddled in generic stews. It's worth recalling that Italian peoples, historically separated by mountain ranges and expanses of water, never supported monolithic rule long enough or strongly enough to forsake their parochial identities. Even now, long after former kingdoms, principalities, duchies, and lilliputian republics metamorphosed into twenty regions comprising nearly a hundred provinces, ethnic peculiarities remain in customs, speech, and cooking. The local flavors of Italy's *trattorie, osterie, locande, taverne, pizzerie, pasticcerie, botteghe,* and *mercati* are often imitated but rarely duplicated elsewhere. In more than thirty years of dining in the country, the meals I've most savored invariably told a story of a people and a place.

Still, no veteran *buongustaio* would pretend that those once jealously guarded traditions are all going strong. Change was accelerated in the 1970s with the advent of *la nuova cucina,* a parody of French *nouvelle* by Italian restaurateurs, who, if nothing else, mastered the art of serving smaller portions at higher prices. Yet the crusade did help to persuade cooks to use fresher, lighter ingredients where diets were heavy or humdrum, while contributing to a breakdown in the classical north-south division expressed in the "Italy of butter and the Italy of olive oil," with a steady gain in favor of the latter.

Through the affluent 1980s, chefs flaunted creativity while equally pretentious critics invented restaurant guides to lavish them with symbols of success. But a lingering recession in the 1990s has sent fancy eateries and costly menus into decline, giving a new lease on life to trattorie and osterie whose hearty dishes and honest values recall the spirit of the times when dining was the national pastime. The trouble is, though, as surveys confirm, Italians spend less time at the table nowadays and pay less heed to the origins of what they eat and drink. But then alimentary standards have been falling throughout Europe in the path of the fast-food blitz that has swept across the continent from America.

Degeneracy has been hastened by the European Economic Community mandate to unify member nations' commerce and industry in a consumer society of homogenized tastes. This dreary dream is becoming all too true around the EEC as supermarkets from the Faroe Islands to the Peloponnesus push ubiquitous brands of canned and packaged goods for quick and easy consumption. It seems especially ironic that Italians, with their local prides and prejudices, have become staunch advocates of a European market that more than ever qualifies as common. For no other people, not even the French, have such a wealth of culinary treasures to defend.

The Italian government has built a rather frail line of defense on the laws of *denominazione di origine controllata,* abbreviated DOC, to protect names and origins of foods typical of certain areas. The program, which began with wines in the 1960s, has been extended to cover cheeses, prosciutto and other preserved meats, *aceto balsamico,* and, recently, *olio extra vergine di oliva.* DOC can be a distinguishing factor in zones where producers share a commitment to quality, though frequent failures have been due to apathy or lack of trust in institutions. Uniform regulations are hard to apply to foods and wines made by producers large and small with diverse and sometimes conflicting interests.

In the end, though, collective appellations are never as trustworthy as individual credentials: the experience, skill, and integrity that no government could control or guarantee. Yet these human qualities are often overlooked in a food industry dominated by conglomerates, which spare no expense in promoting goods or molding EEC and national policies in their favor. Their tactics deliberately discourage craftsmen by imposing sophisticated and costly production standards that can't always be met on a small scale. Artisan specialties have been routinely replaced on markets by mass-produced replicas at popular prices.

Vanishing from the countryside are the perennial suppliers of premium produce, the family farms, and with them the *contadini,* the rural folk who over centuries tamed Italy's rugged contours into landscapes of civilized grace. Today hand-hewn terraces across the land are being reclaimed by brush and brambles. For few farmers can make a living on small and scattered hillside plots when competitors work from vast, mechanized spreads where chemical fertilizers, pesticides, and herbicides boost crop yields while aggravating Italy's overdose of environmental pollution.

Flagrant disrespect for the wisdom of the ages has been shown in new hygienic norms that in some cases prohibit practices followed by craftsmen for generations. Certain cheeses and meats, for example, were always matured in places where propitious bacteria, yeasts, or molds that accumulate naturally over time in an ambience could endow them with aromas, flavors, and textures that can't be duplicated in the aseptic laboratories now required by law. It's worth recalling that some of the microorganisms now systematically destroyed by chemicals or heat treatments were uniquely beneficial to the digestive system. Bacteria must be controlled, of course. But connoisseurs may ask why authorities, instead of condemning antique methods and shops, couldn't verify the sanitary condition of finished products before they are sold. They protest that the modern obsession with alimentary purity has gone too far when rules, rather than safeguarding consumers, violate the right to enjoy traditional tastes.

It seems, though, that connoisseurs, like craftsmen and contadini, are too independent-minded to raise their voices in unison. That probably explains why their causes have found few champions in the press or protectors in public office. Italian officials, whether influenced by big business lobbies or ignobly unconcerned about the issues, have left practitioners of the gastronomic arts and crafts to fend for themselves as industrialists march down the EEC route toward a brave new world of food.

And yet, despite the odds against them, artisans endure. They seem to thrive on strength of character, inspired not so much by profits or critical acclaim as by pride in workmanship, artistic zeal, and the pleasure of sharing their wares with customers and friends. I've watched them work their wonders in many parts of Italy, from the edge of the Alps to the far reaches of Sicily. They include butchers, bakers, cheesemakers, vintners, coffee roasters, millers, farmers, and cooks, among others, spirited individuals whose attitudes about food and life have varied as vividly as the dialects I've heard along the way. Yet everywhere, as I've come to know these masters of taste, I've been struck by how much skill, devotion, and just plain hard work distinguish a bona fide original from a slick copy.

My mission began as a quest for the best, but I soon found that in crafts that follow seasons and markets and performance levels of virtuosos, merits can't always be measured in absolutes. Some artisans have maintained quality or even improved on it by revising archaic procedures or introducing labor-saving techniques that allow them to persevere and, with luck, to prosper. But if they're too modest or too busy or too isolated from the mainstream to seek publicity, their handiwork may be coveted by cognoscenti but overlooked in print.

With no *Who's Who* in the food arts to fall back on, I often turned to local *intenditori* to lead me to the hidden providers. But once there I relied on my own investigative devices. For, as I see it, a reporter can dig for facts anywhere his appetite may lead him: while tracking truffles in Piedmont, sniffing balsamic vinegars in Emilia, devouring a pizza marinara in Naples, or picking olives on a Tuscan hillside for his own oil. The following reports of my adventures were founded not on scholarly deliberation but on journalistic candor in interviews and observations pieced to-gether in profiles of artisans at work.

Some encounters were so enlightening that I considered tai-loring the text to fit a travel format so that others might follow my trails. But I dropped that idea when I realized that few of the small-scale enterprises involved would be able to host car-loads, let alone busloads, of gourmets. There are, however, men-tions of local restaurants and shops where foods may be tasted or acquired.

The notion of a cookbook, on the other hand, didn't tempt me at all. Now, I'm capable of the occasional kitchen exploit and wouldn't deny a knack for working the grill. But, like so many food devotees in Italy, I rely more on mental notes than written recipes. So, for better or worse, there are none in this book. In recompense, I've reviewed traditional uses of foods, while sup-plying tips on buying, storing, and serving them. I've also at-tempted to trace histories back to their roots, sometimes in antiquity, though reminiscences of Italy's gastronomic past often provide more in the way of color than credibility.

Throughout the chapters, I've kept the focus on the current state of Italy's food arts as illustrated by the words and deeds of the craftsmen themselves. I've witnessed their daily trials and triumphs, admired their spirit and skills, listened to their philos-ophies, complaints, and dreams. I've even had the privilege of learning some of their trade secrets. And yet, though I recognize the tastes, I'm not sure I could ever define those artisan touches that through the ages have lent the magic to the makings of a feast.

# Tartufi Bianchi d'Alba
## *Roving with the spirits of the night*

*T*hose who have never tasted or, more to the point, smelled a white truffle of Alba might wonder how a subterranean fungus of negligible nutritional value, a root parasite, could rank as the most exciting and expensive of foods. Sniffed out by dogs in the night woods of southern Piedmont and dug up by truffle hunters, or *trifolau,* these ''white diamonds'' emerge looking like gnarled potatoes with mud caked around their irregular lumps, wrinkles, and pocks. Only after they have been brushed clean and shaved raw into tawny flakes over hot, buttered noodles known as *tajarin* or mounds of steaming cheese fondue do *tartufi bianchi d'Alba* emit aromas and flavors that, for lack of earthly likenesses, may be described as celestial.

Truffles belong to the branch of the fungus family known as *tuberales,* of which Europe has some thirty species, the most prized being the white (or beige to ocher) *Tuber magnatum* and the black (or dark brown) *Tuber melanosporum*. Italy is a major source of both, but the preference for white truffles is such that most of the black are willingly exported. Although white truffles of various types are found in the root systems of trees in places along the Italian peninsula as far south as Calabria, they have their mecca in the northwest, at Alba, the ancient market town that is also the capital of Barolo and Barbaresco. The bouquets of those regal red wines are reputed to comprise the scent of truffles, along with the requisite violets, vanilla, and tar.

When conditions are right in the foggy chill of late autumn and early winter the calcareous clay soils of the Langhe and Roero hills around Alba render what is reputed to be the most splendidly scented of truffles, a noble variety distinguished from the rest as *Tuber magnatum Pico*. To Piedmontese and numerous other devotees the tartufo bianco (or *trifola*) d'Alba is the ne plus ultra of gourmandise. No other food is so venerated or subjected to such wild price speculation. Yet scarcity in the face of mounting demand has made it an ever more elusive luxury. Its once indisputable supremacy has been undermined by an influx of tartufi bianchi from elsewhere, raising doubts about authenticity on the Alba market, Italy's most active.

But then truffles have always been surrounded by mystique. The ancient Greeks, who coveted them as epicurean delights and stimuli of erotic desires, were neither the first nor the last to consider them gifts of the gods. The Roman satirist Juvenal believed that they grew where Jupiter made lightning strike. Pliny the Elder, after observing growth patterns, described them as miracles of nature. Truffles have continued to fascinate Europeans, who between the sixteenth and eighteenth centuries formulated the science of mycology to study how various mushrooms grow. Yet even today in Piedmont the adventures of the trifolau are linked to mythology and the occult, to tales of forest dwellers and treasure hunters and spirits of the night.

Truffles were known in Latin first as *tuber terrae,* then in the late Middle Ages as *terrae tufolae,* both of which referred to swellings in the earth. Terms evolved to *tartuffole* and on to *tartufo* in Italian and from *truffle* to *truffe* in French and *Trüffel* in German. The ancient term *triffola* or *trifula* or *trifola,* still used for truffle in dialects of Piedmont and Umbria, seems to be related to the term *trifle,* perhaps indicating that servings have always been beguilingly slight.

While establishing lofty status in the continent's cuisines, truffles also came to be associated with trickery and deceit, since their rarity and often inflated prices subjected them to shady dealings. In Italy, where *furbizia,* or cunning, is admired in business as in politics, terms for truffle tend to have humorously upbeat connotations. But to the French, *truffe,* aside from truffle, means swindle or farce. The Molière character Tartuffe was the archetypal hypocrite.

The Piedmontese might attribute this negativism to the fact that their neighbors across the Alps have habitually consumed *Tuber melanosporum* (or the lesser *Tuber macrosporum*), not realizing that black diamonds, normally cooked, aren't worth the fanfare or the price. Years ago the English author Elizabeth David, in *French Provincial Cooking,* noted the superiority of "the wonderful white truffles of Piedmont" and concluded that "it is perhaps the spirit of patriotism which causes the majority of

French gastronomic writers to ignore their existence or to dismiss them as being unworthy of notice.'' But Italians don't seem to mind. Most of their black truffles—found mainly around the Umbrian towns of Norcia and Spoleto, but also in Piedmont—are charitably shipped to France to become *truffes du Périgord* or similar.

In defense of black truffles, it must be said that they add a certain something to tarts, omelets, and soufflés, while providing the focus for such culinary extravaganzas as Paul Bocuse's *soupe aux truffes.* When cubed they look dandy in aspics and pâtés. But habitual users of *Tuber magnatum Pico* (or, in the more descriptive Italian, *Tubero di Afrodite*) vow that once you've had white truffles, raw, you'll never go back to black.

The color of truffles is not distinctly white or black but covers a spectrum of light to dark earthy hues. The surface of the magnatum should be buff to pale gray, tending toward ocher or walnut or lightly burnished brass, through shadings vary according to the soil and type of root the truffles derive from as well as their condition and age. The melanosporum has a dusky brown crust strikingly close in appearance to a chocolate truffle. The less prized *Tuber macrosporum* and summer truffle called *Scorzone* have dark surfaces but pallid interiors.

The Italian composer-gastronome Gioacchino Rossini referred to Alba's white truffle as the Mozart of mushrooms, though in his long exile in Paris in the mid-nineteenth century he usually had to be content with the black truffles that decorate the *foie gras* in tournedos Rossini. Tartufi bianchi d'Alba are more amply flavored than any type of black truffle, but their glory is aroma. You have to get close to pick up the odor of a melanosporum, but a sharp nose could sniff out a ripe magnatum from across a spacious dining room.

Still, even among as expressive a people as the Italians, the consensus seems to be that the odor of white truffles is so distinct that it's undefinable, beyond the elementary *profumo di tartufo,* of course. Those who associate it with garlic, herbs, underbrush, certain ripe cheeses, armpits, or methane gas are not doing justice to this most evocative of the earth's odors. (Yet the tale of the truffle in a carry-on bag that had an airline crew—obviously not Italian—searching for a gas leak across the Atlantic seems to be authentic.)

Alba, founded by the Romans on the Tanaro River about 35 miles southeast of Piedmont's capital of Turin, lies at the center of what has ranked as Europe's premier truffle territory since 1780, when the Polish count Jean-Michel de Borch wrote his influential *Lettres sur les Truffes du Piémont* and the Piedmontese mycologist Vittorio Pico gave his name to the most exalted variety of *Tuber magnatum.*

The excellence of Alba's truffles is attributed to the particular terrains and climate of the Langhe and Roero hills in the upper Po basin, where the cooling effect of the nearby Alps is more influential than the dry heat of the Mediterranean that filters across the Apennines from the south. Woods where oak and linden prevail provide the vegetation favorable to white truffles, which thrive in light-complexioned calcareous soils in valleys or rolling terrain near streams. They will grow on high slopes with enough clay to hold humidity, though they are rarely found at more than about 2,000 feet above sea level in Piedmont.

White truffles from parts of the Monferrato hills to the east in

Asti and Alessandria provinces can be equally esteemed. Various types of *Tuber magnatum* grow between the Po and the Apennines in Lombardy and Emilia-Romagna, as well as in several regions of central and southern Italy. The towns of Acqualagna in the Marches, Gualdo Tadino in Umbria, and San Miniato and San Giovanni d'Asso in Tuscany have become known for white truffles, though it is hardly a secret that the choicest find their way north to Piedmont to become pricy tartufi d'Alba. In the winter of 1992–1993, prices ranged from 2 million to 3.5 million lire a kilogram (2.2 pounds) and occasionally higher.

Alba remains the main arena, but demand has increased everywhere, persuading landowners in many parts of Italy to acquire trained truffle hounds and to plant trees to favor growth. As a result, truffles have been found increasingly elsewhere while Alba and Asti have had dwindling crops. But the Piedmontese maintain the truest tradition of the truffle, which more than a culinary curiosity represents a sociological phenomenon unique in Italy or anywhere else.

This authentic folk culture revolves around the trifolau, or *trifulau,* an aging but by no means dying breed. Often members of family dynasties that date back generations, they have been described as "phantoms of the night," "minions of the moon," and "knights of darkness," while being depicted as reclusive, suspicious, egocentric individuals. Yet in talkative moments they might credit success to the talents of their dogs, *cani da tartufo,* usually mongrels born and raised to sniff out truffles.

Each *paese* around Alba has a legendary trifolau or two, subjects of colorful yarns even if details of their exploits have rarely been confirmed by witnesses. Most go about their work in the dark or the fog to shield them not only from rivals but from the *fisco,* the revenue agents who would dare to violate the canons of an ancestral livelihood by making them pay taxes on earnings. Yet, in spite of complaints about official intrusions, truffle shortages, and growing competition, the rewards can be handsome. Many of Alba's trifolau are reasonably well off.

To dedicated hunters, truffles are not just a food to be dug up like potatoes as a handy source of income but treasures to unearth with ritual respect and to cherish, if fleetingly, like fine gems. To the normally circumspect Piedmontese, tartufi uplift the hearty winter diet with a rare touch of extravagance, suggesting sensual experiences and to some perhaps even spiritual adventures. (They are not, however, known to be hallucinogenic, as some mushrooms are).

White truffles have ennobled *la cucina piemontese* since the early eighteenth century, when the Savoy family began its ascendancy over the region's counties, marquisates, and duchies on its way to becoming the royal house of an Italy united by the Risorgimento. *Tuber magnatum Pico* has come to be revered by cults and convivial societies, the most prominent being the Ordine dei Cavalieri del Tartufo e dei Vini di Alba, whose headquarters are at the Castello di Grinzane, home of the nineteenth-century statesman Camillo Benso di Cavour.

Local savants point to subtle distinctions in aromas between tartufi that originate in the marly clay soils of the Langhe, south of the Tanaro, and those from the lighter, sandier clay soils of the Roero, to the north. Truffles are found in much of the vast Langhe range that extends from where the Apennines meet the Maritime Alps at the border of Liguria north along the Tanaro and Belbo valleys as far as Alba. Its upper reaches, Alta Langa, are mainly woods and pastures, but the lower tracts around Alba consist of waves of steeply rounded rises crowned by patriarchal citadels and cloaked by the manicured vineyards of Barolo and Barbaresco, as well as the more familiar red wines from Dolcetto and Barbera. Roero, named for a noble family that long possessed the territory, is a more compact group of hills topped by villages whose medieval castles and bell towers loom over slopes cleaved by fissures and ravines, where vineyards devoted mainly to red Nebbiolo and white Arneis alternate in irregular patterns with grainfields and woods.

Alba's truffles, like its wines, have good years and bad, though an outstanding vintage for Barolo (invariably hot and dry) may well be a mediocre one for tartufi. Dampness is needed for fungi to grow, but if it rains in August and September, as truffle fans desire, that bodes ill for wine. Nobody has reliable figures on Piedmont's annual truffle trade, since most of the activity is part of a flourishing underground economy. But, because of drought and other factors, the region's truffle crops have been scarce for years. Meanwhile, Alba's vaunted red wines had been favored by a series of exceptional vintages between 1985 and the early 1990s.

White truffles take from six weeks to three months to grow. The first examples are usually ready for the Fiera Nazionale del Tartufo at Alba in October. The fair, held since 1929, attracts curiosity seekers, including those who come to watch the donkey race known as the Paglio degli Asini. But connoisseurs avoid the early offerings, knowing that truffles reach peaks of aroma after the first snows, between mid-November and the end of the year.

Prices hit the ceiling during the holiday season, when virtually every restaurant that counts in northern Italy offers tartufi d'Alba on its menus.

Experts submit that the best Alba truffles—aside from having superior aroma—can be distinguished from others by rounder form, smoother surface, and a more compact, blemish-free interior. The finer and more subtle the internal veining—a tawny brown and pale ocher marbling—the better the quality, they say. If the truffle is spherical but somewhat flat (like a river stone), it probably grew deep down in soft earth. If it has twists and bumps, it probably came from compact soils.

Size is a selling point. A large, healthy truffle is worth more by weight than two small ones, because it makes a better appearance in a restaurant or shop and is easier to shave. Truffles can be as tiny as peas, though those of commercial value range from the size of a walnut to larger than an apple or, occasionally, even an Idaho potato. They say the biggest on record in the Alba area weighed about 4 pounds, but that was probably a freak: two or more truffles joined like Siamese twins. Size and appearance are not always decisive quality factors. Small, stunted truffles sometimes have better aroma and texture than big, smooth ones, which are more likely to have lost aroma from being over-ripe or having hollows inside. The finest are often in the small to medium range, 1 to 3½ ounces.

Astute buyers rely on smell, knowing that white truffles are invariably at their optimum right after being dug from the earth. The feminine gender is said to be more exquisitely perfumed and, among aesthetes who can tell the difference, more prized than the masculine. Like all fungi, white truffles have traces of vitamins and minerals, but their nutritional value is minimal. They are more gratifying to the senses than to the alimentary system. White truffles are rarely cooked, since anything more than gentle heating reduces aroma and flavor. So adamant are the Piedmontese that if a local chef dared to simmer a fine tartufo bianco in a soup, he would probably be run out of town (though he might get by with sacrificing a black one).

Around Alba, as well as Asti, trade in truffles continues after the October fair, though business is largely clandestine. Daily activities begin toward dawn as the trifolau arrive with their night's harvest loosely wrapped in cloth napkins. At Alba they congregate along the central Via Maestra and adjoining piazzas, waiting expectantly with their hands in coat pockets bulging with their treasures. Deals are done surreptitiously following a rigid code of omertà. Trifolau are required to carry a tesserino, an expensive annual license to hunt and sell truffles which not all possess, and sales must be officially registered with a receipt for payment that includes a steep value-added tax. Sellers and buyers alike prefer to avoid such inconveniences, so the street market is risky, since a potential customer could turn out to be the fisco in civilian clothes.

Before revealing his wares, the trifolau may slip off to a side street or into the shadows of an archway. Truffles are often presented in batches previously weighed, but some buyers carry portable scales to double-check the accuracy of claims. The exchanges between the trifolau, who tend to be stubborn, and dealers, who tend to be shrewd, are carried out in Piemontese, a Francophone patois that outsiders have to struggle to comprehend, apart from the lire figures that are bandied about in the millions.

Bargaining can be prolonged, but the best truffles sell quickly, no matter what the price.

Though wary of strangers, the trifolau, if approached, will start by showing the smallest or least desirable truffles, moving upscale only if he figures he's dealing with someone who knows the difference and will pay the price. Impostors may acquire old truffles cheap from other places and try to sell them as newly unearthed. Some have been known to add synthetic odors. But smart buyers are able to judge freshness and quality by an instant sniff and feel. And by now the best truffles from Acqualagna, San Miniato, and other respected sources have established their own channels in Piedmont's elaborate black market.

Many trifolau deal directly with restaurants and shops, accepting less than top market prices for the security of doing business behind closed doors. But when the sales tax is excluded, as is often the case, restaurateurs and merchants risk heavy fines if the revenue agents, who have stepped up raids on their premises lately, find truffles without receipts.

Still, when members of Alba's truffle establishment talk about the good old days, it isn't just because they're under mounting pressure from the fisco. If anything, business is better than ever. Gourmet tourism has increased and demand for tartufi bianchi d'Alba has spread through Italy and beyond. The trouble is that the genuine article is in ever shorter supply.

Meanwhile, growing quantities of white truffles from elsewhere in Italy make their way to Alba. Even educated eyes, noses, and palates would have trouble distinguishing the best of these specimens from a normal *Tuber magnatum Pico*. As a veteran local dealer, who preferred not to be named, put it: ''We always used to say that if a truffle wasn't up to snuff it came from Acqualagna. But these days, if we're smart, we keep our mouths shut. For the truth is that if it weren't for those others, Alba's truffle trade would be in a real crisis.''

As if supplying the home market weren't enough, local dealers also have developed a brisk export trade. Long-distance shipping presents a challenge, because the aroma and flavor of truffles fade from the start, and unless they are kept cool and nearly (but not quite) dry and partly exposed to air, they deteriorate rapidly. Some shippers guarantee delivery by air anywhere within twenty-four hours. The main markets, aside from neighboring Switzerland, Germany, and France (where *les truffes blanches du Piémont* have become chic recently) are the United States and Japan, though requests arrive from as far away as Chile and New Zealand.

Shipping across borders can be a threat, since it's hard to predict how a customs official who has never known its charms might react when confronted with Aphrodite's tuber. Even when packed in jars of rice or wrapped in layers of aluminum foil (neither practice advised), that profumo di tartufo can pervade a room. Yet, despite the risks and prohibitive prices, some restaurants in foreign lands manage to offer fresh white truffles for at least a few days a year.

On balance, though, none of the world's cuisines is so delectably suited to tartufi as is Piedmont's or, more precisely, Alba's, though Asti's cooking presents a close rival. In no other region of Italy are traditions of food and wine so staunchly defended. The flavors come into their own after the harvest when fogs roll up the hillsides from the Tanaro Valley, snow covers the distant backdrop of the Alps, and the nip in the air builds appetites for substantial country fare. Yet, for all the inherent vigor in its autumn and winter menus, *la cucina albese* keeps the focus on the ultimate delicacy of the truffle.

Among several noted restaurants in the area, none casts a warmer glow on a frosty evening than La Contea at Neive, a hill town with fortified walls and a medieval castle overlooking vine-yards of Barbaresco. Tonino and Claudia Verro maintain their cozy inn as a replica of Savoyard Piedmont. The dining rooms have hand-painted designs on walls and ceilings, plaster cornices, lace curtains, terra-cotta floors, and waxed antique furniture, the ensemble heated by wood fires in carved stone hearths. Tonino, an affable host who punctuates quips and anecdotes with an in-fectiously gleeful chuckle, is known beyond Alba for expertise with truffles and wines. But if La Contea has become a rendez-vous for gastronomes of international caliber, it's because Claudia cooks sublimely whether truffles are in season or not.

When they are in, Tonino, like other restaurateurs, uses a *tagliatartufo* or *affettatartufo,* a small plane with a razor-sharp blade, to shave them in paper-thin flakes over dishes. Some hosts, to avoid expensive misunderstandings, ask guests to tell them when to stop shaving. Then there are specialists in making a miserly bit of truffle seem to go a long way. But Tonino, not one for trifles, lets up only after shearing layers whose worth might be measured in grains of gold.

A recent meal at La Contea at the height of the truffle season gave no indication of a shortage. Tartufi proliferated over antipasti of *carne cruda* ( raw veal in a sort of tartar ) and *fonduta* ( fontina and egg fondue ), served with a Dolcetto d'Alba from Gastaldi.

They flattered a plate of tajarin (slender egg noodles) and a sampling of creamy *risotto alla piemontese,* served with Nebbiolo d'Alba Vignaveja from Gaja. They dignified a classic *brasato,* beef braised in and served with a Barbaresco Santo Stefano from Bruno Giacosa, with an endive flan on the side. Tonino even scattered a few priceless flakes over a wedge of soft white sheep's cheese known as *tuma.* Claudia had not yet invented a dessert for the trifola, so I had to settle for a *bonèt* of coffee cream caramel decorated with chips of another local specialty, *torrone* (nougat), served with a glass of fragrantly pétillant Moscato d'Asti from Rivetti.

When the other guests had gone, Tonino sat down and talked about truffles, drawing on experiences as a dealer that preceded his restaurant career. He described the status quo of tartufi d'Alba with a candor not to be found in written works, which tend to embellish rather than explore. I had gained rare insights into the workings of Alba's street market on predawn buying sprees with the late Giacomo Bologna, an extraordinary winemaker, truffle dealer, and instigator of Rabelaisian adventures. My experience in the field had been limited to a couple of nighttime rounds, one accompanying an aging trifolau who spoke passable Italian when recounting war experiences but who talked truffles in heavy Piemontese, the other tagging along with a taciturn type evidently more at ease with dogs than with people. What I needed to accomplish my mission was to meet a trifolau willing and able to talk about trade secrets.

Tonino brightened. "I've got your man," he said. "Vaschetto." He pulled a portable *telefonino* out of a pocket and, refusing to be dissuaded by my plea that it was almost midnight, dialed a number and got a quick response. They spoke in dialect, but I gathered that the trifolau had just returned from a round and wouldn't be going out again until morning.

"He'll be here to pick you up at about six," said Tonino, putting the phone back in his pocket. "It'll be okay in the morning, there's a fog." He explained that Teresio Vaschetto wasn't an ordinary trifolau but president of the regional association. "Nobody could give you more up-to-date information," Tonino assured me before I made my way upstairs to bed.

The alarm sounded at five-forty, rousing me from a deep slumber. After making the day's first decision, that I wasn't going to bother to shave, I groped through the dark to the window and opened the shutters to check the weather. Neive seemed to be engulfed in a cloud. Through the haze in the piazza below beamed a car's foglights illuminating the figure of a man leaning against the hood with arms folded in a way that suggested he was waiting for someone.

I called down to inquire if he might by chance be Signor Vaschetto. "Sì, sì," came the reply, "perhaps I'm early." In decorous Italian he told me to take my time. After pulling on layers of available clothing, I hurried down to the piazza, where Vaschetto, who looked to be about sixty, greeted me with a smile as dignified as his buon giorno. He was outfitted in an ample field jacket and loose trousers, both in thick corduroy, with a wool stocking cap pulled down over his ears, a red kerchief around his neck, and rubber boots reaching up almost to his knees.

"Tonino tells me you've been truffle hunting before," he said with a trace of doubt in his voice, perhaps observing that I was hatless and wearing only lightweight suede boots in the damp cold. I told him I had some research to do and I hoped he wouldn't mind if I asked a few questions. ''Not at all,'' he said. ''Well, then, let's get going.'' He suggested that I follow him with my car, because he had to go off in another direction for an appointment later that morning.

Vaschetto sped ahead in his worn compact Renault 4, down the hill from Neive and north across the bridge over the Tanaro. The fog was even thicker in the valley, but he drove through it at such a pace that I lost sight of the taillights of his car until I nearly rammed into it when he stopped at the crossroads at Baraccone. A couple of minutes later, after passing a sign for the village of San Giuseppe di Castagnito, he turned down a packed gravel path through a wooded area and pulled up at a clearing. There he told me to wait while he went to get his dogs.

The first light of dawn barely penetrated a mist so thick that I could see only the silhouettes of nearby trees and their few remaining leaves in amber, yellow, and brown. Dampness hung in the air, intensifying a chill that, despite my vigorous motions to speed circulation, invaded ears, hands, and feet. The trees, many of them recently planted with earth mounded at their bases, stood in rows at regular intervals in the rolling terrain. Puddles had formed in gaps and furrows in the pale brown soil, heavy with clay that caked onto boots and turned hard as it dried.

Maybe five minutes had passed when through the gloom came the sounds of dogs on the move, their shrill yelping and baying echoing down the hillsides. The first to reach me was Stella, a copper-colored crossbreed with a white stripe on her breast, leaping from the murk to lick my hands and nuzzle my jacket pockets while smearing pastel mud over my previously clean jeans. Soon the others arrived, four of them, including a puppy whose plump black-and-white body writhed with excitement.

Vaschetto appeared, calling for order while feigning threats to rap them with a wooden cane, the trifolau's standard *bastun*. ''They think you've got food. Don't pet them. Don't even talk to them, or they'll climb all over you and won't hunt.'' He put leashes on two of the five and assigned them to my command, explaining that on normal night forays he wouldn't bring that many out at once but with my assistance he could give the young ones some experience.

And the hunt began. Vaschetto moved at an easy gait, his breath issuing in puffs of vapor as he voiced commands in vernacular to the dogs, who darted to and fro amid the trees, sniffing and scratching, while my tandem pulled enviously on their leashes. Gesturing with the bastun, he repeated the line: ''*Beica ben, seu, seu, seu. Cerca un po' lì. Seu, che è la paga.*'' (Sniff carefully, c'mon, c'mon, c'mon. Search a bit over there. C'mon, there's a reward.) The reward may be chunks of bread or cheese rinds or, handier these days, dog biscuits carried in a pocket.

Vaschetto, studying the dogs' maneuvers, knew instantly when one had located a truffle after repeated false starts. Stella was the first to hit pay dirt, scratching frantically near a small linden tree. Vaschetto rushed over to join her, dropping to his knees and watching and waiting as the other dogs gathered around, trying to get in on the action.

''Hold on to this one please,'' he said, pushing a male named Briz in my direction. When Stella had dug to the depth of his hand, the trifolau shunted her aside and began probing in the earth, first with his fingers and, cautiously, with a small pick called a *sapet* or *sapin,* which he carried inserted under his belt. Then he let Stella resume for a few seconds, watching her nose to get the bead on the target. When the depth was halfway to his elbow he gave the dog a biscuit to distract her and continued alone, digging alternately with pick and fingers, sniffing samples of earth from time to time as he descended. He explained that the truffle must be located and unearthed by hand because a dog's paw or the pick can break it or scratch the surface.

Five or six minutes after Stella's alert he drew forth a small, mud-caked trifola with his left hand, while continuing to probe with his right on the slight chance that there would be another. (Usually a root yields one truffle a year, but twins do occur.) Satisfied that there were no more, Vaschetto rose to his feet and, grasping the prize in his fist, let Stella sniff it thoroughly before giving her a reward. Then the puppy, a promising apprentice in his kennel of eight, was allowed to nuzzle his fist before getting a biscuit to associate with success. Before resuming the hunt, he gave each of the others a morsel. ''They're typical Italians,'' he remarked. ''One does the work but they all expect to be paid.''

Before moving on, he carefully filled in the hole, packing the dirt with hands and feet and scattering leaves and grass over the bare spot. He said that the point was not so much to cover his tracks as to restore the habitat as closely as possible to its former state, since truffles tend to grow in the same places year after year but won't germinate if the soil has been radically disturbed and roots have been broken or left exposed.

As the fog slowly shifted, the growing daylight provided my first clear image of the trifolau, who had removed his stocking cap, revealing neatly combed brown hair, graying at the temples, and a tan so even that it could have been cultured. He had clear brown eyes under heavy brows, a straight nose underlined by a hint of gray mustache, and a broad mouth that curved slightly downward at the edges. He reminded me of someone, a face from the past; on reflection it turned out to be the English actor James Mason. He even had some of that élan about him, more the manner of a country squire than a *contadino*. In contrast with other trifolau I'd met, he was open in his views, expounding on truffles with conviction and polish befitting a *presidente*.

He reserved his highest praise not for his fellow trifolau, however, but for their dogs, which he described as the real stars of truffles. Many are crosses of setters, spaniels, beagles, terriers, retrievers, and other hunting breeds with what are known as *bastardelli da pagliaio,* ''haystack mongrels,'' the perennial watchdogs of Piedmontese farms. The advantage of mongrels is that they are less nervous than purebred hunting dogs, whose acute sense of smell makes them easily distracted by game. Females are often preferred over males, who will run off if they smell a bitch in heat. Most dogs are small to medium in size, because they're easier to control than big ones. Vaschetto's were all mongrels, except Briz, a compact brown-and-white Breton Español, which, despite the non-Italian name, seems to have been bred locally for truffling.

Like many veterans, Vaschetto trains his own dogs. But some matriculate from the noted ''truffle dog college'' at Roddi d'Alba where the Barot family for four generations has conducted a fifteen-day course. The animals' normal quest for food must be steered toward a craving for truffles, even if they never get a chance to eat them. The penchant is developed through an elementary learning process. Pieces of truffle are buried and the young dogs search them out. Some have the ability and improve with repeated finds and rewards of food; others don't and fail. But continued success seems to depend on the dog's character, developed through nonviolent discipline, infinite patience, and lots of affection. A trifolau will never beat a dog, knowing that if it associates truffles with pain it will run away from its intended quarry.

Any proven young truffle dog is worth at least 2 million lire and, exceptionally, up to three times that. It can earn back its purchase price in a season by locating a few pounds of truffles. Good hunters are so prized that they almost never change owners, though their offspring may be worth plenty. When not hunting, they are locked away in kennels to keep them from wandering and digging up and eating truffles but also to protect them from abduction and harm. Pigs, having even more sensitive noses than dogs, were prized truffle finders in the past, but they are rarely used because they are too heavy and strong to manage when digging.

Vaschetto said that some dogs can detect a truffle underground from the length of a football field away. But, curiously, a truffle emits no odor until it reaches a precise moment of ripeness. That means that a dog may pass over one and not smell it and then, returning an hour or two later after it ripens, it will. Veteran trifolau know the spots and realize when the time is right, relying on secrets passed down by their fathers, as well as on calculations based on phases of the moon. They might smell or at least sense the presence of truffles, but can't pinpoint them the way a dog can. Still, some go out without dogs, following charts or mental notes on past finds.

This secretive and competitive circuit seethes with rivalries, though trifolau usually keep disputes to themselves. Tricks of the trade include placing food at key points to distract another's dogs or leaving highly odorous substances around to throw off their sense of smell. Poisonings of top dogs by jealous trifolau are an all too frequent threat. Vaschetto deplored the harm done by *bracconieri* (poachers), whose hasty digging had destroyed many a truffle bed. In central and southern Italy, the great nemeses are wild boar, which root out truffles and gorge on them. But since boar are rare in Piedmont, Alba has been spared that problem.

As we walked through his property, situated on the lower slopes of the Roero less than five kilometers from the northeastern edge of Alba, Vaschetto talked about his family dynasty. His grandfather Giuseppe (called Giusepin) was apparently the first trifolau in the area to plant trees with the idea of inducing truffle growth. Teresio's father, Fiorenzo, who died in 1992 at the age of ninety-seven, founded a tree nursery with truffle grounds or *tartufaie*. It covers twenty-five hectares, divided into what are called *vecchie tartufaie* (trees at least ten years old), *nuove tartufaie* (trees of seven to ten years), and recent plantings designed to generate truffles.

Vaschetto sells trees from the nursery locally, but he often gives away saplings to develop tartufaie elsewhere in Italy. He will even take his dogs to potential areas to check if truffles already grow there. He hasn't fenced his property, because he favors open hunting for licensed trifolau as in the old days when tartufaie weren't closed off and protected by owners. He encourages honest trifolau to tell him where they find truffles so that he can mark the spots on a detailed map (each of about three thousand trees has a number) to aid his studies of growth patterns. He observed that truffling is evolving from a game of chance into an increasingly manageable activity that approximates agriculture. Yet, even if the requisite conditions for growth are known and can be duplicated, Alba's white truffles cannot, strictly speaking, be cultivated.

Mycologists have explained how they grow. A spore from a previous year's truffle germinates into an embryo fungus, whose vegetative part or mycelium consists of threadlike filaments called hyphae. These attach themselves to tree roots, whose sap nourishes the parasitical truffle in a symbiosis known as mycorrhiza. But vegetation occurs only when conditions of humidity and temperature are right in the season starting in August or September and lasting until January. *Tuber magnatum Pico* grows mainly in lightly alkaline calcareous or siliceous clays. Rocky terrain rich in minerals rarely produces truffles.

Vaschetto described Alba's hills as a "royal ground" for things that grow, expressed in the flavors and aromas of wines, fruit, vegetables, and mushrooms, especially the *porcino,* a type of boletus or *cèpe* that has its moments of glory in the late summer and early autumn before the truffle reigns supreme. As for tartufi d'Alba, Vaschetto agreed with Tonino Verro that the most perfumed come from Roero, whose secret seems to lie in a greater proportion of sand in the soil. Other authorities agree. But since both men are natives of those hills, they might be accused of *campanilismo,* local patriotism, by partisans of the Langhe, who boast that their compact clays not only breed wines of greater stature but equally edify the trifola.

Vaschetto, between episodes of digging as he rotated shifts for the dogs, pointed to what he called the *piante madri* (mother plants) in his tartufaie, describing the types of truffles they engender. Oak in various species favors amply scented, solid truffles of fairly deep color. The linden or lime family is known for truffles of a lighter shade, even more prized for aroma, though they tend to be slightly shorter-lived. Also conducive to growth are different types of poplar and willow, whose truffles are less aromatic, and pine, which is associated with the unremarkable pale white to roseate *bianchetto*. Hazel, which flourishes in the hills as a source of nuts used by confectioners of nougat and chocolate, favors black truffles. Vaschetto admitted that he has no interest in black truffles: ''I dig them up and sell them cheap. Most end up in France.''

His distaste is not shared by all Italians, however. In Umbria, where black truffles prevail, the Urbani family of Norcia has built a commercial empire around them with both fresh and preserved versions sold in volume in Italy and abroad. They pioneered the concept of ''cultivating'' truffles in special tartufaie, whose success indicates that the black species are easier to generate in Umbria than are the white in Piedmont. Around Alba rumors circulated about ''outside black truffle interests'' secretly investing profits locally to develop commerce in white, but nobody seemed willing to confirm that the outsider was Urbani.

Vaschetto observed that the drive to generate white truffles had led to planting of trees with artificially mycorrhized roots, meaning that the spores of *Tuber magnatum Pico* were attached in laboratories. The soil is sterilized before planting to eradicate spores from other species of fungi and foreign substances believed to prevent growth. But he was skeptical about prospects, noting that scientists still hadn't explained to his satisfaction why some trees are regular sources of truffles and others next to them with apparently equal attributes never produce.

He suggested that truffle production around Alba would return to former levels naturally if woods were replanted and pollution controlled. The truffle grounds of the Langhe and Roero have been depleted by construction of homes, factories, and roads. Fires, often set deliberately, have taken a toll of woods and brushland. Some types of trees seem to be suffering from air pollution, whose probable source is Turin's heavy industry. Herbicides and fungicides used in fields seem to have reduced yields of truffles in adjacent woods where they used to abound.

Despite the shortage, Vaschetto estimated that the number of truffle hunters in Piedmont had grown to about eight thousand. But he carefully distinguished between the true trifolau, mainly farmers or villagers who search almost incessantly during the season, roaming as much as 2½ miles night and day, and the amateur outsiders who poke around the woods in their spare time and on weekends—a category that includes the destructive poachers.

Alba's commercial truffle interests have avoided sounding the alarm, fearing damage to the local reputation and business if problems should be aired in the national media. But Vaschetto deplored their caution. ''Tartufi d'Alba are a national treasure,'' he stated, his voice rising with emotion as he paused for a moment under an oak tree and gestured vehemently with his bastun.

"The question of saving face is nothing compared with the challenge of saving a heritage."

Trufflers may be legendary loners, yet Vaschetto had managed to organize 2,900 of them, all licensed, in the Unione Associazione Trifulau Regione Piemonte. They have been lobbying regional and local governments for emergency programs to replant suitable trees in areas historically known for truffles and to encourage reforestation elsewhere. "This isn't just for the benefit of us trifolau," said Vaschetto, noting that the campaign had gained backing from ecologists, wildlife groups, and the area's tourist board. "Cleaning up the environment is in the interest of everybody who eats, drinks, and breathes."

The trifolau also support a bid to have Tartufo Bianco d'Alba controlled and protected by a geographical denomination, like wines, though the proposed DOC zone would extend beyond the Langhe and Roero to take in the Monferrato hills of Asti and Alessandria provinces. Advocates admit that whatever the zone, distinguishing one's white truffles from another's is a formidable challenge. Origins can't be verified by expert examinations of odor alone, nor is tasting practical, since sliced truffles could hardly be sold. Suggestions that geographical origins could be authenticated by testing each truffle's soil radioactivity sound like science fiction.

Doubters wonder how effective a DOC might be anyway for an ephemeral food whose spontaneous origins—like, in a sense, most of its market activities—take place underground. Some fear that rigid supervision of hunting and commerce would steal the romance from truffles, and what other edible, they may ask, so inspires fantasy, ingenuity, affections?

Vaschetto, agreeing that DOC was still remote, noted however that true trifolau have shown a new sense of discipline in the drive to save their unique heritage. Their union might have been founded for reasons of self-defense, but once the trifolau got to know each other, a feeling of camaraderie arose. They now gather for dinners and parties and hold simulated truffle hunts, awarding prizes to diligent dogs. They even have an anthem entitled *Viva la trifola*.

Another sign of change is in eating habits. Vaschetto said that in the past, trifolau invariably sold all salable truffles, consuming only tiny ones or broken bits chopped up with ricotta cheese or butter. But now, in prosperous times, they'll eat truffles as other people do. Still, of course, the most valuable will be sold, or perhaps given to someone worthy of a special favor.

Our morning hunt had turned into a rambling interview. But Vaschetto, between discourses and disclosures, had also unearthed five truffles. Stella and Briz located two each and an older dog, who seemed to have a streak of setter in her, found another by sitting on the spot and uttering anticipatory noises but not bothering to scratch until her master arrived. "She has a sharp nose," he said, "but she's never been much of a go-getter." He let the puppy dig for that one.

Vaschetto, saying he had to get to his appointment, led the damp and muddy entourage at a fast pace to his home. Before closing the dogs in the kennel, he gave each a last biscuit and an affectionate pat on the head. As I prepared for departure, he beckoned me into the kitchen, where he took the tartufi from his pocket and wrapped them in a checkered cloth napkin. "Take these to Claudia and tell her to cook up something tasty," he said, conveying regrets that he couldn't join us and scoffing at my offer to pay for the truffles as he hurriedly said good-bye.

The fog had shrouded the passing hours. Only after crossing the Tanaro and ascending through the mist swirling upward on the way to Neive did I see the day's sun. It seemed to be about noon. But with the celestial profumo di tartufo inveigling my senses, no fact so mundane as the exact time was needed to remind me the nearness of lunch.

Piedmontese insist—and who would presume to fault them?—that tartufi d'Alba are intended to be eaten close to home. By now cooks in other parts of Italy, and to some extent abroad, can imitate the rituals, but they could never duplicate the atmosphere or, more broadly speaking, the culture of truffles found in the gastronomic temples of the Langhe, Roero, and Monferrato.

Piedmontese eat truffles as fresh as possible, shaved raw over foods whose flavors and aromas are known by tradition to be complementary. Specialties range beyond the fonduta, carne cruda, tajarin, risotto, and brasato savored at La Contea. Whatever food or wine accompanies them, the rule is to make it elegant but keep it simple. For instance, perhaps nothing so flatters a truffle as a fresh egg, lightly sautéed sunny side up in butter. Fresh porcini mushrooms sliced thin with a layer of tartufi over them bring together flavors of the earth in a marriage that might have been made in heaven. Piedmont's famous agnolotti, made with either a light meat filling or spinach and ricotta, take naturally to truffles, as do many other pastas, risottos, gnocchi, or even polenta, simply laced with butter or cream and possibly some grated Parmigiano or melted Fontina. Tartufi dignify roast or stewed beef, veal, and poultry, as well as feathered and furry game, though sauces or gravy should never be strongly flavored or spicy.

Elsewhere truffle customs vary. Umbrians shave them (white or black) over *tagliatelle* with meat ragout, a practice Piedmontese deplore. A rare version of cooked white truffles acceptable to epicures is *tegamino alla lodigiana* (layers of tartufi and Parmigiano heated slowly in the oven), though that comes from Lodi in Lombardy, not Piedmont. Creative truffle dishes abound, but experiments seem to work better from level-headed chefs than from showmen.

The wines to serve may rely more on other ingredients in a dish than on the truffles themselves. Some meats and game call for aged Barolo or Barbaresco, but mellower reds, such as a plush young Dolcetto d'Alba or supple Nebbiolo from Roero, often harmonize better.

White truffles, if acquired fresh for home cooking, require special care. Claudia at La Contea cleans the surface with a slightly damp toothbrush, whose bristles are small enough to enter the crevices, then pats them dry with paper towels. They can be stored in a cool cellar, in theory for a week or two if wrapped in cloth napkins or paper towels, changed daily, though they will lose odor steadily. The lower part of a refrigerator could serve as an emergency deposit for a day or two. White truffles should not be kept in jars of rice (a once-frequent practice), since they dry out, nor in plastic or metal wrappings. They may be preserved in olive oil or butter, or even kept frozen, as the black often are, but only to gratify desperate out-of-season cravings.

The one way to be sure of eating tartufi at their best is to make the late-autumn or early-winter pilgrimage to the temples of Alba and Asti. Recommended are Giardino da Felicin at Monforte d'Alba; Belvedere at La Morra; Brezza at Barolo; Da Cesare at Albaretto della Torre; Falstaff at Verduno; La Pergola at Vezza d'Alba; Dell'Arco at Alba; Da Guido at Costigliole d'Asti; Il Cascinalenuovo at Isola d'Asti; San Marco at Canelli; Gener Neuv at Asti.

# Pane Toscano
## The pride of out-of-the-way places

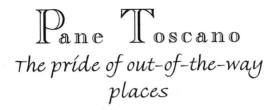

**W**hile people in other parts of Italy expanded culinary repertoires with such staples as pasta, rice, and polenta, Tuscans through the ages maintained an almost Biblical attachment to bread. Their staff of life was saltless *pane toscano*, prodigious loaves baked in wood-fired ovens and eaten warm at the mid-morning *colazione* when scents of soured leavening mingled with a smoky sweetness and thick crusts, parched to tawny hues, enveloped a pale beige pulp flecked with irregular holes. Such bread remained fragrant and moist with a cushiony resilience to the bite for several meals beyond, though it kept well for a week or so, getting firmer but not stale as it became the base for the thick soups that Tuscans habitually favored over *pastasciutta*.

The sanctuaries of pane toscano were the inland provinces of Florence, Siena, and Arezzo, taking in the hills of Tuscany's heartland of Chianti. There every stream once powered a *mulino* with stone wheels to grind flour and every village had a wood-burning *forno* to supply the daily bread and a warm place to exchange the morning gossip. Some towns even provided communal ovens for housewives to bake their bread after preparing the dough at home.

Each farm had a forno attached to the house, where the *massaia* made her *pane casereccio* once a week, preferably on Sunday mornings when the still-hot oven could be used to roast meats and simmer beans in terra-cotta pots for the noon meal. Each time she would set aside a portion of raw dough so that yeasts would ferment to become the *madre,* the starter for the next batch, kept in the *madia,* the bread cupboard that symbolized the rural kitchen. The madia was usually built of chestnut wood with an upper section that opened at the top like a steamer trunk and served as a trough for kneading and leavening the dough. The lower part, with paneled doors, had a shelf or two used for storing flour and a week's supply of baked loaves.

Italy boasts an inestimable wealth of breads, some as distinguished as pane toscano. Yet to me nothing so evokes the savor of those days when country food was genuinely delicious and irresistibly cheap. In Chianti and environs, bread, of course, was perennially linked to wine. In rural places the *osterie* or *trattorie* were often located, half hidden, behind grocery stores. As you sat down at the table, hosts greeted you with a flask of Chianti and a basket of bread. It was not so rare in my youthful days to finish off a tumbler or two of that vivacious ruby nectar and a slab or two of that habit-forming sourdough before the antipasto arrived.

But my taste for pane toscano wasn't shared by all. Most Italians, north and south, have historically eaten salted bread, so to them the Tuscan type could be *sciocco,* bland or insipid. To Tuscans, on the contrary, salt in bread detracted from the flavors of wine and other foods, which were anything but sciocco. Even if pane toscano represented an acquired taste, the absence of salt seemed to me to enhance the vaguely nutty flavor of stone-ground grain and the mellow sourness of natural yeasts. As the exiled Florentine Dante Alighieri complained in the *Divine Comedy* nearly seven hundred years ago: ''how it tastes of salt, the others' bread.''

It has been alleged that the Tuscan tradition dates to the Middle Ages, when salt carried a hefty sales tax and the notoriously frugal Florentines made their bread without it. But it probably began much earlier, with the Etruscans, whose bread was supposedly considered bland by salt-craving Romans. Even then mills in central Italy ground flour *a secco* (dry or plain), while in other places it was often ground *a salso* (with salt).

Italy remained divided for centuries between advocates of salted and unsalted bread, though the latter represented a distinct minority confined to the regions of Tuscany, Umbria, and the Marches. It isn't certain just why those not otherwise close-knit neighbors formed a united front of saltless bread. But so adamant was their abstinence that visitors there were sometimes known to sprinkle salt on slices on the sly so as not to offend the natives.

Tuscans, as the most assiduous of bread users, ate it with every meal, keeping the firm *pane raffermo* as the essence of many a recipe. The basic snack for infants and adults alike was *pane e olio,* prized extra vergine, of course. This became antipasto as *fettunta* or *panunto*, bread toasted over coals, rubbed with garlic, and soaked with oil—also known in parts of Tuscany and elsewhere as *bruschetta*. Thin-sliced *crostini*, sometimes lightly toasted, were topped with pâté of chicken livers and milt or anchovy paste or chopped tomatoes. A summer treat was *panzanella*, a salad of sorts, made of bread soaked in water, squeezed dry, crumbled, and mixed with raw onions, tomatoes, cucumber, basil, oil, and vinegar.

Variations on *minestre* were legion. The classics were *zuppa di pane* (vegetable and bean soup thickened with bread that became more concentrated in flavor when reheated, or reboiled, to become *la ribollita*) and *pappa al pomodoro* (literally a bread pap stewed with tomatoes and onions). Bread figured in soups with black cabbage, onions, and sage and garlic, in *minestra di pan grattato* (bread crumbs in broth beaten with eggs and grated Parmigiano), and *acqua cotta* (''cooked water'' flavored with vegetables and herbs and sometimes wild mushrooms). Around Arezzo, *scottiglia* was a stew of meats and poultry, vegetables and herbs served over grilled *pane abbrustolito*. Tuscans normally nibbled away on bread with meats, fish, and vegetables, and used chunks unabashedly to sop up sauces. Bread even made its way into desserts, such as *budino* (pudding) flavored with honey, fruit, and nuts.

For centuries bread and wine had symbolized the rustic elegance of the Tuscan repast. But then, a couple of decades ago, pane toscano began a rapid decline, a consequence of the migration of country folk to the cities and the degeneration of traditional values and tastes. Most of the small, water-powered *mulini* had closed down by then, replaced by larger mechanized mills. Many village bakers tore out their wood-burning *forni* and replaced them with multiple ovens that could bake all kinds of bread, including types made using salt and bleached flour for a fluffy, snow-white pulp that turned stale in twenty-four hours. These days even the aging *massaie* rarely bother to fire up the forno, except on occasions when relatives gather to remember old times. A new generation of farm wives seemed only too happy to sell their flour-caked *madie* to antiques dealers and equip their once rustic kitchens with shiny metal and plastic components.

Meanwhile, cosmopolitanism has crept into Tuscan restaurants, where menus may suggest the likes of smoked salmon, foie gras, spaghetti alla carbonara, risotto alla milanese, steak au poivre, lobster, soufflés, and mousses. For diners who can't afford—or can't abide—such creativity an alternative is the pizzeria, by now a fixture in every Tuscan town.

Still, though no one seems to be doing much to halt the corruption of local cooking, it's hard to find a Tuscan over forty who won't vouch that bread and virtually everything else tasted better back then, especially if made by Mamma. It must be admitted, though, that here and there in these legendary hills, osterie or trattorie still provide tastes of the past at something approaching reasonable prices. Nor has the true pane toscano completely disappeared, though it owes its precarious survival to the sort of local pride found mainly in out-of-the-way places.

One such place is Loro Ciuffenna, a town nestled into the foot of the Pratomagno range of the Apennines on the edge of the Arno Valley midway between Florence and Arezzo. Loro is dialect for *lauro*, laurel or bay, a shrub that grows wild hereabouts, and Ciuffenna is what the Etruscans called the stream that tumbles down from wooded hills through a gorge of impressive depth but narrow enough so that the Romans could build an arching stone bridge over it. Just upstream from the *ponte romano*, almost in the shadow of a reinforced concrete span that bears today's traffic, is one of the few functioning water mills in Tuscany.

Giuseppe Parigi, owner and operator, doesn't consider his mulino a musem, though the Belle Arti, the official protectors of fine arts and architecture, have declared it a historical monument. Parigi, an unassuming fellow who would like to spend his remaining years quietly milling grain as he has for half a century, complains that he's under pressure from authorities. "On the one hand, the Belle Arti tell me that I must preserve everything exactly as is, which is fine with me, but then the USL [Unità Sanitarie Locali, which enforces health standards] insist that I make the place 'hygienic' with tiles on the walls and floors and machinery that can be cleaned efficiently. Well, I'd close down rather than do that, so I hope the Belle Arti prevails."

Parigi shrugged bewilderedly when asked about the mill's future. "I'm getting old, and there's nobody waiting to replace me, so it can't go on much longer," he admitted. "But for now it's worth keeping up. Water power is free and ecological, it doesn't pollute." As he described the workings of the mill, his sad eyes brightened.

When the Ciuffenna is flowing, as it is most of the year,

he lets water build up in a reservoir and then opens a gate so that the stream rushing under the mill splashes against the paddles of an entirely hand-hewn wooden wheel, an antique turbine that spins at dizzying speed and powers three millstones inside. Grain is funneled down from an attic into basins where the stones grind flour, the "cold milling" that allows it to retain more food value than "hot" mechanical processing would. This coarse flour, whether unsifted as *integrale* or lightly sifted as *tipo 0,* is carried to a bin through a series of belts, hoists, and chutes, a system powered entirely by water or gravity that looks as if it might have been conceived by a local predecessor of Rube Goldberg. But it works just fine and costs virtually nothing to operate.

Parigi also grinds corn for animal feed and in the winter passes chestnuts, roasted and peeled, through the works to make a sweet, golden flour for *castagnaccio,* a flat cake baked with pine nuts and rosemary. But the irony is that the nutritious integrale flour from this monument to milling is rarely used by local bakers. He said that this is not just because it costs more than refined flour but because dark bread isn't much in demand anymore. His stone-ground tipo 0 also makes fine pane toscano of an off-white color. Parigi sells some flour at his shop beneath the new bridge, but the bulk goes to middlemen, so he doesn't know where it ends up.

Loro was once renowned for traditional bread, but the two remaining bakeries in the center of town no longer have wood-burning ovens. What is known locally as *pane cotto a legna* (wood-baked) comes from the hills, from artisan forni in the localities of Trappola, Trevane, and Gorgiti. Bread from all three is commendable, but to my taste the huge loaves from Gorgiti most faithfully uphold the past glory, with their thick, crunchy crusts and weighty pulp riddled by fissures and holes, and the smoky sweet-and-sour sensations in aroma and flavor.

Carlo Cocollini, the fornaio there, seemed pleased to hear my impression. "We do things pretty much as they did a century ago," he told me, though he admitted that about twenty years ago he quit using whole-wheat flour from the mill at Loro. "With the coming of *benessere* [well-being], people decided that dark bread was too heavy," he recalled. "So from then on we've used tipo 0, which makes a substantial bread with some of the color of the grain. But the whole-wheat bread had stronger flavor and it lasted longer. I preferred it, but we have to cater to the market."

I had met Carlo Cocollini a few days earlier while he was delivering bread to shops, and I asked if I could come to see the baking. "Sure," he said, "but I start at four-thirty in the morning, so I hope you're an early riser." On the appointed day in early July, I left Loro just after four and drove the strip of asphalt road that winds up something over 4 miles along the Ciuffenna stream to Gorgiti. That secluded hamlet, surrounded by the dense Pratomagno woods noted for chestnuts and *porcini* mushrooms, straddles the Ciuffenna in two sectors linked by a narrow footbridge. The main gathering place for its sixty or so residents is the complex of stone buildings that house the Cocollini family forno, general store, tobacco shop, bar, and osteria under a sign "Alimentari & Vini" partly camouflaged by wisteria spilling over an arbor.

The glow of a fluorescent lamp guided me to the Cocollini kitchen, where Carlo was waiting with a sleepy smile on his round face. "Right on time," he greeted me, and apparently feeling no need for further formalities in the predawn solitude, suggested that we get to work.

We walked up a path of well-worn stones and into the compact building that houses the forno. He had readied the oven the evening before, piling in bound bundles of brush, a few branches of oak, and some scrap paper, to which he casually touched a match. The fire was soon roaring, with flames lapping through the arched aperture and smoke belching out in such volume that only a fraction seemed to be following its intended course up the narrow gap of a chimney above the arch, while the rest shrouded the baking hall and drifted out the front door.

The fornaio, ignoring the fumes, hurried into the adjacent room to make the dough. Carlo recalled that in the old days bakers did the kneading by hand in the madia. But he uses a mechanical mixer or *impastatrice,* "a great labor saver when you're making sixty to a hundred and twenty loaves a day." In the stainless-steel cylindrical tub, which is never washed but scraped clean with a spatula after each use, he had left a quantity of the previous day's dough—about 22 to 26 pounds—to ferment and become the madre. This starter had been augmented the previous evening by about $10\frac{1}{2}$ ounces of packaged beer yeast to bolster the buildup of natural yeast fungi, which on their own can ferment to become too acidic and sour.

Carlo, wearing loose-fitting denim trousers and a short-sleeved cotton shirt that covered his girth but exposed his beefy forearms, worked with a quickness so casual that it seemed to be guided by instinct. At a corner sink, he filled pails with first cool and then warm water and dumped them into the mixer, adding quantities of flour, which he scooped from two large, heavy paper sacks. He said that in winter to get the yeasts working faster, he increases the portion of warm water. He flipped the switch that started the tub turning the mass while the *tanaglia,* rotating wishbone-shaped tongs, kneaded the dough.

He uses only tipo 0 flour but from two different mills, to cut risks that might arise from one batch being in less than top condition. Tipo 0 is rich in glutens, the grain proteins which during kneading cling to one another to give the dough a rubbery sort of elasticity. As he added the flour, purely by eye, he said he would make about 320 pounds of dough for 265 pounds of bread, noting that considerable weight in moisture evaporates during baking. He said that texture and flavor depend on how thoroughly the dough absorbs moisture and then gradually expels it while cooking, pointing out that Gorgiti's pure spring water is a key quality factor.

As he worked, he explained steps with summary phrases voiced in a singsong tenor using the local idiom that echoes the Florentine aspiration of the hard C to sound like a guttural H. Although Loro Ciuffenna and its scattered *frazioni* lie in the province of Arezzo, the Loresi, like other inhabitants of this stretch of the Valdarno Superiore, have felt stronger historical ties to Florence. Yet Arezzo, whose domain had been Tuscany's prime source of grain since earliest Roman times, has better preserved the remnants of its bread tradition than Florence, whose local customs have been compromised by the growth of tourism and industry.

While the impastatrice turned, I asked Carlo whether he ever added anything else to the dough, like salt or oil. "No, never," he said, eyeing me as if I'd arrived from outer space. "It wouldn't be to our taste." Then he qualified his statement, noting that *panelli,* the flat breads better known elsewhere in Tuscany as *schiacciate* (literally squashed), are topped with olive oil and salt. "But the dough itself is always pure: flour, yeast, and water."

He went out to attend to the oven, using a long wooden pole to shift around the burning branches and reddened coals. By then the bit of smoke they emitted flowed smoothly up the flue. The oven, whose circular interior is a little over 7 feet in diameter with a vaulted dome about a yard high, was built by specialized craftsmen using small firebricks on the walls and ceiling and square tiles on the floor. Carlo said it is ready for baking when the ceiling bricks, corroded to jags and dents by nearly thirty years of fires, turn white (actually pale gray) from the heat. "I never measure the temperature," he said. "A fornaio knows at a glance when it's ready."

After the dough had been worked for about twenty minutes, he tested it by stretching a wad into straps like warm taffy. "It's set," he said, turning off the machine. He began pulling clumps of dough from the mass, rapidly weighing each on a scale, dusting them with flour, and gently patting them into ovals called *pagnotte.* First he made forms of just over 2 pounds of dough each, to be used for panelli and the 1-kilo loaves that a few customers demand. Then he formed about fifty pagnotte for the heroic 2-kilo loaves typical of his forno.

I noticed that he hardly worked the dough with his hands

at all. "It doesn't require more kneading—the *lievito* does the work," he said, pointing out that the more yeast a bread contains the quicker it rises and the greater its nutritional value. He placed the pagnotte, preceded by sprinklings of flour, onto layers of jute cloth arranged on aluminum shelves in mobile racks with wheels. He said that in the past they used wooden shelves, preferable because they hold steady temperature, which metals do not. But the hygiene inspectors don't permit wood because it can harbor bacteria. "What difference it makes, I don't know," he said. "Baking purifies bread on the outside anyway."

When the pagnotte were set, he used a blunt knife to score the upper surface of each to give the finished bread an identifying sign of two parallel grooves. He said that each fornaio tends to make his own mark, a practice that probably began long ago at communal ovens to distinguish one family's loaves from another's. Carlo draped cloths over the loaves, leaving them to rise as he stoked up the fire by adding another bundle of brush. Then he set a heavy metal panel against the aperture and propped it with an arched rod, leaving a crack for air to enter and smoke to escape while the oven built heat. He said he could somewhat regulate the heat by controlling the size of the aperture, but the key is to have the fire right from the start.

It was five-forty-five under a cloudy dawn sky when he shut the door to the building, complaining that it was necessary to close the place to hold the heat inside in what had been an unusually cool, damp summer. "Well, anyway, it's good weather for porcini," he said, pointing up to the edge of the forest where those prized *funghi* thrive. We went across to the kitchen, where he made us each a coffee at a gleaming espresso machine and lit up a cigarette, cursing the habit he took up to while away waiting time.

He related that the family bread tradition began in the early 1950s when his mother, Iole, widowed young in her native town of Grosseto, near the Tuscan coast, moved her family to Gorgiti. She started the forno on her own in what had been a stall adjacent to the kitchen, where she kneaded dough in the madia. Carlo gradually took over, though Iole still bakes bread occasionally while doing most of the delectable home cooking for the family osteria.

They built a new forno in 1964 and installed the impasta-trice, but Carlo purposely kept the dimensions small. Now in his mid-forties, he takes good-natured pride in his work, which he performs every day except Wednesday (when the Cocollini complex closes for a rest) and often twice on Saturday to meet demands from weekend visitors. I conjectured that he goes to bed early. "No, not usually," he said. "There's always something going on here until late with the osteria and bar and friends playing cards. Anyway, three or four hours of sleep are enough for me, though I'll admit there are days when I don't feel like hopping out of bed."

Asked if he had anyone to succeed him as fornaio, he looked uncertain. "My son Davide is just seven, so who knows? But I doubt it. There aren't many young people left in these hills. They find work in the cities and come back in summer to visit their families and breathe some fresh air. You know, though it might be lonely here in winter, I wouldn't trade it for city life for anything. Here you're your own boss and, within limits, you can do what you like: hunt for mushrooms, fish for trout, keep a garden and fruit trees, some rabbits and chickens. We raise most of the food we eat and serve in the osteria, and it's all natural.''

Carlo's wife, Grazia, who arose at her normal six, arrived in the kitchen with a cheery smile and a condemnation of the weather. Short, stout, and dark-haired, with a reserve of restless energy, she was soon bustling about sweeping floors and dusting the already spotless surroundings. She scolded her husband for not offering something to eat. ''We're waiting for panelli,'' he said, and went across to the forno to check the rising bread, only to find that the coolness had slowed progress.

Finally, about six-twenty, he opened the oven and used a metal paddle to slide the hot coals into a pile at the left-hand side. He took a pole with a clump of chestnut leaves tied on as a broom and swept the forno floor free of ashes. He began with the panelli, made using nine of the small pagnotte. One by one, he placed them on the flat blade of a wooden *pala* ( baker's peel ), pressing them into fairly flat, irregular rectangles. After dousing them with extra vergine olive oil and a liberal sprinkling of salt, he slid them into the oven. He closed the aperture for five or six minutes and then, using a smaller peel, gave each a deft 180-degree rotation so that they would brown evenly. He replaced the panel for a few minutes more, and when he opened it again they were done to a gleaming tan. He used the pala to remove them and place them on shelves.

Panelli resemble pizza, though they are thicker and more breadlike because of slower baking. Carlo's forno, though similar in form to the classical pizza ovens of Naples, is larger and de-signed to generate relatively moderate heat ( 500° to 535°F ). In

Naples, pizza bakes in a minute or two in ovens which get much hotter (715° to 750°F) and hold heat longer, because of their compactness and the special firebricks used.

As Carlo prepared the oven for bread, Grazia came to help, wheeling a rack full of pagnotte into position. She grasped each in the palm of her left hand, flipped it onto a wooden scoop shovel held in her right, took a few steps, and plopped it down in the original position onto Carlo's flour-sprinkled peel. He slid each into place in the oven with easy precision, forming circular rows until the entire floor was covered with loaves separated from one another by no more than the width of his thumb. Three pagnotte were left out. "Better than usual," said Grazia. "Some days we have as many as fifteen."

Carlo replaced the panel, lit a cigarette, and announced, "Now we wait." He explained that large loaves cook more slowly than the small, developing a thick, protective crust that keeps the interior moist, retaining the vitamins, minerals, and proteins that have made bread the essence of the Tuscan diet for centuries. "You know that bread is *vivo* [alive, as he put it] when you can smell the natural yeasts. They not only enhance the flavor but aid digestion." He said most bread from modern bakeries is sterilized inside and out from hot baking in vaporized ovens.

Grazia had cut open a panello and filled it with slices of mortadella, providing a hot breakfast that indeed seemed to melt in my mouth. After about twenty minutes, Carlo opened the oven and with brisk motions of the smaller peel rotated loaves that had begun to brown on the side facing the coals so that they would cook evenly.

Between maneuvers he recalled that a decade or so ago wood-fired ovens for bread baking were supposed to have been banned because the traces of ash that remain on the crust were considered unsanitary under new health norms. The use of natural leavening was also under threat. ''We were worried,'' Carlo recalled, ''because our livelihood was at stake. But I kept making bread just as I always had and nobody ever did anything about it.'' Some time later the USL told him that everything was okay again, offering no excuses or explanations. ''Buh?'' he muttered, the verbal equivalent of a shrug. ''Maybe our enlightened bureaucrats realized that if ash and natural yeasts were poisonous there wouldn't be any Tuscans left.''

Grazia, who wore a colored dress, said that, technically speaking, they are required to work in white outfits with aprons and bakers' hats. Carlo, with his high-pitched chuckle, added that the lower walls and floors of the baking hall must be lined with tiles, as they are, and the upper walls and ceilings painted—all immaculate white, of course. ''Well, we dutifully whitewash the place four times a year,'' he said, ''but after three or four days of smoke, it's all gray again. People who make these rules ought to have some practical experience.''

As the baking proceeded, he spent more time shifting loaves that were nearly cooked to cooler parts of the oven, turning them on their sides or upside down and shifting others to take their places. This made space for the three extra loaves, which by staying nearer the coals came out baked with the rest of the batch. Carlo said that he could manipulate the loaves so that all would be cooked to more or less the same degree, but it isn't worth the effort, because some customers like bread well done and others lightly cooked. "Why, there's a lady who phones up most days and tells me she wants a kilo loaf baked just so," he said. "I do it to her specifications, but I'm glad there aren't too many of those requests."

After about ninety minutes, Carlo took the peel and began extracting loaves from the oven, starting with those of a kilo, which had baked at the coolest point near the aperture. He wore suede gloves to handle the hot bread and used a linen cloth to dust ash off the bases. The big loaves were the size of pillows with mottled shadings of tan, powdery buff, and charcoal amid welts, ripples, craters, and crevices that resembled relief maps of the surface of the moon.

He placed about a dozen loaves onto shelves to be sold on the premises and arranged the rest on their sides in large plastic baskets for delivery. Carlo's sister, Carla, who lives in the adjacent quarters, had arrived to tend the food shop with its small bar. She and Grazia lugged baskets down the stone walkway to the roadside and loaded them into the back of a compact white Fiat van that Carlo uses to do his morning rounds.

Before he left, the fornaio ate his first food of the day, a stand-up colazione in the company of friends who had returned from hunting mushrooms. Carla cut thick wedges of warm bread and made panini for them, sandwiches filled to order with salty mountain prosciutto or finocchietto (the local salame flavored with wild fennel) or creamy fresh pecorino cheese, or mortadella. They drank tumblers of rough red wine from the plain below Loro and exchanged views on porcini and the weather, which had taken a temporary turn for the better as feeble rays of sunlight filtered through the clouds.

Carlo stepped out onto the terrace and between bites talked about his calling. ''Baking bread is lonely work and the hours are dreadful, but I can't complain. I was in Grosseto recently and saw one of those automated bakeries. You know, they told me that bread there is never touched by human hands, and they seemed proud of the fact. Well, I'll bet it tastes that way, too. It'll go stale almost as soon as it's cut open.''

He gestured toward his friends, chewing contentedly on sandwiches. ''After all these years, they still compliment me on my bread. On weekends people drive all the way up here from the valley to buy a loaf or two because they say the bread tastes like it did in the old days. Sometimes they can't wait to get it home, so they rip off chunks and nibble on them. It's little things like that that make it worthwhile, when you know that something simple that you create daily with your own hands gives people such pleasure.''

The Cocollini family osteria serves delicious meals at moderate prices in the best Tuscan country tradition, though only if ordered a day ahead of time so that Mamma Iole can prepare dishes in the forno after the bread is baked. Her favorite is rabbit stewed with wine and herbs, though the wood oven also brings unmatched succulence to pork, chicken, lamb, duck, stewed *fagioli* (haricot beans), and pan-browned potatoes. Each day she makes a fruit tart or flat cake. She uses firm bread as the base of chicken-liver crostini, ribollita, and pappa al pomodoro, and for panzanella in summer, when customers can sit outside under a pergola. Otherwise meals are served in an ample dining room above the kitchen. The telephone is (055) 9704001.

Carlo's pane cotto a legna is available each morning at Gorgiti and at neighboring Modine, where another sister, Franca,
runs a general store. It can also be found, while supplies last, at
the Conad grocery at Loro Ciuffenna and on Monday mornings
at the open-air market in the center of town, where Giuseppe
Parigi's mill may be seen in operation.

# Pasta
## The unifying force of spaghetti

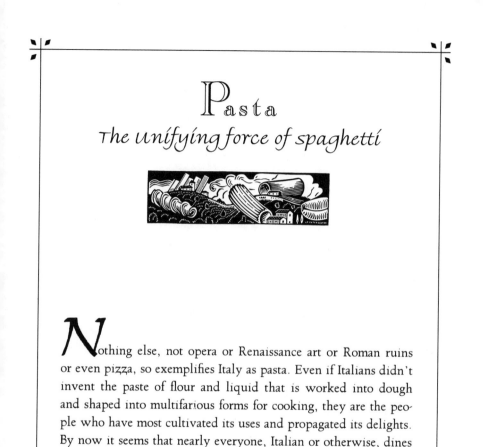

Nothing else, not opera or Renaissance art or Roman ruins or even pizza, so exemplifies Italy as pasta. Even if Italians didn't invent the paste of flour and liquid that is worked into dough and shaped into multifarious forms for cooking, they are the people who have most cultivated its uses and propagated its delights. By now it seems that nearly everyone, Italian or otherwise, dines with some regularity on spaghetti or lasagne or ravioli or just plain noodles that are amassed within what must rank as the western world's favorite category of food.

Pasta's popularity owes much to the fact that it is inexpensive, easy to store and cook, and remarkably versatile. Historically a humble food, everyday sustenance in the southern half of Italy, it was long appreciated more for its cheap and filling attributes than for its dietetic or aesthetic virtues. Over time it had been criticized as starchy, hard to digest, and fattening, especially in northern Italy, where it nonetheless gained steady favor among chronic consumers of rice and polenta. Southern Italian emigrants introduced it abroad as a novel carbohydrate in amusing shapes that gained prominence as spaghetti and meatballs doused with tomato sauce and macaroni smothered in melted cheese. But with the emergence of the Mediterranean diet as the smart way to eat and the rise of *la cucina italiana* to the heights of international cuisine, pasta has been placed on a pedestal by nutritionists and epicures alike.

Its secret of success may be culinary simplicity, but *pasta alimentare* is an institution of encyclopedic complexity. So varied are its shapes and sizes, methods of making it, and modes of flavoring, dressing, and serving it that literature on pasta is often confused by classifications and definitions. Authorities, however, do not all agree on details or terms, a situation further complicated by the fact that names of identical types of pasta often differ from one place to another.

In confronting pasta's infinity of forms—strings, strips, sheets, tubes, shells, rings, spirals, cartwheels, stars, ears, noses, belly buttons, butterflies, envelopes, pillows, and hats, among others—it is useful to note that it comes in two elemental types.

*Pasta secca* (dry) is made primarily from semola (coarse durum wheat flour) and water into dough shaped mechanically by being forced through slots of varying sizes and patterns and cut and dried to be preserved for weeks, months, or even years. Pasta secca may be subdivided as *lunga* (long like spaghetti), *corta* or *tagliata* (short like penne), and *pastina* or *minestrina* (minuscule pieces), further defined by shape (solid or hollow) and surface texture (smooth or ribbed). Hollow forms may also be *da ripieno* (to be filled or stuffed).

*Pasta fresca* (fresh) is usually made from soft wheat flour and eggs, rolled and shaped by hand or using simple machines, to be cooked within hours or, at most, a couple of days (though vacuum packing or freezing prolongs storage). A distinct variation on the *fresca* theme is *pasta ripiena,* applying to numerous filled or stuffed types such as ravioli and tortellini.

The term *pasta asciutta* or *pastasciutta* refers to any pasta scalded and drained and served dry (*asciutta*) as opposed to *pasta in brodo,* cooked and served in broth. Pastina or minestrina, whether dried or fresh, is normally cooked in broth or soup. What distinguishes pasta from such other flour-based foods as breads and pastries is that the primary cooking of the unleavened dough is in liquid, whereas the others may be baked, roasted, grilled, or fried.

Italians today generally regard pasta as a *primo,* a first course or *minestra,* which also takes in dishes of risotto, polenta, gnocchi, or soup. That does not mean that the primo will necessarily be the first dish to arrive at the table, however, since in most regions antipasto is served before the regular part of the meal begins. It does suggest, though, that a *secondo,* or main course, would ensue: usually meat, poultry, game, or fish, with a side dish of vegetables or salad. A complete meal might be followed by cheese, fruit or dessert, and *caffè.*

These dining customs, which vary from region to region, sometimes confuse foreign visitors used to eating pasta as a main course. Restaurateurs who insist on serving the entire ensemble might be ignoring the fact that to many Italians in the not so distant past a heaping bowl of pasta with sauce and grated cheese (or in hard times with a few drops of olive oil and a hint of seasoning) was a meal in itself. But then it's surprising how little is known about the background of a food so prominent in modern Italy.

There is no concrete evidence that Italy's ancient peoples ate pasta at all. Etruscan drawings of banquets indicate that something similar to lasagne might have been consumed, but that's archaeological speculation, since the practice was not continued by the Romans who conquered them. The early Greeks in Italy, as well as the Romans—who faithfully recorded recipes and menus—ate strips of dough that resembled lasagne before cooking. However, this *laganum,* as the Romans called it, was not cooked as pasta in liquid but roasted on hot stones or in ovens and served with cheese and other flavorings as a sort of tart or pizza.

Pasta may have originated in the Orient, since the Chinese are believed to have eaten noodles as early as the first century B.C. But the long-held notion that Marco Polo introduced pasta to Italy on his return from China in 1295 has been dispelled. It probably arrived in Italy from the Near East, during the Arab conquests between the seventh and thirteenth centuries. The first written evidence of pasta's presence was a Genoese merchant's inventory in 1279 describing a shipment of *macharonis,* probably from Sicily. The Genoese are credited with spreading the use of pasta to coastal regions of Italy and beyond. The cult had crossed the Apennines to Emilia by the fourteenth century, when Giovanni Boccaccio in the *Decameron* wrote that people there ate ''maccheroni and raviuoli'' in broth with grated Parmigiano.

To this day Emilians remain the champions of pasta fresca. But Sicilians, with their Arab links, were the first Italian masters of dried pasta, or what came to be known in much of the south as *maccheroni* or *maccaruni* or *maccaroni*. Those terms may have come from *maccare*, meaning to squash or flatten, in reference to the dough. Neapolitans claim to have invented maccheroni, but trade records indicate that until the early nineteenth century they imported most dried pasta from Sicily and Sardinia. Then came the "maccheroni revolution," coinciding with the rise of the tomato, or *pomodoro*, which dressed it so tastily. Italy's first sizable pasta industry grew up along the Gulf of Naples. The noted center was the hillside town of Gragnano, close to the grainfields of Campania and favored by pure mountain water and a sunny climate for open-air drying of strands draped over cane poles.

Maccheroni has remained a generic term in the Mezzogiorno for pasta secca. This takes in such diverse types as the tubes known as *penne*, *perciatelli*, and *ziti*, the spiraled *fusilli* and the shell-shaped *conchiglie*, all typical of Campania. It might also include pasta lunga such as spaghetti and the slimmer strings of *vermicelli*, though to Neapolitans maccheroni signifies pasta corta. To the north, maccheroni often refers to a specific type of short, ribbed pasta tube.

The traditions of Liguria and Emilia-Romagna had influenced other northerners to fashion local versions of pasta, usually fresh. But late in the last century, dried pasta gradually broke its bonds as southern soul food to win admirers up to the Alps and beyond. General Giuseppe Garibaldi, on liberating Naples in 1860, announced: "It will be maccheroni, I swear to you, that will unite Italy." But the unifying force turned out to be spaghetti, which surged to prominence after the Risorgimento to become the closest thing Italy has to a national dish.

The advantage of dried pasta over fresh was that it could be produced on a large scale and packaged and distributed with little risk of spoilage. The Italian market for pasta secca has become increasingly focused on a dozen or so types, with spaghetti accounting for about 40 percent of sales. In recent times, hundreds of small *pastifici* around the country have been closed or absorbed by the large firms that now dominate production. Campania remains a major producer, but pasta is big business in neighboring Apulia and the central regions of Abruzzi, Molise, Umbria, and Tuscany, as well as the northern Emilia-Romagna, Liguria, and Lombardy. Domestic consumption of pasta, after reaching highs in the 1960s, has leveled off at about 55 pounds per capita annually (enough for 250 normal servings). But demand from abroad has made it a key growth sector in the Italian food industry.

Under Italian law, pasta secca must be made only from *semola di grano duro,* which renders a stiffer dough and firmer finished product than soft wheat flours do. Most pasta is made from semola and water alone, without salt, though *paste speciali* may include whole eggs (fresh or frozen), which make it yellower and tenderer, or spinach or tomatoes (fresh or dried and powdered), which make it green or pink.

A fair amount of durum wheat is grown in southern Italy, though the pasta industry relies heavily on imports from Canada, Argentina, and the United States. In other countries packaged pasta is often made from soft wheat flour or blends with semola, resulting in lower costs and markedly inferior quality. After resisting Common Market orders to permit imports of such pasta, Italy finally was forced to allow them in with the open European market in 1993.

Mass-produced pasta meets generally good standards in Italy, even if some firms seem to put more stock in appearance (a buttery yellow color) than in taste or food value. Still, though pasta is limited in vitamins and minerals, nutritionists point out that its complex carbohydrates are a rapid and enduring source of energy, especially useful for athletes and physically active persons. They have also deflated the long-standing myth that pasta is fattening, commending it as an essential of the Mediterranean diet because it balances so well with small portions of other foods, filling the stomach while providing calories more readily burned than from fats.

But beyond pasta's generic attributes lie specific distinctions in quality. Here and there in Italy artisans use semola from choice grains and follow traditional methods of slow drying that give extra dimensions of flavor, texture, and digestibility. A few force the dough through *trafile di bronzo,* the old-style brass drawplates whose unlined slots give the pasta a rough, porous surface that better absorbs sauces than industrial types pressed through smooth Teflon slots.

Certain artisan pasta I had tasted was unquestionably superior, but I never gave much thought to the reasons until I was introduced to ''La Pasta'' of Latini. My friend Paolo Magnoni of Bologna, who sells that pasta along with wines and spirits, sent a carton containing a dozen types to my home. With the samples came descriptive notes so clear, concise, and credible that I actually read them—all four pages—and in minutes reaped more knowledge about the niceties of pasta than I'd gleaned in nearly half a century of eating it.

An intriguing point in the notes was that the company, Azienda Agraria Latini, is based on a farm, where the producers grow their own special types of grain. Also apparently unique among Italy's pasta makers is the practice of hand-numbering each of the artistically designed half-kilogram packages. The Latini pasta proved to have those extra dimensions. So I asked Paolo to put me in touch with the owners, Carlo and Carla Latini, a young couple at Osimo, a town near Ancona in the east-central region of the Marches.

When I phoned to ask if I could visit the pastificio, Carlo Latini was cordial but hesitant, which made me wonder if he was being modest or had something to hide. The magnanimous Magnoni intervened, though, and set up a visit a few days later. On that mid-May morning I met Paolo at Cupramontana, at the Colonnara cellars whose fine Verdicchio Classico dei Castelli di Jesi is the mainstay of his selections. After a tasting and a late start for our lunch appointment, we drove east past the town of Jesi and then up over rolling green hills to the Musone River valley, where we sped past fields of grain toward Osimo until Paolo pointed to the Latini farmhouse, a white building flanked by tall trees and a neatly kept garden.

The house fronts directly on the main valley road, but there was no sign of a pastificio or any other kind of business. Carlo Latini met us at the gate with a gentle smile that seemed to excuse our tardiness. With his infant daughter, Teresa, clasped in one arm and son, Michele, tugging on the other, he led us inside to meet Carla, whose compact kitchen regaled us with odors of simmering sauces and roasting meats. Though both are in their early thirties, they looked younger in their different ways. Carla, a classical Mediterranean type, is trim in stature, with large dark eyes and long black hair revealing her Sardinian origins, but Carlo, with close-cropped reddish-blond hair, pale blue eyes, and solid frame, probably could trace part of his ancestry to points north of the Alps.

Carlo quickly got us seated at a long table and served chilled Verdicchio with a mixture of antipasti, while Carla prepared the pasta. "You like it *al dente,* I assume," she called from the kitchen. And al dente it was, penne as firm to the bite as any pasta I could recall, dressed with a smattering of meat ragout and a sprinkling of Parmigiano. As we bit in, I glanced at Paolo, whose expression seemed to reflect my doubts about whether it would be considered "to the tooth" or underdone. But our hosts chomped away so contentedly that we followed suit. By the third mouthful I was getting used to the firmness and complimented Carla on the flavors.

Carlo took that as a cue. "We've noticed that most people don't think of pasta as having any particular taste, and they're usually right," he said in his amiable way. "To them the only flavor is in the sauce." He pointed to an almost bare penne tube in my bowl. "There, try that piece alone," he suggested. I bit into it and tasted what reminded me of the crust of freshly baked white bread, though when well masticated it became mellower, vaguely like puff pastry. "Now, test the aroma," he prompted, pointing to another piece. Aroma in pasta? I wondered. But he wasn't kidding. Similar if subtler sensations came across to the nose.

As we polished off our penne with new gusto, Carla brought a bowl of spaghetti dressed only with a deep green local olive oil and a hint of parsley and tomato sauce. The strands were so rigid that they didn't wrap easily around our forks, but we were learning to savor the sturdiness. Carla explained that minimal cooking not only retains flavors but that the chewing makes pasta more digestible. Well-cooked noodles contain more water, which dilutes digestive juices, said Carlo, adding that only the best pasta secca could be cooked to the lower limits of al dente without becoming gummy or crunchy as some industrial types tend to be.

The Latini's promised ''simple country lunch'' had become a feast, with the arrival of roast duck and rabbit, garnished by raw and cooked vegetables, all from their garden, and served with a supple Rosso Conero from vineyards just over the hill. But even over dessert our focus remained on pasta. Carlo pointed out that theirs, thanks to selected grains, is unequaled for its natural content of glutens: 16.5 to 17 percent, compared with the normal 12 to 14 percent. Beyond their nutritional value, these grain proteins also contribute to the firm, even texture. He added that their pasta has a few calories less per serving than normal, due to extremely low contents of starch and lipids, the vegetal fats present in grain.

''But we're not promoting it as diet pasta,'' said Carla, with a trace of irony in her broad smile. She said that after experiments they were about to release a pasta from semola with some wheat germ and bran. ''But all of our pasta, including integrale, has to meet the same standards of flavor, texture, and cooking performance,'' reminded Carlo. ''No exceptions.''

The meal ended toward evening, as Paolo, still running late, left for Bologna, and Carlo invited me to tour grainfields. Carla stayed behind with the children as we drove off in his vintage Mercedes-Benz station wagon west along the Musone and up along narrow lanes of packed clay and gravel into the softly rolling hills. As he drove, he talked about their background. They met as students in Ancona, while taking part in a theater group. Carla, who studied engineering, also played guard on Ancona's women's basketball team. Carlo got a diploma in agricultural science. When they were married in 1984, they decided to move back to Carlo's family farm to join his father and mother in growing premium-quality vegetables and fruit to sell on local markets. They also grew wheat, which sparked Carlo's idea that they could raise choice grains for their own pasta.

"But we didn't actually come out with our first pasta until April of 1990," he said. "It took years of research and experiment before we were satisfied that we had something truly special. But by satisfied I don't mean to say that we can't do better." He turned to me with a smile that exuded youthful optimism. "At first we wanted to build our own pastificio, but that would have cost well over a billion [lire] and we couldn't afford it. Still, you know, even if a pastificio would be a great convenience, it isn't top priority. I've come to think of myself primarily as a grain grower more than a pasta maker. Any pastificio with the right equipment can make artisanal pasta. The secret of quality is in the grain."

We ascended the valley 6 to 12 miles inland from the Adriatic past vast estates with castles and villas that in many cases have belonged to the same noble families since the Marches was part of the Papal States. Carlo said that the owners rarely get

directly involved in agriculture but lease the land to grain growers with the machinery to work ample spreads. Many contadini,
the former sharecroppers, have moved away to the towns, leaving
behind empty farmhouses, substantial brick buildings of impressive architecture that if located in more glamorous regions such
as Tuscany or Umbria might be worth small fortunes. But it seems
that the local patriarchs prefer their rural solitude to profits from
real estate speculation.

Carlo said that his family has only a little more than 12 acres
of fields, but as the business expanded he has convinced farmers
to grow grain under his supervision. He stopped the car beside
a sloping expanse of wheat and invited me to follow him as he
hiked into the chest-high waves of green. Though calm and precise in expression, Carlo discussed grain and pasta with the sort
of enthusiasm that young oenologists devote to vines and wine,
often drawing parallels between grapes and wheat. He extolled
the recently recognized benefits of low crop yields, the impor-
tance of varietal selection among the many types of durum, and
the care that must be taken in storing, milling, and pastification
to preserve the essence of the grain.

We reached a place where stalks had bent over or collapsed.
''Allettamento,'' he called it, saying it was caused by wind or
rain or hail. ''That's the flaw of Senatore Cappelli,'' he said.
Senatore? I inquired. ''Yes, the variety was named for a politician
from the Marches by the father of modern grain growing in Italy,
Nazareno Strampelli.'' Carlo pronounced the name with reverence, explaining that around the turn of the century Strampelli
developed grains immune to the maladies that had nearly destroyed Italy's wheat crop, causing famine. He also bred produc-

tive, early-ripening strains of wheat that have been planted worldwide.

"For much of this century the main purpose of grain in Italy was to combat hunger by providing the maximum possible quantities of flour for pasta and bread," said Carlo. "So it was normal to seek prolific types." He pointed to plots with other varieties: Grazia, Ulisse, Duilio, Tresoro. "They're good grains, but Cappelli is the best for pasta because of its extraordinary gluten content," he said. "Of course, it's also the least productive. Yields are a half to a third as much as others, and since farmers grow it to our specifications, we pay much more per ton than the others do. So far we've had to use other grains in our pasta, but we'll soon make some batches exclusively from Cappelli."

As we rambled through the tall grass, Carlo puzzled over why more pasta makers don't select superior grains. "Consumers are increasingly conscious of ingredients, but so far the pasta industry hasn't been very responsive," he said. "We seem to be almost alone in upholding the merits of grain. But connoisseurs will pay the difference for quality. Our pasta costs more than double the standard types, but that comes to only two or three hundred lire more a serving, the price of a pack of chewing gum. I'd welcome more competition at our level, especially if it stimulated grain research. And if somebody comes up with a pasta better than ours, more power to him. It would make us try all the harder."

Not that the Latini have many idle moments. Carla, between the bookwork, the housework, and the children, designed the handsome paper box in a dappled garnet red with streaks of leaf green and an oval window to show the pasta. She also helps her mother, who lives nearby, with the hand-numbering of tabs that sealed 380,000 half-kilogram packages in 1992. Carlo, beyond his grain and pasta duties, directs sales and what he described with a self-conscious grin as public relations. When I praised his writing, he admitted that he, too, had been an author. After high school he wrote a guide to Italy's discotheques—a self-financed printing of four thousand copies, of which more than three thousand remain in the attic. "I've had more luck selling pasta," he acknowledged, "but someday I'd like to write another book, maybe about grain."

On the way back I asked when I might be able to see pasta being made. Carlo looked uncomfortable. "Not for now," he said. "The pastificio is in the Abruzzi, quite a way from here. We make our pasta there under contract, using our own equipment. Maybe you didn't know this, but pastifici, even small ones, almost never let outsiders see their operations." I tried to reason, promising that I wouldn't reveal trade secrets, that I merely wanted to describe the process by seeing it firsthand. But Carlo wouldn't budge. "We still hope to have a pastificio of our own some day," he said. "When we do, I swear you'll be the first to see it."

I left late that evening after agreeing to return in July for the grain harvest. Carlo promised in the meantime to get me complete documentation on the pasta-making process. To my surprise, though, he phoned in early July to announce that he'd persuaded the owners to let me visit the pastificio. "It must be because you're a foreigner," he said. "They've never let me bring anyone else near the place before."

When I arrived at the Latini farm a couple of days later, I was told that the pastificio was the second item on the agenda. First was a visit to Cesare Maliani, the eminent grain researcher. At that point, the idea of delving deeper into cereals seemed an impediment to exploring the intricacies of pasta. But Carlo and Carla spoke so highly of Maliani that I went along with them on the promise that we'd move on as soon as possible to the Abruzzi.

We drove up the graceful slopes to the town of Recanati and down again toward the Adriatic, past whitewashed houses and amber wheat fields flanked by poplars and cypresses, scenes radiated by midsummer sunlight that reminded me of Van Gogh's depictions of the Midi. We turned down a dusty lane and left the car in the shade of a large olive tree, where we waited for a gaunt figure of a man approaching us through the waves of grain. Cesare, with his ambling gait and serene smile, had a spiritual air about him, like a Franciscan monk who for the occasion had exchanged his frock for a short-sleeved blue oxford shirt and neatly pressed beige cotton slacks.

He spoke that way, too, softly, in a high-pitched voice that cracked frequently, yet he had the gifts of clarity and brevity, and a gentle wit that made his accounts of genetic grain engineering fascinating to follow. Carlo described Cesare as a ''pure researcher'' who, despite his erudition, had always shunned academe, preferring to make his living on commissions and royalties from the many varieties he's developed. ''I might have retired by now,'' admitted Cesare, who had just turned sixty. ''But Carlo showed up one day, and with that enthusiasm of his, got me interested in solving the Cappelli problem and developing new strains of durum. He not only inspired my research but he's turned me into a pasta fanatic.''

We walked from plot to plot on Cesare's sanctuary, plucking off *spighe,* the ears of grain, and rolling the dry husks between our palms to separate the kernels, which we munched on much the way winemakers sample grapes. There were marked differences in what Cesare described in Latin as *Triticum durum* and *Triticum vulgare,* the soft or common wheat whose flour is used for pasta fresca and, of course, bread. The larger, darker, smoother durum kernels proved to be richer in flavor and firmer in texture than the vulgare, which crumbled and melted in the mouth. Cesare had me try a kernel of the Cappelli developed with shorter stalks through cross-breeding. When I said it seemed the richest of all, Carlo beamed like a proud father.

''We're going to make pasta from pure Cappelli,'' he said, ''but the research won't stop there. We're hoping to come up with other superior types. There are varietal wines, so maybe someday there will be pasta named for the types of grain.'' Cesare, patting his young colleague on the shoulder, cautioned that it takes years to develop a new variety. He pointed out, though, that some shortcuts had been devised since the days when Nazareno Strampelli and his successor, Cirillo Maliani, Cesare's father, led the field.

Cesare invited us to lunch at his home in the center of Recanati, a tranquil town noted above all as the birthplace of the poet Giacomo Leopardi and the lyric tenor Beniamino Gigli. ''Great men,'' said Cesare over his risotto. ''But I sometimes wonder why there's no monument in the Marches to another eminent son, Nazareno Strampelli, whose grains fed millions of hungry people around the world. To me he deserved a Nobel Prize, as the American Norman Borlaug did for his green revolution.''

''You'll always be unsung heroes,'' Carlo reminded his mentor as we left for the Abruzzi and Carla headed back home. ''Maybe one day you'll have a pasta named after you.''

It took an hour and a half of hard driving on the Adriatic autostrada to reach Francavilla al Mare, a seaside town just south of the Abruzzi's main port of Pescara. Along the way, the grain harvest was in full swing, as the reapers that do all the labor with grim efficiency crept up and down the fields like mammoth robots. Carlo reminisced over his boyhood when the *raccolto del grano* was one of the year's events, as neighbors grouped into teams and went from farm to farm to cut and bundle wheat by hand and feed it into the huge, box-shaped threshers that were hauled from place to place by teams of oxen. The *trebbiatura* was exhausting manual labor in the hottest weeks of summer, but in the evening the host family provided a banquet with generous servings of pasta and roast meats and cooked vegetables and demijohns of young wine to be drunk copiously to restore those vital body fluids. ''But now, like the grape harvest, it's just another country routine,'' said Carlo. ''The folklore is gone.''

As we approached Francavilla, he briefed me on the steps leading up to *pastificazione,* the pasta-making process. After the harvest, the grain is stored in requisitely dry, cool rooms to maintain freshness, usually in cellars where temperatures vary naturally from about 40°F in winter to 50° to 54°F in summer. Then, never more than twenty-four hours before the pasta making, the Latini take the grain to a mill near Osimo. There it is ground by modern machines and sifted into what might be considered either a coarse flour or, better, the fine meal known as semola di grano duro, from the heart of the durum kernel without the germ or bran. (Those by-products are sold by the millers, usually as a base for animal food in a country where even dogs eat maccheroni).

The Latini make their pasta periodically, according to market demands. Early on the morning of each scheduled session, Carlo loads sacks of semola into the family van and drives the 90-odd miles to Francavilla to the Pastificio Mennilli, a drab concrete building on the Via Adriatica. Since ours was merely an observation tour, we arrived there late, after five in the evening. Carlo reminded me of the significance of this first visit by an outsider as we went inside to meet the owners, a couple of generations of the Mennilli family, elderly brothers and their sons.

After introductions, one of the sons, wearing a white T-shirt and jeans, invited us into the drying rooms, opening a heavy steel door with the comment: "If you think it's hot outside, wait'll you step in here." We entered a dim, steamy room in which a series of long, rectangular metal shafts were linked by a series of tubes, an oppressive place where the temperature and humidity seemed roughly equivalent to a sauna. We stayed just long enough to open a couple of side panels in the shafts to see strands of still-moist spaghetti draped over wooden rods. "We work up to sixteen hours a day in these conditions," said young Mennilli. "It's worse in the winter when we're constantly moving in and out from hot to cold. As you can imagine, we've all got problems with muscles and bones and lungs and raspy voices."

The drying-room ordeal over, I asked when we could see the pasta being shaped and cut. "Oh, you're too late for that," said Mennilli. "Too bad you didn't get here an hour or two earlier." Noting my chagrin, Carlo remarked on the side that they probably wouldn't have let me see the operation anyway, though he said it was slightly different from his own. Instead he described the process.

On arrival at the pastificio, the Latini deposit their semola into metal containers known as *semoliere*. There is one for pasta corta and one for pasta lunga, because each type is put through a separate network, though the basic working principles are the same. In the semoliera the contents of different bags are blended for uniformity and lightly sifted to remove any lumps before being drawn through pneumatic tubes to the *impastatrice*. In that stainless-steel vat, semola and water are mixed at the rate of about six to one (with slight variations for lunga and corta) and worked by paddles into a stiff, smooth, elastic dough. This is transferred by a spiral conveyor that functions like a meat grinder as it propels the mass into a reinforced metal container called a *testata* with a thrust that builds pressure to about 100 atmospheres and forces the dough in a continuous flow down through holes in thick brass drawplates or dies, the trafile di bronzo.

The Latini, like an elite few other artisan pasta makers in Italy, use the unlined brass trafile to keep the exterior rough and porous, though nearly all pastifici of a certain size, including Mennilli, use Teflon-lined slots to give the pasta a smooth surface. Carlo showed me some trafile, which for pasta corta are thick disks with relatively large holes and for pasta lunga are elongated rectangular plates with many more slots.

Each type of pasta has its own trafila with holes of uniform size and pattern to shape it and rotating blades underneath that automatically cut it to length. Among pasta lunga, spaghetti and the slimmer spaghettini are forced through round holes; spaghetti and spaghettini *alla chitarra* through square ones; *trenette* and *taglierini* through slender rectangular ones. The exiting strands are cut long and draped over *canne*, which refers to the cane poles that were used for drying in the past, though today rods of acacia wood are used for the *essiccazione*.

Most pasta corta is tubular, so the dough is compressed in the slots and then forced out through closed circular apertures, leaving it hollow in the middle. Each piece is cut to prescribed length and angle by revolving blades. The same trafila is used for both the ribbed maccheroni, cut short and straight at the ends, and the even shorter *maccheroncini*. Likewise, penne and the shorter *pennette*, ribbed tubes trimmed obliquely, share a trafila. *Conchigliette* are ribbed tubes forced through curved slots to form arcs. *Strozzapreti* (''priest stranglers'') in the Latini version are a solid, smooth pasta cut short and wrapped into twin furls. There are two types of minestrina: *stelline*, six-pointed stars, and *semini*, which resemble grape seeds.

The ultimate step that distinguishes the pasta of Latini and a few other artisans from the industrial types is the traditional slow, gentle drying. During the first phase, known as *incartamento*, the freshly cut pasta is blown by warm, dry air for about ten minutes to firm it up and prevent pieces from sticking together. Pasta lunga remains draped over canne, but the freshly cut pieces of pasta corta and pastina drop onto belts that keep them in motion in the closed chamber so that they dry uniformly.

Uneven or excessive heat can make them hard and brittle. Then they are transferred into the *essiccatoi*, ventilated shafts where temperatures are gradually alternated between 95° and 120°F. Pasta lunga stays there for forty to forty-five hours, pasta corta somewhat less because its hollows facilitate drying.

Carlo praised slow or static drying as the key to maintaining flavor and aroma. He pointed out that by contrast industrial pasta usually undergoes dynamic drying in which hot, dry air and steam are alternated in rapid sequence—a process that takes only two to four hours. Open-air drying of pasta, once common in sunny places, is no longer allowed for hygienic reasons, but, as Carlo said, it wouldn't be practical anyway, even for small producers. He noted, though, that during static drying, temperatures must not remain so low that the moist dough begins to acidify and take on a sharp or acrid taste, a defect found in some artisanal pastas.

The essential moisture content of pasta secca is limited by law to 12.5 percent maximum, since more could favor bacterial development. Good artisanal pasta should retain 11 to 12 percent humidity through months of storage, remaining firmly flexible, never dry and brittle. Such pasta also holds shape and texture in cooking, during which the boiling water should not become turbid from an excessive release of starch. Cooking increases the weight by about 150 percent, so that 100 grams of dry pasta will become 250 grams cooked.

Carlo said it takes them eight to ten hours to make 2,000 to 4,000 kilograms of pasta in various versions and put it through the incartamento. Three days later, when static drying is complete, the pasta lunga is cut to length, though the curved ends that were draped over canne are maintained in double strands. The long pasta is inserted by hand into heavy cellophane wrappers; pasta corta can be packaged automatically. The measure for all types is 500 grams, though pasta lunga takes a long box and pasta corta comes in two squatter sizes.

Carlo and Carla haul the boxes home to their small depository recently built onto the back of the house, where they apply the numbered seals over the top flaps and pack them into cartons of twenty. Carla admitted that the hand numbering is tedious, but she sees it as a guarantee of the personalized care that distinguishes their pasta from the rest. By making pasta at calculated intervals following demand, they avoid long storage. Carlo said that freshness is a factor in the flavor of dried pasta, which ideally should be eaten within sixty days, though a couple of months longer won't make a marked difference. They are required to stamp a preferred consumption date of two years hence on the package, though Carlo admitted that that's much too long.

As we headed back toward Osimo, driving against a brilliant setting sun, Carlo apologized for the limits on my visit, but observed that for the Mennilli family it signaled a new openness that he found encouraging. "When I first showed up and talked about special grains and trafile di bronzo and static drying, they thought I was crazy," he recalled. "But they went along with it because, like many family pastifici, they needed the extra revenue. Since we've been working together, we've developed a mutual respect. Of course, they've got their market and we've got ours, but I wouldn't be surprised if they moved upscale some day."

The Mennilli sell much of their pasta directly at the plant in sixty-three competitively priced types. "La Pasta" of Latini is distributed by Paolo Magnoni to specialty food and wine shops and sold directly to choice restaurants in Italy. Carlo and Carla have gradually built exports, which began when Fauchon, the Parisian food purveyor, requested exclusive distribution to shops in France. They also ship limited quantities to northern Europe and the United States.

"The business has gone better than we expected," admitted Carlo. "In fact, we're still kind of amazed by the success. But we're determined to keep it small and absolutely family-run, no matter what the demand. Of course, our main emphasis will always be on the quality of grain. When we come out with a pure Senatore Cappelli, that will bring a new strategy to the pasta market. I can't wait to see the reaction."

Nor could I, I assured him, as we sped past grainfields toward Osimo. And someday, I added, trying not to sound impatient, I hoped that Carlo and Carla would build that pastificio of their own so that I could witness the full production cycle for pasta, including the intimacies that had so far taunted me as forbidden rites.

Perhaps the most complete survey of the pasta field is *Pastario* by Eugenio Medagliani and Fernanda Gosetti, an "atlas of Italian paste alimentari" that covers the basic categories of secca, fresca, and ripiena. The index includes nearly five hundred names (many synonyms for the same type), but the authors admit that the 1989 edition of their catalogue is not exhaustive.

To those accustomed to dining in Italy, pasta outside of the country, however tasty, never seems quite the same. For one thing, non-Italians often fail to comprehend the advantages of al dente, which admittedly takes getting used to, especially when dealing with the degree of firmness favored by the Latini. But Italian chefs working abroad, who themselves wouldn't eat pasta secca any way but al dente, often compromise by catering to customers who grew up with the notion that noodles are by nature mushy.

Beyond the degree of cooking lies the art of making sauces with the unmatchable ingredients found in Italy: extra vergine olive oil, special types of vine-ripened tomatoes, basil, sage, chili peppers, garlic, onions, wild mushrooms and truffles, the freshest of Mediterranean shellfish, select meats and sausages, and well-matured Parmigiano or pecorino for grating.

Carla Latini keeps her pasta dishes quick and simple. She boils the pasta in plenty of water (about 6 quarts to 1 pound) with a couple of tablespoons of sea salt thrown in, though only for flavor, since salt isn't necessary in the cooking. Although the Latini pasta comes with advisory notes on cooking times, she suggests sampling during the boiling and relying on experience to satisfy personal concepts of al dente.

Carla and Carlo, who eat pasta at least once a day, prefer an extremely light touch on sauces or dressings, which they almost always make using their local olive oil. Their favorite ingredients are fresh, seasonal produce—tomatoes, zucchini, peas, artichokes, eggplant, basil, and porcini mushrooms, for example—or fresh seafood from the Adriatic. But their cooking is so spontaneous that recipes haven't been written down.

The Latini don't sell their pasta directly at the farm. But

travelers in the Marches, which is one of the most pleasantly civil of all Italian regions to visit, would be able to taste it at the following restaurants: Symposium at Cartoceto; Giacchetti at Portonovo; Giardino at San Lorenzo in Campo; La Grotta del Frate at Staffolo.

# Olio Extra Vergine di Oliva

## Anatomy of an almost perfect virgin

*T*he Italy of olive oil, as opposed to the Italy of butter, covers the Mediterranean sphere of the peninsula and islands. The heavy olive oil producers are Apulia, Calabria, and Sicily in the deep south. In the north, oils tend to be milder by nature, though olives grow only where winters are temperate: along the Ligurian Sea and the Gulf of Trieste, in the Adriatic hills of Romagna, and in the lake country, mainly around Garda. To my taste, though, *olio extra vergine di oliva* has found its promised land at the nation's heart, in the hills of Tuscany, where climes compel the tree of the gods to show all of its venerable mettle.

My preference, if shared by a quorum of critics, reflects a stubborn bias, since I cultivate olives in Tuscany for my own oil. Or, I should say, *our* own oil, for the token production is a family affair. It's for home use only, but if it were for sale the price would be prohibitive. Not because ours is necessarily the world's greatest olive oil, but because, as the pride of do-it-yourself *olivicoltori,* the time and effort behind it exceed rational limits. Still, even when made with a measure of efficiency, a true Tuscan extra vergine rates appraisal as liquid gold.

The most vaunted of virgins come from olives picked by hand on cold days of late autumn in groves of shimmering silver-green that embellish the terraced hillsides around Florence, Siena, Pistoia, and Arezzo. By tradition the olives were bundled in sacks and brought to the *frantoio* to be ground under massive stone wheels into pulp, then layered onto circular mats and pressed cold to render only a fifth to a tenth of the original weight in oil.

Tuscans, and Tuscans by adoption, savor oil fresh from the frantoio, when its vivid green color is still murky, its aroma is pungently vital, and its flavor is said to *pizzica,* pique the tongue with the artichoke-like nip of underripe olives. After months of storage in cool cellars in *giare,* portly terra-cotta vases with wooden lids, its aromas and flavors mellow into harmony as it settles to become almost limpid with golden highlights, reminiscent of emerald or jade.

More than the most wholesome of comestible oils, pristine extra vergine is the most pleasing to the eye, nose, and palate. It is best used raw as a condiment or mixed discreetly in dressings or sauces. Tuscans sop up *olio* with their unsalted bread and dribble it into certain soups and pastas, using it as a garnish for vegetables and greens, as well as for the legendary *bistecca alla fiorentina* and *fagioli,* stewed haricot beans. When the oil of a particular hillside or farm shows its innate personality, then extra vergine compares to a standard olio di oliva as a *grand cru classé* relates to a blended and pasteurized jug wine.

Full-flavored oils of similar type are made in neighboring Umbria and occasionally in the Marches, the Sabine hills near Rome, and in the Mezzogiorno. But they must come from olives picked early to have the key quality factor of low acidity. The other prominent style of oil is lighter in color and subtler in aroma and flavor, as made from fully mature olives in Liguria, in coastal places of central Italy, and points north.

Whatever the origins, it must be extra vergine (also written *extravergine*). That distinction doesn't always denote the paragon of virtue, however, even if it does convey the curious conception that virginity in olive oils may transcend a state which in mortals is considered absolute. Italians tend to overlook the apparent contradiction, maybe because, living in a land where almost anything that ranks a notch or two above the norm carries the suffix *issimo*, they've become inured to superlatives. Anyway, it's common knowledge among them that a label claim intended to distinguish the purest of oils from an ordinary vergine or a mere olio di oliva has been roundly abused by blenders and bottlers.

More than 90 percent of the world's olive oil comes from Mediterranean lands. Italy makes a quarter to a third of the total, depending on the fortunes of each harvest, though its output has been surpassed in some recent years by Spain. Italians, as the most prolific users of olive oil at 12 liters a head per year, import a share of their needs from Spain and Tunisia.

As the essence of the Mediterranean diet, olive oil of all types continues to gain favor in a country whose historic culinary division is no longer so clear-cut. Northerners, impressed by the message that rates of heart disease, digestive disorders, and obesity are lower in the Italy of olive oil, have learned to reconcile it with or substitute it for the habitual butter and lard.

Extra vergine represents more than half of retail sales of olive oil in Italy. But the presence of suspiciously cheap versions of uncertain origin has tended to level a market dominated by a dozen brands, including some that sell in supermarkets for as little as 5,000 lire for a standard bottle. In contrast, an estate-bottled Tuscan extra vergine might cost more than five times that much in a shop and represent truer value. Many Italians still regard wine and oil as cheap commodities. But discriminating buyers, following a pattern set with fine wine over the last couple of decades, are coming to appreciate that the choicest oils are worth the elevated price. Although extracts from vegetables, seeds, and nuts dominate the market, Italy's elite extra vergine has become the most coveted of the world's comestible oils.

A key step toward clarity in labeling and consumer trust came with a recent law to establish zones of *denominazione di origine controllata* (DOC), where extra vergine or vergine may carry a geographical name only after passing a panel tasting for authenticity. Quality won't be guaranteed, but at least DOC, as it takes effect in coming years, should serve as a guide to the types of oil found from one region to another. In the meantime, though, confusion reigns in Italy and abroad about the official classifications of olive oils.

Extra vergine must be extracted from the first pressing of olives by mechanical means only (without use of chemicals) and must contain less than 1 percent of oleic acid. Next in rank comes vergine, with the same rules of extraction and a maximum of 2 percent acidity, though that is already well above the limits of finesse. Then comes olio di oliva, from blends dominated by inferior oils chemically rectified, deodorized, and deacidified to 1.5 percent maximum (and sometimes exported all too grandly as ''pure Italian olive oil''). There is also a utilitarian market in Italy for *olio di sansa di oliva,* from rectified dregs of pressed olives.

Unscrupulous bottlers of ''extra vergine'' had managed to skirt rules about extraction up to now by blending first-press oils with lesser types while remaining under the limit of 1 percent acidity. But new European Community norms require detailed chemical analysis of all grades of olive oil following criteria that range beyond acidity. Estimates are that as much as half of what had been labeled extra vergine—or the equivalent in Spanish, French, Greek, or other languages—would be demoted. The new standards should also assure that anything labeled olio di oliva derives entirely from olives, as was not always the case before.

The lesser oils are best for cooking, though like extra vergine they contain the oleic acid that derives mainly from the fruit of the olive as a monounsaturated fat that tends to lower the so-called bad blood cholesterol and reduce the risk of arteriosclerosis. Being easily digestible, olive oil is more readily assimilated as a source of energy than are saturated or polyunsaturated fats, a favorable factor in weight control. Extra vergine oil, when extracted cold, as it should be, retains integral vitamins, nutrients, and even an element that seems to combat the aging of cells in the human body. But among connoisseurs, health considerations bow to questions of taste. They insist that the only olio di oliva worthy of the name is a pedigreed extra vergine.

It's sometimes said that the better the oil, the more complex its personality. Nuances derive primarily from the plant: the terrain and climate in which it grows and the varieties of trees. Italy has more than a hundred cultivars that produce olives of diverse size, shape, color, texture, and flavor. These include table varieties, grown mainly in the south, though most cultivars are designated for oil. Each region has its preferential types, which are often blended to give the oil composite tones. Since each year's crop differs in quantity and quality of olives, vintages for extra vergine oils can be as important as they are for premium wines.

Beyond nature's variables, the style, class, and durability of an oil rely on the timing and method of harvesting. Hand picking of underripe olives is time-consuming and costly, but when pressed immediately they render superior oil. Yet much extra vergine comes from mature olives caught in nets as branches are struck with poles or trunks are shaken by machines. The bruising and battering can cause oxidation, but such oils are usually better than those from olives gathered at low cost in late winter after they finally drop from the trees. As olives ripen, their acidity rises. Oleic acid is scarcely perceptible on the palate, but as a rule the lower an oil's acidity—ideally from 0.2 to 0.4 percent—the fuller the aroma and flavor.

The ultimate determinant of quality is the method of extraction. Stone crushing and mat pressing are now rare in Italy, practiced mainly in small frantoi in Tuscany and choice other places where oils are prized. A few artisans use the *sinolea* technique to render *olio fiore,* an unpressed, free-run oil. But most of Italy's extra vergine is extracted by mechanical mashing and centrifugal pressing. Such processing at moderate temperatures can produce good oil, but if heat rises or hot water is added to facilitate the operation, the consequences are a loss of aroma and flavor and a bitter aftertaste that becomes more pronounced with age.

Nearly all oils are filtered before bottling to rid them of *morchia*, brownish dregs that cause stale odors. Artisans prefer cotton filters, but commercial firms use the more thorough cellulose to satisfy the mistaken notion that clarity signifies purity. If exposed to extreme cold, some oils develop clots like cheese curds, though these disappear with no lasting effects. An unfiltered extra vergine, if carefully separated from its dregs, retains more flavor and food value. If it has low acidity (under 0.5 percent), it should remain slightly opaque, a favorable sign as color turns from lively hues of green toward muted shades of gold.

That enticing youthful piquancy will fade, but a fine extra vergine should stay fresh for a year or more if stored in a cool, dark place. Although virgin oils contain natural anti-oxidants, exposure to heat and light cause rapid deterioration. Oil doesn't improve with age, but as it grows milder it becomes more agreeable to some palates. The flavor of a mature oil should strike a balance between bracing and mellow, with velvety texture and firm body, neither thick nor thin, and never flabby, greasy, or cloying.

Although Tuscans describe their best oils as fruity, associations are often with vegetables or nuts, such as artichokes, celery, green tomatoes, hazelnuts, or almonds. Scents suggesting fruits, such as bananas, ripe apples, or melons, indicate that the oil is turning rancid. Moldy odors indicate oxidation, also revealed by hints of rusting metal or lubricating oil.

Production standards vary widely, yet experts generally agree that the class of extra vergine has risen overall, even if Italy could do much more to realize its potential for excellence. So, for that matter, could Spain, Portugal, France, Greece, and the few other countries that boast an active olive oil industry. Demand for fine extra virgin oils seems destined to mount as modes in western cuisine turn increasingly back toward the millennial roots in the Mediterranean.

The wild olive or oleaster seems to have been domesticated in the Near East around 6000 B.C. But the olive, unlike other stone fruits such as cherries and plums, isn't pleasant to eat fresh, so ancient peoples learned to assuage its bitter-acrid flavors through cooking or seasoning or steeping in brine. It came to be valued above all for its oil, which served not only as a cooking medium, condiment, and preserver of other foods, but as a base for medicines, ointments, soaps, and cosmetics, as a lubricant for machinery, and for centuries as the primary fuel for lamps and burners.

Egyptians, Hebrews, Greeks, and Romans granted sacred status to a plant that grows slowly but whose roots have a seemingly perpetuous capacity to regenerate and yield fruit in the arid, stony soils around the Mediterranean. Trees, which may be as majestic in stature as oaks or as diminutive as holly bushes, have contorted trunks that with time develop cracks, dimples, and hollows, enlarged where growers carve away dead wood. Their scraggly, supple branches bristle with slender, leathery leaves of evergreen with a substrata of silver, a sign of prosperity in Mediterranean lands and a venerable symbol of peace.

The Greeks, to whom the olive was a gift of the goddess Athena, spread its culture to their colonies of Magna Græcia in southern Italy. Yet *olivicoltura* may have been practiced as far north as Tuscany 3,500 years ago, since a tree in the Maremma near the Tyrrhenian coast is purported to be that old. If so, it would have preceded not only Greeks but Etruscans.

The Romans, with customary enterprise, developed the commerce of olives, classifying oil in five types. Olive oil, often flavored with aromatic herbs and spices, was used more lavishly in Roman times than in the centuries that followed. The author Columella, who ranked the olive first among trees, described methods of cultivation and extracting oil. These changed little until modern times, when the donkeys that turned the stone crushing wheels in slow motion were replaced by motors and pneumatic compressors made obsolete the *torchio,* the heavy wooden press that now serves as the centerpiece in many a country museum.

After the empire's fall, the olive was nurtured mainly by Benedictines, who coveted its oil in their frugal repasts, while rationing out enough to anoint foreheads at confirmation and extreme unction. A gradual revival was recorded in the late Middle Ages, though olives only began to thrive again during the Renaissance, especially in the south. Tuscans grew olives as one of several essential crops following patterns of farming pioneered by their ancestral Etruscans, who also evaluated oil more in terms of quality than quantity.

The provinces of Florence and Siena, taking in the hills of Chianti, became the focus of wine and olive oil production, as slopes around fortified castles, abbeys, and hamlets of what was long a battleground were converted into peaceful farms. With time, estates known as *fattorie* were established by the titled and well-to-do, whose castles and villas with shaded gardens and cypress-lined lanes became abodes for gracious living. But Chianti's enduring appeal lies in a cultured rusticity achieved over centuries of toil by *contadini*, whose stone houses, terraced fields, and manicured woods pose pictures of rural harmony.

Each fattoria was tidily portioned into fractions where crops were grown in mixed or what was quaintly described as "promiscuous" culture. The contadini, as they hewed the stony slopes into terraces, positioned the *olivo* or *ulivo* on the outer rim, interspersed with fruit and nut trees and willows and poplars purposely stunted to support vines, while leaving a strip between rows so that they could pass with teams of oxen to plow for field crops.

The status of country folk changed little as systems evolved from serfdom to sharecropping, the *mezzadria* that weathered reforms until after World War II. But the trials of tenant farming endowed contadini with a savvy that allowed them to eat better than the landlords, at least when times were good. After all, they had the first pick of produce and game, the know-how to store vegetables, fruit, grains, and meat beyond their seasons, the skills to make bread, cheese, and wine as the good Lord intended. Oil was provision and protector, preserving tomatoes, artichokes, mushrooms, salame, and little forms of pecorino cheese in vases *sott'olio* and even sealing wine, since it naturally rose to the top of flasks and demijohns. Although it never played a lead role at the table, olio was valued above all other products of the Tuscan farm.

An age-old rule of thumb had it that the best olive oil was worth more by weight than the choicest cut of beef or veal. But mass distribution has blunted the oil market so that these days a liter of fine extra vergine from the Florentine hills would cost no more than three-quarters the price of a kilogram of prime filet. Even the most expensive oils are in a sense underpriced.

Other regions of central Italy produce admirable oils, especially Umbria, where the extra vergine of Spoleto and the Nera Valley can be outstanding. But over the years I've absorbed enough of the native pride and prejudice to pronounce Tuscan oil tops, though only if made following the strictest rules of the craft from olives grown in special places.

The Eden of extra vergine covers much of central Tuscany: the Chianti Classico zone between Florence and Siena and the adjacent slopes along the arching course of the Arno, extending from Pistoia and the Montalbano hills west of Florence up the valley past Pontassieve and Incisa to the Chianti and Pratomagno ranges on the edge of the Apennines.

Trees there are always planted on hillsides, still often terraced, in calcareous soils that need to be well drained, since olives require moisture in small doses during the season. Summers are usually sunny and mild, though droughts sometimes persist long enough to reduce the crop. At heights of about 1,000 to 2,000 feet, occasionally higher, winter temperatures approach the limits of cold that the plant can tolerate. This inhibits production, so that the average yield per tree is about 22 pounds of olives for at most 2 liters of oil. Along the Tuscan coast, rates regularly double that, though in parts of the south where olivicoltura has remained unafflicted for centuries, yields of 220 to 330 pounds per plant are recorded.

Since appreciation may be as much a matter of habit as of taste, I can understand why some prefer the riper, sweeter flavors of oils from warmer places, such as the wine towns of Monte-pulciano and Montalcino to the south, or the maritime hills stretching from Lucca and Pisa down along the coast past Livorno to Grosseto and the Maremma. But I'm hopelessly addicted to the oils from the region's core, where slow ripening seems to account for an extra dimension of fruitiness in aroma and flavor, better balance, and greater durability. There seems to be something to the adage that olives must struggle to produce great oil.

But the annual struggle has been lost more than once, as in January 1985, when arctic winds battered the region, freezing 17 million of 22 million olive trees. They were subsequently leveled, a scenic disaster for a landscape identified for centuries by the olive and the vine. Since then, renewed growth from the surviving roots and fresh plantings have come to fruition, so the countryside has regained some of its former splendor, but oil production was dealt such a crippling blow that previous quotas may never be reached again.

Many farmers abandoned olives, and small frantoi shut down. Yet some Tuscans look back on the great freeze as a bless-ing in disguise, since it encouraged more practical methods of cultivation. New groves have been planted in neatly spaced rows with irrigation tubes strung between trees, now pruned to levels that allow them to be harvested by hand from the ground, mean-ing that pickers no longer need to resort to ladders or feats of climbing.

The revival has set off rumblings of a renaissance, as the extra vergine of Chianti and environs draws increasing praise from writers, restaurateurs, and gourmets. Moves to establish DOC zones for extra vergine were advancing in the central hills, de-

spite some discord over denominations. Meanwhile, the aristocratic trademark Laudemio emerged for extra vergine made by
fifty-five fattorie in the area under strict, self-imposed rules to
be sold in a uniform octagonal bottle in a carton to protect it
from light. These elite *olivanti* include the historic wine houses
of Marchesi L.& P. Antinori, Marchesi de' Frescobaldi, Barone
Ricasoli's Castello di Brolio, and Ruffino, though oil sold as Laudemio must come only from their private estates.

But even producers with marketing clout face an uphill battle
in convincing the public that their august oils are worth that
much more than the ubiquitous supermarket brands. Today few
fattorie can afford to maintain a private frantoio, as processing
becomes centered in larger plants with modern equipment. Still,
the cost of making oil from hand-picked olives is so elevated that
it can't be sold at competitive prices. Since genuine extra vergine
is the sine qua non of *la cucina toscana,* estates often present it
with their wine and other home-grown produce to generate prestige rather than profits. But to growers so amateurish as to disregard the economics, olivicoltura could only be a labor of love.

My passion for extra virgins dates back decades, though only
as affairs became intimate did I realize how much patience is
needed to procure one. The early lessons were learned at a place
called Teverina, in the lonesome hills above Cortona, where my
wife, Nancy, and I bought a run-down farm in 1969, envisioning
a relaxing vacation retreat.

While stonemasons renovated the house, we set out to spruce
up the land on which sadly neglected olive trees were scattered
over a sizable tract of precipitous terraces. Forget the rest and
recreation; our sojourns turned into sweaty bouts of liberating

olive, fruit, and nut trees from encroaching brush and brambles, which only reattacked with greater vengeance. Those sporadic labors delighted the neighbors, who took advantage of our autumnal absences to strip the now accessible trees of olives and add the bounty to their own supply of oil, rewarding us with a jug or two when we showed up for the holidays.

But in 1977 we surprised them and settled in with aspirations that went beyond writing, housekeeping, and raising kids, to trying our hands at farming. Enthusiasm can substitute for know-how in some facets of agriculture, but not with olives. Our modest goal of making enough oil for family needs would never have been met without a little help from our friends.

One morning in March we spotted the neighbors pruning and decided to follow suit, taking up shears and saws with reckless determination. Luckily, Gino, an amiable meddler from a farm across the way, noticed our efforts and hurried over to warn us that the pruning of olives took a God-given knack with which he had been blessed but we evidently hadn't. He took up our cause with energy that belied his advanced years, rambling from tree to tree as nimbly as an orangutan, trimming branches with rusty shears and a billhook, a double-bladed hacking tool used locally since prehistoric times.

It was hard to keep up with either his tactics or his helpful hints, because Gino, whose nickname, Bossolo, refers to a shotgun cartridge, worked almost as quickly as he talked. His soliloquy was salted with folk sayings and peppered with expletives that ranged beyond the usual Tuscan oaths linking saints with animals to terms he'd picked up as a POW in England during the war.

As he clipped and chopped, he'd blurt out the choicest in comic English with a lusty laugh that reverberated through the valley.

Eventually he managed to get across to us that he was shaping the trees like chalices so that the sun's rays would reach the leaves not only around the rim but also at the center. He said, though, that pruning must be kept to a minimum because the goal of all conta-dini—including us, presumably—was maximum annual produc-tion. Before he left for home, after downing several tumblers of a rustic *vino rosso*, Bossolo reminded us that our trees needed an invig-orating dose of fertilizer, recommending bags containing pellets of potassium, nitrogen, and phosphorus in lieu of hard-to-get manure. He also warned with a puckish grin and a show of his gnarled, cal-loused hands that olives need plenty of hoeing.

Bossolo's pruning took a few hours; the hoeing seemed in-terminable. The Tuscan *zappa* is not your country gentleman's garden utensil but the most earnest of a yeoman's tools. Its hefty handle, hewn from a chestnut sapling, supports a wide cast-iron blade with an axlike cutting edge to be wielded like a weapon in assailing earth packed with clay and stones and riddled with sinewy roots of broom, heather, briar, and thorns. First the fer-tilizer needed to be buried deep in a circle. Then, during the season, brush and weeds needed to be cleared and the packed earth loosened so that any precious rain that fell over the summer would soak into the subsoil. There were suckers to cut away from the base of the trunk and along the limbs. And when there was drought, the younger trees required water hauled down the hillsides on foot.

Production gradually increased. But, as we came to realize,

no matter how hard you push them, olives set their own agonizing pace: feast one year, famine the next. There were times when they seemed to be more trouble than they were worth—on a sweltering afternoon of hoeing, for instance, or during a frustratingly light harvest. But those moods passed, perhaps because olives have a soothing permanence about them, an aura of eternal youth that seems all the more magical if you hail from the prairies of Minnesota or a suburb of New York.

Some trees are ample and proud, others scrawny and shy, but as you get to know them they reveal staunch individuality in an antique anima that renews itself with each year's cycle. The exuberant new growth of spring culminates in garlands of tiny, pale yellow blossoms that fall away as the fruit emerges like microscopic peas that expand ever so slowly to assume the shapes and sizes predestined for each cultivar. The evolution accelerates with the first chill of autumn as skins turn toward violet, brown, verdigris, sometimes blotchy or streaked, until November, when some become plump and shiny and others turn to ebony and start to shrivel. That signals harvest time in Tuscany, the exhilarating climax of the olive's enduring year.

On sunny days, picking could seem like a picnic after the previous toils. But by December, when we began, the cold could numb fingers and turn rain to snow. Olives must be harvested dry; moisture induces rancidity. In our territory most pickers used the *brucatura a mano*, which involves ''milking'' each branch with tugs of the fist that cast a few olives at a time into a basket bound by a belt around the waist. A fast picker in a compact grove can harvest well over 220 pounds a day, but we rarely reached half that amount. It took time to make the rounds of our awkwardly dispersed trees, some of which had reached heights that required acrobatic scrambles up trunks and limbs to reach the higher branches.

It took three or four days to gather the olives, which we stored by spreading over a brick floor to keep cool and dry before packing them into burlap sacks and toting them to the frantoio. But in the erratic workings of the old mill there was often a lapse of a day or two before crushing, while the olives moldered in the attic. Since our batches were small—our record at Teverina was 320 pounds of olives for 30 liters of oil—they had to be done with larger lots.

The enticingly raw odor of crushed olives pervaded the frantoio, but witnessing the oil-making process required a long wait in the oppressive noise and heat generated by machinery working around the clock. The olives, after being rinsed with cold water and drained, were fed through a chute to a device known as a *premolitore*, where jagged metal rollers split open the skins and pits. This break expedited the crushing between solid blocks of carved granite used both in the tandem of wheels, known as *molazze*, and the circular base on which they revolved within a tub whose metal rim gave it the shape of a soup bowl. The *frangitura* or *molitura* took about a half hour, grinding the olives into a lumpy, khaki-colored mush.

Then a slot was opened on the side and the mass was raked through into a long vat, where it was kneaded for about twenty minutes by gyrating steel paddles. During this *gramolatura* the pulp became smoother and warmer, as minute drops of oil accumulated into larger ones that were more readily extracted as the fluids were separated from the solids in the pressing or *spremitura*.

Workers rapidly spread the paste onto circular mats of woven hemp (now made of synthetic fibers) with holes in the middle to hold them on a spindle as they piled them head high. Metal disks had been inserted at intervals to keep the column rigid as a pneumatic press applied force that built to nearly 400 atmospheres over an hour or so, constricting the *fiscoli* like the pleats of an accordion and squeezing out brownish-yellow liquid that oozed down the sides.

A vintage-model centrifuge separated the oil from the olive's waste vegetal water. Some *fattorie* with their own *frantoi* then still separated by decantation, as the lighter oil rose and was drawn off the top, a process repeated through a series of descending tanks. But that took days or weeks to render a pure oil. When our batch was ready, a weary *frantoiano* filtered it through cotton, weighed it, and, with the aid of a pocket calculator, divvied up the spoils after working out his fee (based on the original weight of the olives, not the oil).

After the vigil, the new oil offered immediate satisfaction with a finger-licking taste as it was poured from a copper pitcher in a golden-green stream as dense as dairy cream swirling through a funnel into our demijohn. That evening there would be a *festa* at home, with grilled pork sausages, roasted chestnuts, and slabs of bread toasted over wood coals, rubbed with raw garlic, and doused with the pungent oil that for once forsook its supporting role to become a primadonna. The toast, known as *bruschetta* at Teverina, was called *fettunta* or *panunto* a short distance to the north in the Arno Valley, where we moved in 1982.

The transfer toward Florence was intended to bring the chil-

dren closer to schools, but it also placed us at the eastern edge of
the Eden of oil, on the slopes of the Pratomagno range in a hamlet
with the propitious name of Oliveto. Once there had even been
a frantoio, but it had been dismantled, its stones probably used
to build walls of a house that had been pieced together in stages
since the 1500s. The drawback was that we now possessed just
a parcel of cultivable land with a working base of a mere fifty
olive trees in need of revitalization.

We kept doing things contadino-style: hoeing in standard
fertilizer, hiring people to prune, and using the frantoio down
the hill. Oliveto's oil outshone Teverina's, but supplies had
barely begun to meet our needs when hopes were dashed by the
freeze of 1985. It was a bitter blow for local growers. I'll never
forget Eletto's voice choking as he told us how it felt to lose the
company of lifelong friends, or Mario's grim visage as he toppled
the wilted cadavers with a chain saw, taking solace in the fact
that we'd have some extra firewood.

Yet scarcely had the winter's mourning subsided when from
the stumps sprouted shoots that became bushes over summer with
a flourish that reminded doubters that old olives never die but
are resurrected from their secular roots. The survivors protruding
amid weeds on our terraces heralded yet another new beginning.
But this time we decided to get expert advice, turning to Maurizio
Castelli, renowned as a winemaker, though equally worthy of
note as the architect of some of Chianti's finest estate oils.

Maurizio, a philosophical type with the stature of a body-
guard, listened with a vaguely bemused expression as we voiced
our desire to make extra vergine as close to perfection as fate

would consent. He took our mandate with a charitable grin that twitched his bushy mustache, but he warned that we faced some challenges as he weighed the pros and cons.

At nearly 2,000 feet above sea level, Oliveto is close to the olive's upper bounds, though full southern exposure creates a reasonably cozy habitat. Winters are too cold for the dreaded *mosca*, the fly whose eggs cause some olives to drop prematurely while lending a distinctly unpleasant odor to oil from the rest. So there would be no need for pesticides or other chemicals. But the soil needed a buildup through a studied blend of fertilizers over a couple of years to achieve a balance. After that, though, it was to be manure and more manure, however costly. And that meant, as if I needed to be reminded, hoeing and more hoeing.

The traditional mixing of cultivars favors cross-pollination between trees, helping to build yields. Also, since each variety performs differently from year to year, strengths and weaknesses tend to compensate for each other in the blend of oil. Maurizio said that our trees were dominated by Moraiolo, source of a creditably suave oil, followed by Leccino, somewhat milder. There wasn't enough Frantoio, he observed, pointing out that it contributes much of the fruity zest to the best oils. We found space for a dozen seedlings: Frantoio and Pendolino, a prolific variety whose bowing branches make it easy to pick. But, as the maestro cautioned, it might take a decade for our miscellaneous band to become a sonorous orchestra.

Maurizio, who took a degree in agronomy in his native Milan before settling in Tuscany, is a more sophisticated pruner than was Bossolo. But he's also more ruthless, shaping limbs along the new lines of keeping everything within easy reach. After years of watching tree surgeons operate, I've never felt that enough of the providential knack had rubbed off on me to risk imitating them. So, as Maurizio cuts, I keep busy clipping suckers, while Nancy, still determined to learn, sighs and groans through the amputations.

Slowly but surely our olives came back, though for years we suffered the humiliation of buying oil from places in Umbria and along the coast where trees hadn't been frozen. In 1987, we resumed with 7 liters of oil as treasured as Alba truffles. But through it all we were compelled to mix our pickings with a neighbor's to meet the quota at the local frantoio. Only with the 1992 harvest did we finally have enough olives for an oil all our own.

Maurizio booked us in at the new frantoio at Castello di Volpaia, with its revelationary sinolea system. He insisted that we pick early for an oil of low acidity and maximum fruitiness, even if that meant having a little less quantity than from riper olives. We had sworn off ever again letting olives sit in bags to ferment and oxidize, after admitting that our oil at Teverina was sometimes a bit funky. Maurizio, promising that at Volpaia our olives would be crushed *presto,* supplied stackable plastic crates to keep them dry and ventilated.

We were ready to go in mid-November, but that autumn's monsoon-like rains didn't let up until late in the month. Then, in warm sunshine amplified by reflection off a pillow of fog in the Arno Valley below, we picked our bumper crop in two days. The olives, if unavoidably riper than desired, looked glowingly healthy. Filled with optimism, I loaded the crates into the van and drove across the valley into the hills of Chianti, past Badia a Coltibuono and Radda and up the curving lane to the stone-walled aerie of Volpaia.

The frantoio had been tucked into the base of a building whose facade, with wooden shutters flanking doors and windows, looks like a typical house in the medieval hamlet. For, like all the components of an estate that occupies about half of Volpaia's intimate spaces, it was designed with tact and taste to fit the ambience. Inside the compact mill, lined with blue and white tiles, great stone wheels churned a testimonial to the past amid gleaming apparatuses that mirrored advances in olive oil's state of the art.

Saverio, a bearded young man in green coveralls, arrived on a motorcycle to show me where to take the crates. Within minutes, his eager crew had weighed in our olives. The 754 pounds, I reckoned, would render a liter of oil for every week of the year, with a bit left over for friends. Our olives didn't need washing, because cleanliness is the first rule for pickers under Maurizio's command. Nor had we ripped away many leaves, the way some do, having taken to heart the messages that chlorophyll from the foliage adds an acrid taste to the oil and that darker green isn't a sign of quality anyway, despite myths to the contrary.

The olives were dumped into a receptacle with a spiral conveyor to propel them through a chute straight to the molazze, without the initial splitting done in most frantoi. As the rolling stones pummeled them in a pitiless assault, our multicolored gems were reduced to a rubble of pulp, pits, and skins that soon became a khaki-purple pudding. Purple? I wondered. That wasn't the usual hue. Not to worry, said Saverio. He'd seen that anomaly a couple of times before and the oil had turned out okay.

I was fretting anyway when Carlo Mascheroni showed up. His wife, Giovannella Stianti, is named on labels as Castello di Volpaia's owner, but Carlo is the financier, investing earnings from his accounting firm at Monza, near Milan, in a model wine estate with an annex for vinegar. The latest folly, as he put it, was the frantoio. "Among all options the sinolea system was the most expensive," he confided with a wry grin. "We'll never earn back our investment. But it enables us to make oil in the best traditional style without the usual drawbacks and doubts."

Granite wheels were chosen over more expedient mechanical hammers and rollers, because the stones crush the olives at moderate temperature, essential for conserving flavor and nutrients. They're also gentler, since the molazze don't totally smash the olive pits, meaning that the oil cells release larger drops that are more readily extracted by sinolea. Another benefit is that the granite as it grinds together cedes traces of silica, a mineral compound that not only aids extraction of oil but is credited with heightening its aroma.

After kneading in a standard *gramolatrice*, our batch was ready for the sinolea extraction. The crew spread the puce-tinted pâté in layers on trays within the apparatus, an open-sided metal box whose interior parts are all stainless steel. As it clattered into action, Carlo explained that during the process known as *percolamento* thousands of laminated blades penetrate the paste at the rate of six thrusts a minute, emerging with a filmy liquid that contains more oil than vegetal water. With each exit they deposit a few drops into two elongated sheaths from which the liquid drains into a vat. No more than half an hour had passed when Saverio stopped the machine and announced rather uneasily that the extraction was over. Only a light centrifuging was needed to separate the free-run oil from the waste water.

Carlo pointed out that sinolea's unique drip method is quicker and cleaner than mat pressing and the oil doesn't undergo the trauma of pressure. Temperatures during the process rarely rise above 68°F (the limit for cold-pressed oil is 100°F). Blessed with the olive's inborn powers of self-preservation, this olio fiore is as close to pure and natural as oil can be. But since sinolea doesn't extract all of the olives' potential oil, the remaining paste is centrifuged at slightly higher speed and temperature to bring the total yield up to normal. This second extraction compares favorably with much traditional oil and is a healthy cut above mass-market ''extra vergine.''

Carlo admitted that if mat pressing is done in an initial soft phase, the oil that runs off from a gentle squeeze may also qualify as fiore and can compare to sinolea's. But few frantoi can take the time to stop and start over. Still, most of Tuscany's upper-echelon oils are made under the old system by frantoiani with the integrity to let up before the paste requires extreme unction. The remains, called sansa, are usually sold to industrial firms which use chemical and heating treatments to extract the lesser oils. But faithful artisans are all too few in an industry ruled by giants, some of whom publicize the virtues of extra vergine while selling oils that need to be ''corrected'' to be palatable.

Tuscany's persevering olivanti gallantly buck the tide of cheap oils. Castello di Volpaia may soon complement its excellent extra vergine with pure ''varietals'' from the cultivars of Frantoio, Leccino, and Pendolino. Badia a Coltibuono, one of the name estates that use Volpaia's frantoio, sells a rare unfiltered extra vergine from its *cru* of Albereto. As they explain it, what olio drains away from profits it replenishes in prestige.

Public relations were the least of my concerns as I waited for our oil. Soon Saverio arrived with the air of an intern bearing hard news about a patient. The yield was 11 percent, he said, or 38 liters of oil. That wasn't too bad, since rates from rain-swollen olives were running at only 10 to 14 percent that year, compared with the normal average of 17 percent. The odd part was that the percentage of sinolea to second-extraction oil (ideally 75-25, rarely lower than 60-40) was an even 50-50. "That's the lowest I've ever seen," he confessed. "But I'm not sure why. You'd better ask Maurizio."

Is it purple? I asked, bracing for the worst. "No, it's a healthy green," he assured me, and poured our meager rations into canisters to prove it. I took an apprehensive lick of the sinolea. Not bad. No, not bad at all. A second taste tempted me to describe it as elegant, but I settled for suave. It had finely fruity aroma, smooth texture, and mellow flavor with less than the usual bite, but that's a trait of sinolea. There wasn't even a hint of the bitter taste that had marred some oils in the past. Saverio reminded me that it hadn't been filtered, so I'd need to rack it off the dregs in a couple of weeks. "*Coraggio,*" he said, as I departed. "You'll do better next year."

The next day Maurizio arrived with the lab report and an explanation. Moraiolo ripens earlier than other olives, as its usual pale verdant flesh turns ruddy: hence the color. The pulp was so waterlogged that it prevented oil from massing in the big drops extracted by sinolea, which explained why Saverio stopped the process early.

But the good news was that the analysis was normal. That listed the likes of *acido lignocerico, brossicasterolo,* and *delta 7 stigmesterolo,* terms that meant as much to me in Italian as they would have in English. But the gist was that with acidity at an enviable 0.3 percent, ample polyphenols, and minimal oxidizing components, our oil had fine balance and keeping potential. ''Clinically speaking,'' beamed Maurizio, ''it's *quasi perfetto.*''

That's nice, I agreed, if only we had a little more of it. To that end, he prescribed a couple more loads of manure over the winter. ''Next year you've got to pick earlier,'' he admonished. Okay, so next year we'd do sundances at harvest time. In the meantime, though, there would be clearing and pruning and, of course, the joyous rituals of the hoe.

The axiom that veritable extra vergine is best young and at home is not a Tuscan tourist ploy, for oil is sensitive to the heat, light, and motion that it might be exposed to in travel. Still, consumers abroad can be reasonably sure of quality by buying the oil of reputable estates or companies (the group trademark Laudemio is reliable). But always check the vintage or, better, the date of bottling to be sure that it is no more than a year old. Extra vergine should be stored in the cellar with wine, but only to keep it fresh, not because it improves with age. The best exported Tuscan extra vergine should be costly. Bargain prices only indicate inferiority or oil past its prime.

Other Italians rarely use extra vergine as liberally as do Tuscans, who keep the oil bottle (or metal can with a spout) on the table alongside the salt. It's *the* condiment for vegetables and greens, especially fresh tomatoes and basil. It brings unexpected glory to spinach, turnip greens, broccoli, or black cabbage (which makes a wholesome topping for fettunta). Mixed with a little wine vinegar (or, if possible, *aceto balsamico*), it dresses salads or makes a vegetable dip called *pizzimonio*. Although *spaghetti all'aglio, olio, e peperoncini* has southern roots, nothing underlines the zip of garlic and chili peppers like a young Tuscan oil. It's a salubrious substitute for butter in most any vegetarian dish, working wonders, for instance, with baked potatoes.

The favorite Tuscan merenda in April and May is fresh fava beans with pecorino cheese and bread to sop up the olio. A dribble is *di rigore* in the bread soups of *ribollita* and *pappa al pomodoro*. Bistecca and beans can't do without it. Cream and butter sauces tend to mask the flavors of seafood, where a refined extra vergine can only enhance fresh fish flavors, whether grilled, poached, or roasted. It does the same for the seafood cocktail called *frutta di mare,* or even for smoked salmon. But with fish a convincing case can be made for milder oils from Lucca or Liguria. The latter also tend to blend better as a base of mayonnaise, where a fruitier oil might be too conspicuous.

It has been written that prized extra vergine is too good to use for cooking. But chefs tell me that nothing could be further from the truth. Angelo Redditi, whose brilliance illuminates our local restaurant routine, uses only oil from his family's trees to heat vegetable and fish antipasti to their optimum of goodness, to sauté onions, eggplants, or porcini mushrooms, or to deep-fry zucchini flowers or squid.

Angelo is not a *frittura* fanatic, mind you, but when he fries it's with extra vergine. He describes it as the most natural of oils, as well as the lightest, and the best conductor of heat, due to its high smoking point, which accounts for the crispness that seals in flavor. He disputes the popular notion that a *fritto misto* of fish should be a poor man's dish, as it is in places where they use the oil over and over. On his menu it's the most expensive item, because the oil is used only once. Angelo's theories about cooking with extra vergine can be tested at the Vicolo del Contento restaurant at Castelfranco di Sopra, halfway between Florence and Arezzo. Telephone (055) 9149277.

# Pizza Napoletana
## The majesty of street food

*I*t has been said that if Naples had managed to patent the pizza it would now be among Italy's wealthiest cities instead of one of its poorest. Idle speculation, of course, yet Neapolitans could be forgiven for ruminating over the royalties that might be rolling in at even a few lire per serving from a product whose sales in the world's omnipresent *pizzerie* and the like would overwhelm those of hamburgers, tacos, sushi, kebabs, or any other kind of fast food.

But no, pizza isn't a trademark, nor was it even a Neapolitan invention, as historians have so rudely reminded citizens of its adoptive hometown. Yet who could deny that Naples made the pizza famous, starting in the last century, or that its *pizzaioli* at their wood-fired ovens still make the authentic best, with few serious rivals beyond the home region of Campania? That does not mean that elsewhere—in Rome, Venice, Milan, or even New York, London, or Tokyo—one cannot eat appetizing pies called pizza. But it does mean that away from the environs of southern Italy's sprawling metropolis one cannot savor the singularly simple and sublime compositions of colors, odors, flavors, and textures that dignify *pizza napoletana*.

That assertion must be qualified, however, for as I was reminded on my return to the city of sun, sea, and song, there is no consensus in Napoli about what true pizza napoletana is. Still, even if no single pizza is officially known as napoletana, two types stand above imitations and innovations as Neapolitan classics. The most basic may be called *pizza all'olio e pomodoro,* though it is better known as *marinara* because its toppings of oil, tomato, garlic, and oregano could be stowed on voyages so that sailors (*marinai*) of this seafaring city could make pizza away from home. The more glorified *Margherita,* named in honor of Italy's queen on a visit to Naples just over a century ago, combines tomato with mozzarella cheese and fresh basil leaves to symbolize the red, white, and green *tricolore* of the Italian flag.

Defenders of these archetypes include the twenty-six pizzerie of the Associazione Vera Pizza Napoletana, whose members are pledged to uphold statutes that define ingredients, making of dough, and cooking. Each house carries a sign with an image of Pulcinella, the masked Punch of Neapolitan comedy, wielding a pizzaiolo's paddlelike peel. The rules apply not only to marinara and Margherita, but also to *pizza ripieno,* popularly known as *calzone* (trouser leg), filled with ricotta, mozzarella, and pork, and folded over for baking or frying. A fourth is *pizza al formaggio e pomodoro* (grated cheese and tomato), an odd choice since it isn't a classic.

Pizza was essentially a street food in Naples from its earliest days almost to the present, a snack or, for the poor, a meal in itself to be eaten by hand, often folded over. That may explain why Neapolitans still prefer compact sizes, either *pizza a taglio,* cut in squares from a rectangular form and sold over the counter, or disks just large enough to cover a standard plate, as baked expressly in a pizzeria. Away from Naples the format is often larger.

The supremacy of pizza napoletana is founded on the quality of local products. The Mediterranean sunshine and volcanic soil of Campania pack pungency into garlic and herbs and enrich the flavor of tomatoes, renowned from San Marzano near Mount Vesuvius. Pizzaioli here use only the freshest of mozzarella. That cheese, originally made from the milk of water buffalo, also comes from cows as *fior di latte,* whose mild firmness makes it better suited to melting over pizza than the creamy, tangy *bufala* type.

Even with choice ingredients, pizza is an economical dish whose elemental form can be duplicated with apparent ease by anyone who can make bread dough and has access to an oven. Yet, as experts point out, the levels of finesse achieved in the better pizzerie of Naples require the virtuosity of pizzaioli who mastered their craft through a dutiful apprenticeship.

The hallmark of pizza napoletana is a crust of breadlike tenderness that can come only from dough left to rise for hours. When ready, the pizzaiolo pats each form into a flat disk on his marble counter and tops it with the requisite elements, which being mainly raw cook only in the oven. The extreme heat generated by wood embers in the dome-shaped *forno* bake the pizza in less than two minutes as the crust puffs up around the circumference in what is described as a *cornicione*. This contrasts with the thinner, crunchier crust from rolled and flattened dough typical of pizza in Rome and points north.

Neapolitans perfected the contemporary pizza more than a century ago, yet their claims to historical precedence have been widely disputed. The term *pizza* came into circulation in Naples in the eighteenth century to describe a flat bread baked with lard. But the word, whose mysterious roots might be Greco-Roman or Byzantine or Gothic-Longobard, was used as early as the year 997 at Gaeta, a port between Naples and Rome.

Flat breads, referred to generically in Italy as *focaccia* (from the Latin *focus* for hearth), needed only a topping such as cheese, herbs, oil, or lard to become a sort of pizza. Prototypes abounded. The Greeks made *plakous* and *maza* in their colonies of Magna Graecia. The Romans made *laganum* (strips of unleavened dough cooked on hot stones), as well as the hearth breads or pies called *moretum* and *placenta*. Abruzzi had something called pizza in the twelfth century. Calabria made *pitta* or *petta*, Apulia *pizzella* or *pizzetta*, Sicily *sfincione*. Tuscany's *schiacciata* (for squashed) was first roasted on stones by the ancestral Etruscans. Romagna's antique *piadina* is slim and crunchy like the crust of *pizza romana*, which also seems to have preceded the napoletana.

But Neapolitans no doubt produced precursors to pizza too. Greeks founded Neapolis at the site where the siren Parthenope drowned herself after failing to tempt Odysseus to jump ship, thus bequeathing the city its nickname Partenope and just maybe its tragicomic nature. Romans, who conquered Naples in the fourth century B.C., lived luxuriously in its amphitheater of hills, with visions of Vesuvius, Sorrento, Capri, and Ischia as backdrops to a gulf that lived up to the legend that it had slipped from Paradise. They ate well, too, inspired by the consul Lucullus, whose exotic feasts at the Castel dell'Ovo were the envy of the empire.

After its fall the diet no doubt declined as Naples came under a series of foreign rulers ranging from Goths to Byzantines, Normans, French, and Spaniards. By the seventeenth century, the port was the largest city of the Occident and by some accounts its most chaotic and debauched. Only in the next century, with the city under Bourbon rule as the capital of the Kingdom of the Two Sicilies, did pizza emerge, or reemerge, though with not much ado.

Still, even if Neapolitan bakers were slow to stoke up their ovens, once they did they made pizza as never before. The early toppings of lard or olive oil, garlic, and salt soon progressed to ricotta with sugar and spice as well as cheese, ham, anchovies, sardines, mussels, and the tiny goby fish known as *cecenielli*. Most *pizzaiuoli* or *pizzajuoli* worked at hole-in-the-wall outlets called *laboratori* and sold their wares on the streets. From the beginning pizza was considered a humble repast for common people, including the picaresque *lazzaroni*, who ate and often slept in the narrow *vicoli*.

Yet most recorded accounts of those early days involved the aristocratic Bourbons. King Ferdinando IV was so fond of pizza that he had an oven built, ostensibly for his wife, Maria Carolina, near their Capodimonte palace. Bourbon rule was interrupted from 1806 to 1815 by Napoleon's Kingdom of Naples, coinciding with the rise of the tomato. The *pomodoro* (golden apple) was adopted with greater zest in the city than anywhere else in the Old World. In San Marzano's fertile fields it took on the form of a plum, with deep red color and opulent flavor, source of the first of the classics, pizza marinara. The *pummarola,* as it's known in dialect, also became the base of sauces for *maccheroni* and spaghetti, the dried pasta that Neapolitans produced and consumed with unmatched zeal, often using their hands rather than a fork.

As pizza's popularity grew, some proprietors provided benches so that customers could eat sitting down in their laboratori, which were generally regarded as dingy haunts for loiterers and rogues. Gradually, though, some grew into respectable pizzerie with tables and chairs and touches of color from tiles set in patterns on the cupola-like canopies over the ovens. Through the Risorgimento, culminating in Garibaldi's march into Naples to signal Italy's unification in 1860, pizza gradually gained a measure of acceptance among the city's *borghesi.*

But the dish was largely ignored by the nation's food chroniclers until the fateful encounter with Margherita in 1889. The beloved queen, staying at Capodimonte with her husband, King Umberto I, a Savoy, tasted three examples catered by a pizzaiolo named Raffaele Esposito; she preferred the tricolore. The tomato-mozzarella-basil combination was no novelty, swore rivals, yet Esposito not only took credit for creating it but from then on called his family's Pizzeria Brandi ''Regina d'Italia,'' though the queen never set foot in the place. Such pizzazz was normal enough in Napoli, but pizza's flings with royalty were few and far between.

Persistent poverty toward the end of the century persuaded many Neapolitans to emigrate to northern Italy and abroad, taking their pizza and pasta customs with them. Yet in Italy pizza's spread had been spasmodic until the last couple of decades, when production has grown steadily up and down the peninsula. A recent rise in consumption seems due to the fact that pizza remains affordable in a country where food prices, particularly in restaurants, have reached forbidding levels. Italians now eat more than 2.5 billion pizze a year, more than forty-five per person, mainly in the 38,000 pizzerie or other establishments that bake it to order.

Pizza's second home is the United States. Since Gennaro Lombardi, a pizzaiolo from Naples, opened shop in New York in 1895, pizza pie has become as familiar as apple pie to Americans, who often don't seem to know or care that it originated in Italy. Fair enough, since it underwent enough changes in size, form, baking methods, and ingredients to qualify as born again. Americans in Naples might find pizza too basic, delicate, and skimpy, while Italians in New York berate pizza pie as gaudy, gooey, and hard to digest. Yet some of those novel contents, flavors, and colors have made their way from America back to the old country.

Attitudes about pizza vary widely in Italy today. For instance, in Naples it is baked and eaten at all hours of the day, while elsewhere pizzerie function mainly in the evening, serving what is considered a late snack or light supper. But even in its hometown, the restaurant-style pizzeria is a relatively recent concept. Through the last century and well into this one, most pizza and other fast foods continued to be sold or bartered at counters and stalls or from carts wheeled by vendors through the city's narrow cobblestone streets.

Those crowded vicoli run up and across the often steep hills in webs of intersecting canyons, built that way, they say, to block out the wilting summer sun and fend off stiff winter winds off the gulf. Their grimy walls bristle with balconies whose metal railings support clotheslines spanning the heights with laundry which, when it isn't dripping wet, flutters like banners over the impromptu parades through the streets.

My first foray into the labyrinth years ago was like entering a carnival in a tawdry Little Italy of chintzy ornaments and glowing neon lights. But the memories that linger were of sights, smells, and sounds that might have been sensed on a Mediterranean odyssey. Merchant spiels echoed the chants and wails of Arab bazaars, though hawkers were largely ignored by crowds, which might have gathered at one place to cheer a mandolin-strumming troubadour straining with the high notes of O sole mio or at another to mock a minstrel reciting ditties over the wheezing of a concertina, while his foot worked devices to sound jangles and booms.

The Neapolitan dialect would have been indecipherable had it not been accompanied by explicit facial expressions and vigorous motions of hands and bodies. But even if I'd learned the lingo I couldn't have just joined the crowd, for stranieri stood out in this flow of humanity like guppies in a goldfish bowl, or was it jellyfish in a sea of sharks?

Still, even if latter-day lazzaroni were noted as artists of villainy and deceit, they advanced schemes with a measure of good-natured dignity. Even the *scugnizzi*, the street-smart urchins who clung to your forearm and called you Joe while proffering cigarettes or watches or ladies of the night, took refusals with a smile. Any sense of danger soon succumbed to the revelation that life on the back streets was an interminable *scherzo*, a weird and wondrous game.

The bonus for a student whose budget made *Europe on $5 a Day* seem extravagant was that Naples turned out to be a treasure trove of cheap and good things to eat. There were thick sandwiches filled with salame or cheese, hot almond biscuits called *taralli*, baskets of pastries and sweets, fresh ice cream, and the lemon- or coffee-flavored ices known as *granite*. The colors and forms of foods stacked at fruit and vegetable stands, snack bars, and *tavole calde* were as tempting as the smells of shrimp and squid frying in oil, of chestnuts and sweet corn roasting over smoky coals, of tomatoes simmering with onions and garlic for sauces.

Pasta was irresistible to a hungry youth, but Napoli won my heart with pizza. A few coins on the counter commanded a slice from a rectangular slab extracted sizzling from the forno and served folded over in a sheet of brown paper. I usually ate it standing up with wine poured from a flask or drawn from a tap. The zesty white might have been Asprinio and the fizzy red Gragnano, since I learned later that they were once Naples' pizza wines.

After that adventure more than thirty years ago my visits to Naples had been all too few, limited to stopovers on the way to quieter places such as Capri, Ischia, Sorrento, and the Amalfi coast. Italy's third-largest city, after Milan and Rome, offers an inspiring array of things to see and do. But Naples and its province, by far the most densely populated of Italy, are regularly depicted in the press as a rambling inferno of vice and disarray, lorded over by corrupt politicians and overrun by armed hoodlums of the mafia-like camorra. So I suspect that I had been subconsciously avoiding the place. Yet I never could forget old Napoli with its impulsive joys and pristine flavors. So when the quest turned to pizza napoletana, I resolved to carry out my mandate not at some nearby holiday haven but in Paradise Lost itself.

It was well worth the risk. Not only was the pizza unbeatable, but Naples seemed more peaceful than before, even if civic order never could prevail among a people whose intuitive defiance of authority developed over eras when obedience meant bowing to despotic rule. Traffic was intense, if less hectic than in Rome, but as long as one drove through pesky red stoplights as the natives do (if one doesn't, they beep and shout), it kept flowing. Even the weather was welcoming with refreshing breezes off the gulf at Mergellina, where we sat sipping icy lemon granite after our arrival on a sunny July afternoon.

Or perhaps the mission went smoothly because a *napoletano verace* was leading the way: Fabrizio Tomas, a young man from Posillipo, who works as a vineyard consultant in Chianti. Fabrizio, whose calm sincerity hardly fits local stereotypes, grew up in a wildly miscellaneous society whose cultured elements rarely make news. But his native flair came across in a wry sense of humor and unabashed pride in a city that, being quintessentially Italian, has its own peculiar brands of politics and religion, art, music, and food, and a people who have always played the game of life abiding by their own rules.

"Nowhere," he assured me on the drive down from Tuscany, "will you eat pizza as in Napoli." I never doubted it. But since we wouldn't have time for a grand tour of pizzerie, my research had come up with a potential dozen. Fabrizio, while allowing that pizza would be good at any of them, readily pared the list to three. Already excluded was Brandi, where I'd eaten a tasty Margherita years before but found the ambience, with its memorabilia of the queen, altogether too-too. My main requisite, other than pizza at its genuine best, was that the place be Neapolitan to the core. As Fabrizio described Antica Port'Alba, Ciro a Santa Brigida, and Lombardi a Santa Chiara, I detected a lean toward the last. We agreed to start there.

Parking is a problem in the center of town, so we took a taxi from Posillipo. The driver, an amiable fellow with a lively interest in pizza, got so involved in our discussion that he slowed to a crawl in heavy traffic in front of the Teatro San Carlo and, ignoring the wrath of drivers behind, kept turning to face us in the backseat with his hands off the wheel so that he could use them to emphasize points. I was delighted that he considered Lombardi *numero uno* for marinara but just as relieved that he got us to Piazza del Gesù Nuovo without a scrape.

We walked into Spaccanapoli, heart of the old city, noted in guidebooks for its institutes of learning, artisan shops, and narrow, crowded vicoli. But the streets seemed oddly deserted. Fabrizio explained that schools were closed for the summer and on Fridays people tend to pack into cars, buses, and ferries and head out of town to spend the weekend beside the sea. Even street people? I wondered. No doubt about it, then, Partenope had changed.

Visible from far down the Via Benedetto Croce was the sign "Ristorante-Pizzeria Lombardi a Santa Chiara" in blue letters on a white neon background, a beacon that seemed a bit brazen for what had been described as a landmark. But there was also a "Vera Pizza Napoletana" emblem at number 59, where people stood waiting for tables at the plate-glass entrance. "You rarely see a line in July," said Fabrizio, waving to catch the eye of the man behind the cash register, who beamed in recognition and beckoned us inside.

We filed in past the forno, set in a corner fronted by a marble-topped counter with shelves holding bowls and jars of ingredients. Behind it worked a pizzaiolo, short and stout, wearing a white Lombardi T-shirt under his apron and a grin as warm as the glow from his oven. There were displays of fresh fish on ice and platters of vegetables and fruit along the wood-paneled walls of a narrow room ventilated by fans revolving lazily beneath the vaulted white ceilings. The waiters, smiling gamely as they wriggled through with plates of piping hot pizza, wore canary-yellow jackets that more or less matched the tablecloths.

Alfonso Lombardi stopped totting up bills long enough to welcome us and direct us upstairs. He explained that in the usually slow months of summer he alternates work weeks with his brother and co-owner, Luigi, and since tonight was unexpectedly busy he couldn't join us right away. Meanwhile his son, also Luigi but Gigi for short, would accompany us. Gigi, an engineer, introduced himself as the first Lombardi in four generations not to become a pizzaiolo. "I may regret it someday," he mused. "Business is thriving."

The decor in the more sedate upstairs dining rooms struck a nice balance between cozy and functional, tasteful and banal. Most customers appeared to be Neapolitans, discernible by their accents as well as their tendency to eat, drink, and talk with hands in perpetual motion. And if that wasn't enough to satisfy my demands, from a radio somewhere off in the back came the voice of Pino Daniele, whose sleekly modern sounds throbbed with the mystical undertones of the ancient Mediterranean.

In a place that can seat 110, the only empty chairs were ours. Fabrizio, expecting friends, had reserved for eight, but the number quickly reached a dozen and required an added table. They were school chums from Posillipo, now physician, architect, businessmen with wives or fiancées, bright young people whose features and complexions revealed the diverse ethnic lines that converged over the ages on this melting-pot port but whose easy familiarity in speech and manner bespoke that uniquely Neapolitan *joie de vivre*.

The pizza prices, hand-lettered on a list, ranged from 5,000 lire for a marinara to 10,000 for a calzone, below rates in Rome, Florence, or Milan. I had decided to order the classics: marinara and Margherita. Gigi insisted that I also try the specialty *pizza alla Lombardi*.

Fabrizio pointed out that pizza is no longer strictly orthodox in Naples, so menus may include types from elsewhere, such as *quattro stagioni* (four seasons and flavors), *capricciosa* (whims of vegetables and cheeses), or *romana* (tomato, cheese, capers, anchovies). The romana, curiously, is often called napoletana in Rome and points north. Gigi added that true pizzaioli work strictly to order and will meet express requests for toppings that may be exotic, though they'll stop short of sweet and fruity concoctions that seem better suited to American tastes.

Other diners seemed to be drinking mainly soda or beer, but we decided to honor the occasion with wine. The list showed an Asprinio from an unheralded winery at Aversa, in the historic zone to the north. We ordered the wine that the French author Alexandre Dumas, in 1835, had compared to ''an infusion of Champagne with Norman cider,'' though we also requested plenty of fizzy mineral water, just in case. Waiters showed up with platters of antipasti: sautéed eggplant with tomato, daintily brittle deep-fried anchovies, salame laced with *peperoncini*, mozzarella di bufala of the squishy succulence achieved only in Campania, and *provola affumicata*, a related soft, white cheese smoked ever so lightly to a burnished tang.

As the pizze arrived, we split each four ways and shared them. The Margherita, a blissful union of tomato and cheese with a flourish of sweet basil, was indeed fit for a queen. The Lombardi, presented rather grandly by Alfonso himself, melded lightly smoked provola with chopped tomatoes and basil in a pie that seemed—well, why not?—fit for a king. But to my unbending palate the marinara, the humblest-born of the hierarchy, reached the heights of majesty. I ate it before the others and after, lingering to let those splendidly simple sensations of tomato, garlic, oregano, and basil carry me back on a nostalgia trip to old Napoli.

The Asprinio, on the other hand, was so common that we switched. The esteemed Greco di Tufo from Mastroberardino's

Vignadangelo vineyard in the hills near Avellino went nicely, though it was maybe too polished and surely too expensive to be considered pizza wine. As a rule, wines on the light side, including bubbly types, go well with pizza, but in the end those pristine flavors don't require matches any more sophisticated than beer.

Alfonso reemerged to announce that the restaurant could provide main courses of fish, meat, or vegetables, arousing jeers, laughter, and lively repartee in dialect from a crowd happily sated by pizza and in need of nothing more than fresh fruit or gelato or an espresso to round out a meal. Our host, smiling in defeat, sat down and joined us.

Alfonso, in his late fifties, looked the distinguished part of a proprietor, with a deep tan to accent piercing blue eyes and steely gray hair. But he referred to himself as a pizzaiolo from a proud family tradition. That began late in the last century when his grandfather, Enrico Lombardi, opened a forno at the old city gate of Porta Capuana. He ventured off to South America and France to pioneer pizza, before returning home. In the early 1920s his son, Luigi, opened a pizza outlet in a structure set flush against the outer wall of the campanile of Santa Chiara, an imposing medieval Gothic church. There he and his wife, Giovanna, baked pizza for decades, teaching the trade to their sons, Alfonso, Luigi, and Enrico. (''Our family has a confusing repetition of names,'' admitted Alfonso.) In 1961 they moved to the present location, a stone's throw down the street, but kept the reference to Santa Chiara.

Veteran pizzaioli are known as indefatigable raconteurs, but Alfonso traced the family line in calm, modest tones. Other pizzerie often display photos signed by celebrities such as Enrico Caruso, Sophia Loren, or Frank Sinatra, but Lombardi presents its credentials with a few framed press clippings among the paintings on the walls. Most came from local journals, but there was also a full feature with photos in *The New York Times* from 1976.

As I glanced through that, Alfonso reminisced about his father, who among other things created the pizza Lombardi and ate mainly that. He was called Don Luigi, a reflection of his habit of addressing clients as *dottore, professore, conte,* and the like in a city where some took titles seriously and others used them in jest, especially the students who flocked to his forno for snacks. Don Luigi hosted luminaries too, such as Benedetto Croce, who lived at number 12 on the street named after him. But the eminent philosopher, who stopped by almost daily for a pizza and a chat, never got around to signing a photo.

Alfonso recalled that until fifteen or twenty years ago most pizza was still sold over the counter. But as living standards rose, Neapolitans, primarily the young, preferred the comforts of the pizzeria as a place to gather and eat. There was a rapid growth in pizzerie as the pizza became chic, he related. "Now it's eaten at all social levels, at places fancier than this. Still, over all I think we eat less pizza than before. In the past some people practically subsisted on it."

Alfonso and Luigi II remained at Santa Chiara, while brother Enrico founded his own pizzeria, Lombardi a Foria. As business grew, they expanded upstairs and added a kitchen to provide restaurant service, as many pizzerie now do. But Alfonso said that 70 percent of the business remains in pizza, which they produce at the rate of three hundred to five hundred a day. As the business prospered, the brothers became more involved as managers and hosts. The baking was turned over to Giuseppe Mazza, who began as an apprentice *fornaio* at the age of fourteen and has been with them for more than thirty years.

Around midnight, as the party broke up, we went downstairs to talk to Mazza, who was tidying up the forno. Praise for his pizza brought a smile that creased the eyes and puckered the mouth of his roly-poly face, capped by a *berettino,* the standard white baker's cap. As he munched on the remains of a Margherita, he admitted that he ate at least two pizze a day. "It's as genuine a food as you can find," he assured me, "and I know what goes into it."

When I asked if I could come by in the morning to interview him, Mazza looked amazed. "An interview?" he uttered with an impish grin. "Imagine that, just like Maradona!" He referred to Diego Maradona, the diminutive Argentinian who long played soccer for Napoli, where he was known as "il Re." As we parted, Alfonso observed that his pizzaiolo was about the same size as the soccer star but made a little less money.

On Saturday morning the cab sped through nearly empty streets to deposit me in front of Lombardi minutes before our eleven-o'clock appointment. The roll-down metal shutter was drawn tight, but Mazza had told me to just pound on it. In moments he arrived and hoisted it high enough so that I could crouch in under, then slammed it back down into place with a fearsome clatter. He shook my hand eagerly. "We don't open till noon," he reminded me, "so when do we do the interview?" Oh, I'll just tag along and ask questions, I said.

Mazza went right to work. He measured some salt into folded waxed paper and descended to the cellar to mix the dough in a small, white-tiled room much cooler than the cooking area. He said he makes two batches a day—now for that evening's pizza and late in the evening for the next day's noontime batch. The mixing and kneading are done in an *impastatrice,* a revolving tub with a whirling beater, like those found in artisan bakeries.

Naples had always been known for pure water, a factor in the excellence of its pizza dough as well as its espresso. Mazza, drawing a bucketful from a faucet, noted that it was still good in this area, but heavily treated in others. He added the salt and poured it into the mixer, scooping in flour measured only by eye. He used the refined *tipo* OO mixed with lesser amounts of the even finer *tipo* OM (from American grain), scattering bits of beer yeast into the paste. Mazza said that when it's cool some dough is left aside to ferment slowly and become *criscito,* the leavening that lends a slightly sour taste admirers adore. But in the heat it would rise and sour too quickly, so in summer only the safe beer yeast is used.

As the machine turned he went upstairs to arrange ingredients on shelves. The basic purée had been made by passing canned San Marzano tomatoes, peeled but uncooked, through a food mill. There were also chopped fresh tomatoes for the Lombardi. Mazza said that in fall and winter they use small *pomodorini di Sant'Anastasia,* hung in bunches in airy places to concentrate flavors, but they had become a luxury at ten times the cost of fresh.

Bowls held fior di latte and smoked provola chopped into strips and bits, as well as grated cheese. There were leaves of fresh basil, coarsely chopped garlic, powdered oregano, peperoncini, sliced mushrooms and onions, fresh mussels and shrimp, salted anchovies and capers, and containers of tuna and artichokes in olive oil. To one side stood special items for calzoni. Still more things were ready in the kitchen to meet requests.

We returned to the cellar, where the dough had been working for half an hour. After testing consistency, Mazza stopped the machine and removed half the mass to a work table, then started it up again, adding a little more beer yeast. With unerring speed he patted wads of dough into dozens of balls called *pagnotte* of about 7 ounces each—one for each pizza—and placed them in wooden racks stacked in layers. When the first batch was done, he made pagnotte of the second, which he said would be ready sooner because of the extra leavening.

It was nearing opening time as Mazza toted racks of pagnotte made the evening before upstairs to the forno. Pizza ovens in Naples are almost identical in their dome-shaped interiors and arched apertures, but exterior designs express unrestrained individuality. Canopies are often rounded in the shape of a mushroom or onion and covered with tiny tiles as mosaics, but at Lombardi the form resembles a three-sided awning jutting from a corner all bedecked in brown and white rectangular tiles. Standing at the shrine was a youth named Maurizio, one of two apprentice fornai who work alternate shifts. He had been waiting to kindle the fire, a twice-daily routine that my curiosity had transformed into a self-conscious ceremony.

Alfonso showed up too, just in time to give Maurizio the cue to shove a crateful of wood shavings through the aperture atop coals still glowing from the night before. When these *pampuglie* burst into flame, he tossed in pieces of walnut and oak, hardwoods that abound in Campania's hills. The bit of smoke that filtered out under the arch rose through a slot into a flue that angles over the oven and then climbs straight up five stories to the roof. Alfonso explained that these chimneys not only draw smoke but serve as exhausts for cooking odors and heat that would otherwise be excessive in the room.

As the flames subsided, Mazza propped a heavy metal lid against the aperture, saying that the oven would be hot enough for cooking in about fifteen minutes, or when the bricks of the dome turned from dark to light gray. What temperature? I asked. The pizzaiolo shrugged. ''Too hot to hold your hand inside.'' I later read that they reach 715° to 750° F, much hotter than the similarly shaped but larger wood-fired ovens used for bread in much of Italy.

Alfonso said that pizza forni are built by craftsmen whose secrets have been passed down through generations, using firebricks known as *mattoni di Santa Maria,* after a town near Salerno. The interior dome consists of small rectangular bricks set with refractory clay and insulated from the exterior by a layer of fine sand. The circular floor is formed by four large tiles over a base of river sand and sea salt, which hold heat without shifting or shrinking.

So old is their craft that they work without diagrams following dimensions expressed in *palmi*, handbreadths. Alfonso had to get a measuring stick to confirm that one palmo was 10½ inches, meaning that the originator had a large hand. That was the height of the aperture, just enough to permit a pizzzaiolo to maneuver. The interior diameter was five palmi, or 53 inches. The builders must also use smaller units (thumbs perhaps), since the oven was 17½ inches high and the aperture almost 19 inches wide, but Alfonso wasn't sure.

Once conditioned from repeated use, the ovens retain heat from coals and ash that are never completely cleared out but remain in a perpetual pile to the fornaio's left, taking up about a quarter of the floor space. They generate calories so intense and constant that the pizza bakes to perfection on top, bottom, and sides in 80 to 120 seconds, no more. Gas or electric ovens cook too slowly to achieve that fusion of flavors and textures that ennobles pizza napoletana.

At noon a waiter rolled up the shutter and clamped it into place. The first customers in ordered pizza to go. Alfonso explained that they do a brisk takeout business but absolutely will not deliver. Mazza went to work, assuring me with a wink that "making pizza is a pleasure like making music," and he hummed a tune as he prepared a marinara.

After spreading a little flour on the counter, he plopped down a pagnotta, gently spanking it flat into a disk. Then, in rapid sequence, he ladled on a meager coating of tomato purée, sprinkled on some oregano, added a couple of rough cuts of garlic and four basil leaves, and doused the surface with oil from the *agliara,* a traditional copper-and-brass can with a long, narrow spout. Maurizio held a wooden peel next to the counter as

Mazza arranged the disk on the flat blade, stretching it at the edges to enlarge the circle slightly before the fornaio shoveled it into the oven. The preparation couldn't have taken more than fifteen to twenty seconds, for by the time the first one was drawn sizzling from the oven five others had been shoveled in.

The tempo was dazzling, but the procedures raised a couple of doubts. First, why canned tomatoes instead of fresh? And, second, wasn't that oil too pale to be olive? Mazza explained that the purée came from the choicest San Marzano tomatoes, whose flavor is more condensed than the fresh. And, correct, that wasn't olive oil but seed oil, which being virtually flavorless, odorless, and colorless serves more as a lubricant than an ingredient. As I advanced pleas in favor of fresh tomatoes and extra vergine oil, Alfonso intervened, promising to personally bake me what was known as *pizza all'ugl'e pummarol* for lunch.

I was also curious about the dough. Mazza explained that his gentle, hands-off treatment keeps it aerated so that it rises in the oven and stays soft like bread. In Naples, where rolling pins or apparatuses that flatten the forms are taboo, a pizzaiolo is no more likely to sail a disk Frisbee-style in the air than he would be to strut down the street like a cowboy in a ten-gallon hat. It was clear that improvisers in the pizza field make their dough in other towns.

Mazza was fashioning a Margherita, using the same purée topped with dabs of fior di latte and a sprinkling of Pecorino Romano, preferred as saltier and sharper than Parmigiano. He added fresh basil and oil, but no garlic or oregano, which others sometimes use. Alfonso said that neither of the classics includes capers or anchovies, unless requested, but then they wouldn't be classics. He added that the Margherita is the most popular pizza not just of the house but of Naples and all Italy, crediting its superior class locally to the freshness of fior di latte.

Asked if they ever used the true mozzarella di bufala, Alfonso said that a cheese so luscious fresh only loses when heated. Anyway, since it contains more fat and liquid than fior di latte, it melts rather sloppily. Both types are supplied fresh daily, along with smoked provola, cheeses known as *pasta filata* because the pulp is "spun" into strands. Most mozzarella is made where buffalo graze in swampy plains of the Sele Valley around Salerno and Battipaglia to the southeast and the Volturno Valley near Aversa and Capua to the north.

As Maurizio inserted pizze in the oven, he periodically tossed in shavings over the coals, creating flares and sparkles and bursts of heat reputed to raise the cornicione and give it the desired calloused texture with spots that are dark brown but not quite burned. He used a slimmer metal peel to remove them individually and slide them onto plates. In Naples pizza must arrive at the table still too hot to eat, a waiter told me, as he hurried off with three.

Mazza was creating another specialty: pizza ripieno or calzone. He prepared the disk the same way but this time added a smattering of fresh ricotta, bits of fior di latte, cooked ham (salame or pork crackling may be used instead), and tiny lumps of snow-white lard. Then he folded it over, pressing down the edges to seal in the filling, and spread the surface with tomato purée, adding fior di latte, grated pecorino, and basil. Tempting, but too filling for lunch.

Fabrizio had arrived with friends, all planning to catch the ferry to Ischia in a couple of hours. So we ordered just pizza and beer, Peroni Nastro Azzurro, light but refreshing on a hot day. The others had a choice, but I was having marinara both ways. Even if I now knew about the canned tomatoes and insipid oil, Mazza's marinara was as splendid as it had been the night before. Alfonso arrived with his ugl'e pummarol, warning me that the olive oil tends to smolder in the forno's elevated heat, so there might be a hint of scorch. There was indeed, and this time the oil seemed heavy in relation to the delicately fresh tomatoes. The challenge between raw tomatoes and purée remained a toss-up, but next time I had to be sure to bring some Tuscan extra vergine, an oil that could surely stand up to the heat.

By the time we'd finished our pizza and beer, I'd been talked into spending the rest of the weekend on an island by the sea. The abrupt departure left me with the uneasy feeling that I should have tried at least another pizzeria or two. But Fabrizio assured me that on Ischia the pizzaioli all come from Naples, so I could continue research there. Anyway, it was time to run.

On the way out I thanked Alfonso for his hospitality and Mazza for his patience. The pizzaiolo used his apron to wipe flour off his hands so we could shake. "Ciao," he said "Remember to send the interview." I promised to deliver it, a good excuse for a return. He plucked up a pagnotta and resumed working and humming, which reminded me that I mustn't forget his analogy about making pizza and music. I was also thinking, as we hurried down the Via Croce, that after his Neapolitan medleys most other pizza was going to seem pretty flat.

Lombardi a Santa Chiara at Via Benedetto Croce 59—telephone
(081) 5520780—is open weekdays and Saturday from noon to
three-thirty and seven in the evening to midnight, except during
a three-week closing in August. But visitors to Naples needn't
limit pizza experiences to Lombardi, as I did this time, or to the
Vera Pizza Napoletana group. My luncheon companions, who
were raised on it, agreed that over all pizza in Naples has never
been better.

# Parmigiano Reggiano
## The Olympian Jupiter of Cheese

*I*n much of the world "Parmesan" is a pulverized cheese sold in packages with apertures so that it can be sprinkled onto spaghetti and other hot dishes to melt, though some samples provide little more to savor than the sawdust they resemble. Of course, pasta devotees everywhere know that bona fide Parmigiano comes in hard, pale golden hunks to be grated into coarse powder that adds exquisite flavor as it clings to noodles and melds with sauces. But perhaps only those who have tasted bite-sized morsels gouged from a freshly split form in its native Emilia could really appreciate why Parmigiano Reggiano, as it's officially known, has been crowned the king of cheeses.

Appearance is its first mark of majesty. It comes in large, solid drums that can vary in weight from about 53 to 88 pounds. Its thick crust over time takes on a tawny hue and lustrous patina like fine calfskin, on which the brand PARMIGIANO REGGIANO, indented in dot matrix, is repeated in stripes around the subtly convex circumference. With a year of age its rind becomes so leathery-tough that a drum will remain unscathed if struck with a hammer or dropped from a shelf.

Although favored nearly everywhere for grating, Parmigiano is noblest as a table cheese. The form is usually cut and cleaved open using a special knife whose blade is shaped like a laurel leaf with a blunted tip, an instrument designed not to slice the cheese but to first wedge it into large chunks and then carve it into jagged pieces. Classified as a hard cheese, Parmigiano when ready to eat should be compactly firm to the touch yet so brittle that it can be portioned as easily as fresh milk chocolate.

Ripe Parmigiano has a pale straw color with faint flecks of white and minute, almost imperceptible holes in a granular surface that may show hints of *gocciole,* or dewy moisture. A buttery delicacy in aroma carries over into flavors of mellow maturity accented by a scintillating tang on the tongue. When chewed, the cheese should feel *sabbioso,* as if laced with fine sand that melts in the mouth like sugar or salt. With age it becomes almost golden in color, drier and harder with more concentrated flavor, making it ideal for grating. But Parmigiano should never be markedly salty or sharp like the other classical grating cheese, Pecorino Romano, whose pungency is amply suited to the lively cooking of Rome.

Parmigiano reigns supreme in Italy in prestige and price, even if some rare local *formaggio* may cost more per kilogram. Its class, versatility, and longevity, combined with notable nutritional value and easy digestibility, earned it the accolade of Italian gas-

tronome Luigi Carnacina as "the complete cheese, the true aris-
tocrat." Some admirers might even endorse the eulogy of the
nineteenth-century author Giovanni Rajberti that it "stands with
all the other cheeses of the world like the Olympian Jupiter
amidst the rabble of the minor gods."

In 1955 Parmigiano Reggiano was distinguished as a cheese
of controlled origin. The title, which is sometimes hyphenated,
refers to the cities of Parma and Reggio nell'Emilia and their
provinces—a duet justifiably insisted upon by the Reggiani,
though the traditional name Parmigiano or Parmesan regularly
stands solo. Yet the production zone, which covers the heart of
Emilia from the Po River to the Apennines, extends beyond
Parma and Reggio to take in the entire province of Modena and
part of Bologna to the west of the Reno River, plus a slice of
Lombardy in the section of Mantova (Mantua) province that lies
south of the Po.

Despite its singular stature, Parmigiano does not stand alone.
It is one of a family of cow's milk cheeses known as *grana,* after
their fine granular texture, made in much of northern Italy.
Grana—also called *cacio,* an ancient term for cheese—was once
linked to towns where local customs determined distinct styles.
Piacenza and Lodi stood out, though Mantua, Cremona, and Bres-
cia's Bagoss were also well noted. But by now most such cheeses
from outside the Parmigiano Reggiano area are grouped under the
name Grana Padano, whose *zona tipica* covers much of the vast
Po Valley in the regions of Piedmont, Lombardy, Veneto, and
Emilia-Romagna. The northern province of Trento makes Grana
Padano Trentino.

Parmigiano, like all grana, is a hard, semifat cheese made

from partly skimmed cow's milk, gently cooked, pressed, molded into cylinders, salted, and matured slowly—for at least twelve months under official appellations, though often longer. By tradition, cheese made from spring through summer was called *maggengo* (after the month of May), and in the winter *vernengo* or *invernengo,* distinctions that may still apply to Grana Padano. Until 1983, Parmigiano Reggiano could be made only from April to November, though producers could make vernengo in a special category the rest of the year. Then production was extended year round, eliminating vernengo, as well as the categories of the once admired *vecchio, stravecchio,* and *stravecchione,* for forms aged from eighteen months to four years.

Cheese was made in the Parma area in Etruscan and Roman times, as the writings of Apicius noted in praising *caseus parmensis,* a distant forerunner of Parmigiano. Grana may have originated in the twelfth century when monks at the Cistercian abbey of Chiaravalle della Colomba began converting the Po marshlands into pastures to raise cows for the making of cheese. Since Chiaravalle lies in its province, Piacenza claims to have made grana before its Emilian neighbor Parma, whose provincial borderline passes a short distance to the east.

Promoters of Grana Padano state emphatically that their cheese dates back eight centuries. But their archrivals seem less assertive about the origins of Parmigiano. Its cradle was long alleged to have been the plain of the Enza stream, which divides Parma and Reggio provinces—but credible documents indicate that the cheese was first made there only in the early seventeenth century. Much of the best Parmigiano Reggiano still comes from cows nourished on a studied mix of grasses and alfalfa grown on the Enza's irrigated fields around the towns of Bibbiano, Montecchio, and San Polo. But since they are in Reggio's domain, one might wonder why the appellation didn't become Reggiano Parmigiano.

In confronting such puzzles it should be remembered that between the Romans and the Risorgimento the lands of northern Italy changed hands with dizzying frequency, as popes, emperors, kings, warriors, and nobles of various title conquered territories and altered their names and boundaries at will. If there's one thing the literature about grana makes clear, it's that the family history is thoroughly muddled.

Confusion also reigns abroad, where the term *Parmesan* (from French) is used in English-speaking lands to describe not only Parmigiano Reggiano and other Italian versions of grana but most of the ubiquitous surrogates, including domestic prepackaged types. Yet no one, not even in Piacenza, would have the audacity to deny that Parmigiano or Parmesan refers to Parma or that a grana type of cheese was made in its domain long before the seventeenth century, probably by the same order of monks that founded Chiaravalle.

Today's bitter Parmigiano–Grana Padano rivalry might trace its roots to the mid-1300s when Giovanni Boccaccio, in the *Decameron,* depicted a place called Bengodi, where upon ''a mountain all of grated parmigiano cheese, dwelled folk who did nought else but make maccheroni and raviuoli, and boil them in capon's broth; and hence they then cast them down, and he who grabbed the most had the most.'' Boccaccio's jest, besides confirming that the cheese was already used for grating, seemed to have launched Parmigiano on the road to fame. Yet the term *parmigiano* was used generically for grana even then. That is why citizens of Piacenza may still insist that Boccaccio, a foreigner from Florence, was referring to Cacio Piacentino, which was more abundant and esteemed than Parma's cheese. The people of Lodi could put forth similar assertions, since their Cacio Lodigiano was widely acclaimed.

But Parmigiano gradually established preeminence, thanks in no minor way to its universally recognized name. The sixteenth-century chronicler Christoforo di Messisbugo noted that ''Parmeggiano'' had become a prized item on the tables of Italy's aristocracy. It was equally admired in France, where the seventeenth-century playwright Molière in his later years supposedly ate only Parmesan—along with three daily glasses of Port—a diet still cited as evidence of the cheese's benefits for the elderly and infants. Parmigiano has won endorsements since from doctors, chefs, athletes, stars of stage and screen, statesmen, and musicians, led of course by those sons of Parma Giuseppe Verdi and Arturo Toscanini.

Today the Consorzio del Formaggio Parmigiano Reggiano, which exercises sole quality control in the five provinces, emphasizes the natural virtues of a cheese that is an admirably balanced source of nutrition and energy. Despite heavy production, which accounts for about 14 percent of Italy's total, few cheeses are made following such rigid norms. Parmigiano must be made in the morning. No chemical or coloring agents may be used. The only permitted additives are a minute dose of rennet, which causes milk to coagulate and curds to separate from whey, and salt infused discreetly as the new forms soak in brine. Each drum is given a physical exam during aging by the consortium's notoriously severe "cheese doctors," who, at the least sign of a flaw, will stamp stigmatic X's into the rind, condemning it to be sold at low price.

Codes for Grana Padano permit some variations in process-ing, such as the addition of saffron for a deeper shade of yellow (a tradition now largely neglected) and the use of antifermen-tatives (a precaution conscientious cheesemakers avoid). Al-though the zone is much larger and cheeses that carry the name on a diamondlike trademark seem less uniform in character and quality, Grana Padano has rallied forces into a united front against Parmigiano, parlaying lower prices and aggressive marketing into mounting success.

In the face of this competition, the Parmigiano Reggiano con-sortium has stepped up advertising and public relations. Visiting writers are lavished with books, pamphlets, and press clippings attesting to Parmigiano's supremacy. There's even a videocassette, accompanied by chamber music, providing a nostalgic tour of the dairy country with cows grazing in languid meadows around *caselli,* cheese houses that resemble antique chapels. Even if there is something to the notion that each form of Parmigiano is the work of a master craftsman, the image makers might stretch the myth to depict the legendary *casaro* laboring over caldrons heated by open wood fires, following methods unchanged for seven cen-turies.

Yet nowhere in Italy is agriculture more industrialized than in the Val Padana, the great plains of the Po, which have long been the nation's leading source of grains, fruit, vegetables, meat, and dairy products. Emilia's small farms have been incorporated into big ones as new varieties, breeds, hybrids, and clones have boosted yields in produce of all kind. Dairies have prospered as sources of cheese and other products that enabled a local milk company called Parmalat to expand into an international food conglomerate. Italy's largest food manufacturer, Barilla, a specialist in pasta and bakery products, was founded here. Other sectors of the farm economy are less successful. A cooperative group called Riunite, which bottled nearly half of all the wine imported into the United States before the bubble burst on sweet Lambrusco, has been forced to close some cellars as growers uproot vines across Reggio's plains.

At first it seemed that only environmentalists complained that artificial fertilizers, herbicides, and pesticides were upsetting nature's balance. But by now ecology has become a common cause among a citizenry concerned that decades of forced yields have seriously depleted the Padana's natural abundance. Even farmers habitually disciplined by the policy that quantity is more profitable than quality admit privately that bigger isn't better.

After an era of unprecedented growth, the embattled forces of Parmigiano Reggiano have also been pressured into reassessing their concept of progress. Production, which expanded and contracted periodically over centuries when cheesemaking was a cottage industry, increased from 55,000 tons in 1955 to more than 110,000 tons in 1990. At that point the consortium imposed a quota on volume in a so far unsuccessful attempt to stabilize the market and reinforce Parmigiano's image of elite class. While production doubled, the number of caselli decreased from 2,356 to 785, a third of the former total, as cheesemaking became increasingly centered in cooperative *caseifici sociali*. Yet even if Parmigiano ranks as a major industry, the cheese can't be manufactured on assembly lines. That explains why a number of small, independent caselli have managed to survive.

Grana Padano, which tripled in output over the same period to nearly equal its rival in volume, is now often made in two shifts a day by large producers seeking ways to hold down costs without sacrificing quality. It might be said that the upper crust of Grana Padano is comparable to good, bourgeois Parmigiano, whose overall standards have been stabilized by controls that have virtually eliminated former lows. But epicures agree that the finest Parmigiano remains the ne plus ultra, still a monarch even if longtime admirers miss those peaks of mature splendor once savored in vecchio, stravecchio, and stravecchione.

Market analysts maintain that there would be little demand for those rarities among modern consumers, who prefer mellower, more youthful styles in cheese. But veteran casari admit that the classics vanished because the quality of milk isn't what it used to be. They say that even if the demand existed, they would have trouble meeting it, because today's cheeses don't have the substance to improve much beyond two years of age, let alone three or four.

When dairy farms were small and cows were grazed or at least fed on locally grown forage, distinctions were evident in the typology and class of cheeses from different areas of the vast zone. Seasonal variations were determinant when Parmigiano could be made only during the cows' normal lactation period, in the warm months when they ate fresh green grass after giving birth to young. In the winter, when they had dried forage and yielded less milk, vernengo was made as a fresher type of cheese to be sold young and at lower price. But no longer.

Many dairies have been consolidated into networks of stalls, where cows, kept conveniently inside, can be controlled so that births are staggered (through artificial insemination) and herds yield milk fairly regularly year round. Rules stipulate the mix of grasses and straw the cows are to be fed, but forage now comes from many sources, often outside the zone, so local distinctions in cheeses aren't so evident anymore. But if modern Parmigiano is increasingly homogeneous, with less distance between high points and lows, the great levelers have been new breeds of productive cows. The influx has been dominated by the northern European Frisian or Frisona (described locally as a ''milk machine''), which has largely replaced the historical Razza Reggiana (or Vacche Rosse), Parmigiana, Bianca Val Padana, and Montanara.

The native cows produced less milk, but it was richer in casein, the protein that favors greater body and more compact structure in cheeses, giving them the constitution for aging. Attempts have been made to save the fading breeds, and even revive some. A casello at Reggio now makes Parmigiano exclusively from Vacche Rosse after studies showed that their milk gives higher yields in cheese than the ''cosmopolitan cows'' (7.5 percent vs. 6.5 percent). Also, being a rustic breed used as work animals since the Middle Ages, they are healthier and less voracious and cost less to keep. Another incentive to farmers is that their superior cheese (and milk) would be worth more. The Parmigiano Reggiano consortium has agreed to let the Vacche Rosse cheese carry a trademark showing two red cows pulling a cart. But despite such admirable efforts, soundings taken around the dairy country indicate that the future holds little hope for anything beyond a token return to the Parmigiano of the good old days.

The consortium offered its hospitality. But having an aversion to programmed tours, and having seen large caseifici before, I declined, explaining that I'd decided to visit a small casello in the hills south of Reggio belonging to a certain Peppino Mornini. That name raised eyebrows in the public relations department, where I was told that Mornini makes good cheese but warned that his casello's *ambiente* left something to be desired.

The appointment, however, was already set. The next day at dawn at the Reggio exit of the Autostrada del Sole, I met Massimo Casali, a bon vivant who makes my favorite Lambrusco (dry, naturally) in the hills at Scandiano, and his friend Giuseppe Boschi, a young restaurateur who deals in gastronomic items. ''Boschi seeks only the authentic best,'' Casali had assured me over the phone, ''and he says that Mornini makes the Rolls-Royce of Parmigiano.''

We drove off on state route 63 toward the southwest, crossing frost-covered flatlands before ascending along the twisting gorge of the Crostolo stream to the towns of Vezzano and Casina, where we veered right toward the village of Migliara. As we climbed, the views opened onto a panorama that swept from the heights of the Apennines, looming to the south along the border of Tuscany, over a mantle of somber gray smog covering the Po Valley, to the Alps, glittering white in the early sunlight a hundred miles to the north. Casali, who as a boy had attended a school in the area, said such splendors could be seen only on special winter days.

We passed the medieval stone archway at Migliara and followed a narrow, winding road over the hillcrests of an idyllic gap in the Emilian Apennines to Beleo, a locality of small farms set amid steeply sloping pastures and woods. "This is it," said Boschi, as we arrived in front of a building whose plaster walls and wooden doors and shutters obviously hadn't been painted in years. Its sullen exterior made it look abandoned except for a towering TV antenna atop the roof and a couple of well-fed house cats eyeing us warily from a doorstep. We were early for our eight-thirty meeting, and Boschi, after sounding a buzzer and getting no response, strode off toward a barn where a chorus of pigs, squealing and grunting ecstatically over their morning feed, shattered the mountain stillness.

As he ducked through a doorway into the din, I checked out the surroundings. Behind the building, chickens and geese pecked for food amid the soggy remains of haystacks. Across the road a makeshift shelter with corrugated aluminum roof turned out to be a bus stop with a list of five scheduled daily departures. Casali found it odd that a casello wouldn't have a sign outside, or at least the usual symbolic replica of a wedge of Parmigiano to advertise it. I was beginning to understand what the PR people had meant about the *ambiente.*

Boschi emerged from the barn followed by a short, wiry man wearing a tattered laboratory frock over his work clothes and heavy rubber galoshes that seemed to accentuate his limp. His handshake was firm, despite a missing index finger. "Mornini," he introduced himself, surname first, doffing a visor cap with a paint advertisement and exposing a full head of gray hair. "Call me Peppino." He had a lean, weather-creased face with a prominent nose, bright hazel eyes, and a wide mouth that gave in easily to a smile, revealing a remarkably straight set of teeth. "Excuse my attire," he said. "I've been slopping the hogs." And though it was no joke, he conveyed such self-deprecating mirth that we laughed along with him.

Introductions over, he pushed open a creaking wooden door and ushered us into the casello. I had anticipated the sort of archaic sanctum depicted in the consortium's videocassette, but instead we entered a spacious workshop illuminated through windows by sunlight that cast a sheen on the tiles of floors and walls and a gleam on stainless-steel and copper equipment. Peppino hurried about the place, nimbly shifting his gait from hobbles to hops as he pointed out the functions of tanks, vats, pumps, and centrifuges. He seemed to want to describe the entire operation before he went to work on the day's cheese, but I had trouble following his dialect, which to my ear sounded like a mix of medieval Latin and upcountry Provençal.

"Peppino, parla italiano," Boschi reprimanded him. "We can see how the cheese is made later. Right now the writer wants to know something about your background, your career."

"My career?" Peppino chuckled. "Well, what else would a casaro do but make grana?" He laughed with what turned out to be his customary exuberance as Casali explained the pun; grana, besides cheese, is slang for dough or scratch (as in money), as well as for trouble or scandal. Peppino came back: "But in my case it just means formaggio."

Then in dutiful Italian he recited the basics of his background. He was born in 1923 in the nearby town of Castelnovo ne' Monti, where he worked as an apprentice in a casello before going to Parma to become a full-fledged casaro. "Until 1955 we made cheese in hand-forged copper caldrons over open wood fires," he recalled. "We even stirred the milk by hand, with wooden paddles. But that's all folklore now. If you can put a man on the moon, why make cheese over open fires?"

Peppino continued his saga. "Parma was still a *paese* then and those were pleasant years. I had a good position, family, friends. I banged up my leg [in an accident while driving a cheese truck] and lost a finger [while trying to repair a butter machine]. But, Lord knows, such things happen. All along, though, I'd had it in mind to have a casello of my own in the mountains. Here the grass stays green most of the year, so the milk is better, and the pure, cool air is just right for aging cheeses. My son Ugo had become a casaro too, so about fifteen years ago we bought this place. It isn't easy to be independent, but it's the smartest thing I've ever done. Well, I guess that's it," said Peppino. "That's my story."

"Not all of it," Boschi corrected. "He forgot to tell you that he's the leading accordion player in these hills."

Son Ugo arrived, backing a large, white, almost new Fiat Ducato van up to the main entrance. He greeted us with a modest smile and a quick wave and within minutes had unloaded a dozen 50-liter milk containers and was back in the driver's seat ready to go. "Come on along," he shouted over the sounds of music playing on tapes. So I joined him for the last three dairies of his morning round.

Ugo drove the heavy vehicle rapidly up and down steep and

tortuous grades as he talked about cheesemaking. ''We have long-term deals with farmers to provide milk each morning and evening,'' he said. ''But the cows don't take vacations and neither do we. So we make cheese three hundred and sixty-five days a year.'' At each dairy he hoisted a container of milk into the van, clamped it into a frame so it wouldn't slide, and signed the farmer's ledger. He explained that the dairies are paid annually a sum based on records of the quality of cheese their milk makes. But to be sure of getting the best milk, they have to pay more than the cooperatives do.

''This is a tough business, and it's hard for a small casello to compete,'' said Ugo. ''But we're doing pretty well now. For a while we were making just one or two cheeses a day, but we've taken on some new dairies, so we're up to three or four. Never more than six, though. That's our limit. You can't give it your best efforts with more.''

Ugo pointed out that one form of Parmigiano requires nearly 500 liters of fresh milk, roughly the daily yield of forty cows. He cited a series of figures to illustrate why the wholesale price of a cheese aged for a year netted them little over production costs, though he noted that the by-products—butter, ricotta, and hogs fed on whey—accounted for further earnings. ''But our best profits come from selling cheese retail at the casello,'' he said. ''We get lots of customers up here, because Peppino is a natural salesman.''

Ugo, a head taller than his father and solidly built, had sturdy facial features and light brown hair. But there was a resemblance in their hazel eyes, a familiar sparkle when they talked about cheese. ''I've been working in caselli since I was a boy of six or seven, except for a year in the military," said Ugo with a resigned smile. "Here I am in my thirties and still a bachelor. When you're busy from six in the morning till eight in the evening, it's hard to find time to socialize. I'll tell you, being a casaro isn't for everybody. You have to love this life."

Back at the casello Peppino, who had washed and shaved and changed into clean clothes in the family living quarters upstairs, was preparing equipment while bantering with Casali and Boschi in Emilian patois. Ugo reminded his father that they were running late as he tied on a heavy white apron and with a determined air began the operation.

The last evening's milk had been left in large stainless-steel trays overnight so that some cream would rise to be collected and made into butter. They drained this partly skimmed milk through a tube into two caldrons located on a lower level, 500 liters into one and 250 into the other. Using an automatic hoist to lift the containers, they measured equivalent amounts of fresh, whole morning milk into each caldron, explaining that they would make two cheeses in the first and one in the second.

The caldrons, or *caldaie,* are shaped like inverted churchbells, as they were in the past when they were made entirely of copper. But now they are built of cast iron and only lined with copper, the metal which best conducts heat to the mass from steam pumped through a serpentine of tubes in the space between. An electrically powered propeller-shaped paddle inserted in the caldron kept the milk swirling and churning slowly to blend it and keep the cream in suspension rather than rising.

As the milk was gradually heated, Ugo added *siero innesto,* starter whey. This residue from the previous day's batch had been left in a sealed container overnight to ferment and build lactic acid. Ugo tested the pH of whey and milk to determine the amount of starter needed—between 10 and 13 liters for each 500 liters of milk—to balance the overall acidity at 4.2 parts per thousand and regulate the degree of fermentation in the forming cheese.

"If that balance isn't perfect," cautioned Peppino, "*addio.* No cheese, just a little butter and a lot of extra whey for the hogs." The milk must be absolutely fresh and unpasteurized, he said, noting that if it comes from cows treated with medicines it won't make cheese. They pay the farmer for the milk anyway, but don't use it. He observed, though, that health problems are rare at the unpolluted heights of more than 2,000 feet above sea level. "It rains more up here than in the lowlands, so dairies have fresh forage most of the year," he said, adding with a wink that "there are advantages to being close to heaven."

Ugo waited attentively for the milk to reach about 90°F before turning off the heat. A minute later he stopped the paddle as the mass continued to revolve slowly in the caldron. Then he added *caglio,* rennet extracted by a special procedure from the stomach lining of nursing calves. This comes in a powder that is mixed with water in exactingly minute quantities, just enough to induce the milk to curdle over the next twelve to fifteen minutes in the phase known as *cagliatura,* the coagulation of the curds.

Texts explain that rennet is rich in the enzymes known as chymosin (also called rennin) and pepsin that cause the protein casein to precipitate, separating the curds from the whey. Peppino might keep it simpler, since, as he put it, ''We don't have college degrees; we worked our way up through the ranks.'' Divine providence rates a share of the credit for influencing the mysterious phenomena that transform milk to cheese, but no casaro would be so modest as to deny a little wizardry of his own. Each form is different from the next, they say, though not just because of the obvious variables in climate and season. Even cheeses made from the same batch of milk develop distinct personalities and need individual care.

The casaro's legendary curative powers with cheese were also often applied to people, which explains why he played a role in Emilian life somewhere between a medicine man and a magician. This description was written at the end of the last century by an unnamed author in Parma: ''The casaro must be a man expert in his craft, but much more he must be a man of good age, healthy and strong and pleasant and charitable and wise and not irritable and not a curser, but calm in his work, as much in knowing how to make cheese as in knowing how to guide it and care for it.''

Peppino and Ugo Mornini seemed to live up to those commandments, though the difference of a generation reflects in the way they interpret their roles. Perhaps the presence of strangers had put them on their best behavior, but I noticed that, among other attributes, they rarely cursed (as their neighboring Tuscans do with such relish). Instead they often said *perbacco,* a quaint expletive which lexicons translate as ''by Jove'' or ''by gosh,'' but which they extend to cover the likes of ''I'll be darned,'' ''what the heck,'' ''you bet,'' ''are you kidding,'' ''you don't

say,'' or even ''don't mention it,'' if someone expresses gratitude.

As the thickening liquid slowly circulated, Peppino and Ugo
hovered over the caldron like two cats watching goldfish swim
in a bowl. From time to time they dipped their fingers in to
collect coagulating bits and squeeze them into snow-white wads,
waiting for signs that curdling had reached the breaking point.
Then, as the mass ceased to swirl, Ugo began the *rottura della
cagliata*, the shattering of curds with the *spino*, a device made of
steel bars curved into what resembles a spherical birdcage on the
end of a long pole. (*Spino* means thornbush, which was originally
used for the operation). Slowly at first and then at increasing
tempo he agitated the mass by plunging the spino up and down,
sideways, and in rotary motions for three or four minutes while
the heat was raised to about 115°F. This vigorous maneuver frag-
mented the curds into fairly uniform particles about the size of
corn kernels, accounting, so they say, for the finished cheese's
fine grain.

Then came the *cottura*, as the heat was raised sharply for two
or three minutes to 131°F. Ugo explained that this gentle cooking firms up the curds and separates them from the watery whey
at a temperature high enough to kill off potentially harmful bacteria while allowing beneficial microorganisms to survive. When
the heat was turned off, the curds precipitated to the base of the
caldron to form a mass. After four or five minutes, Ugo reacti-
vated the paddle for a last rapid stir of the whey, thus releasing
the tiniest grains of curd (known in jargon as *polvere* or powder) to settle and fill any surface holes or fissures in the form.

While working over the two-cheese caldron, they had been

repeating steps at about ten-minute intervals in the vessel for the single cheese. When that was set, Ugo ladled some of the still-foamy whey from the caldrons into an aluminum vat to ferment and become the next day's starter. Some casari let the embryo cheese rest for twenty to thirty minutes before retrieving it from the base, but Peppino and Ugo leave it for nearly an hour, insisting that this *riposo* makes it more compact from the start.

Ugo, with his first chance for a morning break, invited us to join him for a coffee at the bar in Migliara. But Peppino apologized and said he couldn't go. He had other jobs to do before the final act in that morning's drama. ''We casari need to always keep on top of things,'' he reminded us cheerfully. Beyond collecting milk and making cheese, they process the cream into butter and reheat some of the whey to collect residual milk proteins and fats to become the soft, white ricotta. Most leftover whey, called *latticello*, is mixed with bran and corn and fed to the hogs, whose diet makes them choice sources of *prosciutto*. A little of the acidic starter whey is used with water for cleaning caldrons (detergents create unfavorable chemical reactions). Then there is the dreaded accounting, so complicated in bureaucratic Italy that many small-scale artisans have been discouraged and quit. They are even faced with household duties, which Peppino's wife has been unable to perform since going blind from diabetes years ago. But the veteran casaro had no complaints as he discussed his daily schedule with a shrug and a grin and a glance toward the heavens that chalked it all up to destiny.

As they made cheese, it had become clear that Ugo was in charge. He performed most of the important tasks himself with impressive precision and power, while now and then even issuing his father an order or a mild rebuke. But Peppino, more than a semiretired casaro or titular head of the family firm, prevails as the moving spirit of the place, the resident *personaggio*. And it seems only natural that a man of his age, so endowed with wit, energy, and cheer, would derive as much pleasure from selling cheese as from making it.

More than half of the house production of over a thousand drums of Parmigiano a year is sold at the *spaccio*, a shop with a marble-topped counter and a well-worn grocery scale, cramped into a corner of the building. The Mornini cheese with its sterling reputation costs a few thousand lire less per kilogram than it would at a shop in the valley. The house butter and ricotta are also prized. But the bonus that keeps customers from Reggio, Parma, and places beyond coming back to this remote outpost is unquestionably Peppino. They arrived at intervals through the day, filing into the spaccio, where the casaro held court, while carving and weighing grana. Not only did he prove to be a natural salesman, as Ugo had said, but he was a born comedian. His mannerisms might have befitted a medieval jester, in that knack for poking fun at himself while pleasing the crowd with impromptu gestures or dialect jokes, but he also had a player's sense of timing, of knowing when to ease the comedy and put across a point.

Ugo returned and joined his father at the caldrons. He took a long-handled, flat-bladed wooden peel and cautiously pried the rudimentary cheese from the bottom of the vessel, raising it enough so that with one hand he could roll and coax it into the heavy hemp cheesecloth that Peppino had submerged in the whey. The two men grasped corners of the netting and raised the cheese, which looked like an enormous mozzarella ball, tying the cloth to a wooden pole that Peppino had suspended across the rim. Ugo patted and massaged the white mass before leaving it partly immersed in the whey as they went to retrieve the smaller cheese.

About fifteen minutes later, they hoisted the huge form, weighing about 175 pounds, up near the rim and out of the liquid. Ugo, with a large knife, sliced it in two and kneaded each sector into a ball. He netted the odd form with a separate cheesecloth and eased it into a cylindrical mold known as a *fascera*, pressing it by hand to fill out the space and remove more whey. Still in the cloth, the cheese was left to dry for an hour in the fascera, covered with a heavy wooden slab that holds enough heat in to allow it to cool slowly while settling into the shape of a drum.

An hour later each form was turned upside down, and after another hour the heavy cheesecloth was replaced by a lighter one. This turning of the cheese in the fascera, always covered with a wooden slab, was repeated at two-hour intervals until early evening. Then the cloth was removed and the now quite firm cheese went into a plastic matrix that makes tiny holes in the surface, leaving the permanent imprints of PARMIGIANO REGGIANO, as well as the month and year (e.g., ''Feb 93'') and the casello code number (Mornini is 405). The last of the day's tasks was transferring the form into still another frame, this one of willow wood, where it spent the night.

The next morning, the cheese, by then barely pliable, is placed in a stainless-steel form which is tightened around it to force out any remaining whey through tiny holes. This mold has slightly convex sides that give the cheese its permanent shape over twenty-four hours. Then, finally free of hoops and matrixes, the cheese undergoes a day of drying that further solidifies it while the surface acquires enough of a yellow hue to reveal the lettering on the side. But this pale replica of a drum of Parmigiano still has a long way to go to the table.

The next phase is the *salatura,* the infusion of salt realized through immersing the cheeses in brine for twenty-six days in huge concrete tubs. In this *salamoia,* a solution of two parts water to one part salt, the floating drums must be turned daily to submerge the part of the surface that had been exposed to the air. At the end, salt has penetrated only about 2 inches, but over months of aging it becomes evenly distributed through the cheese. Ugo said that some people seem to think the white, sandy-textured flecks in the aged cheese's grain are salt, but they are really protein deposits which form only if the cheese is matured slowly and evenly. When the salatura has ended, in the cold months the cheese is placed in a moderately heated room—68°F—for a day to "sweat out" liquid before the long aging begins. In the warm months the drums are dried in the sun for a few hours.

Peppino showed us the cellars where cheeses are aged on long rows of shelves reaching from the floor to the ceiling. The newest forms are kept for several weeks on the cooler lower shelves along the interior wall, where they are turned and checked daily. As they mature and the rinds gradually harden and darken, the drums are shifted across the cellar to complete the required year of aging. The Mornini cheeses are kept in the cool of their own cellars, one at Beleo and another at Castelnovo ne' Monti. Natural aging has become rare for Parmigiano, most of which is kept in communal warehouses with exacting temperature, humidity, and ventilation controls. Boschi explained that the mountain environment gives the cheese more compact texture and extra dimensions of aroma and flavor.

During the aging, consortium inspectors check drums periodically, looking for any sign of a defect, which is often only a slightly flawed appearance—a spot or dent in the crust. The worst ailment, bacterial rot, is revealed by a swelling, or *balon* in jargon, indicating that the cheese must be discarded. The "doctors" tap each drum smartly with percussion hammers to reveal any hollows. (Peppino said that even the slightest cavity will produce an echo like that from tapping a watermelon.) Approved forms are branded with a hot iron that leaves an oval stamp with the consortium seal, certifying the year of production. Any form found to be below standard or even suspect will be marked with X's that cover the names all over the crust.

Peppino admitted that they get their share of rejects (about 15 percent overall), but pointed out that some *scarto* is as good as the approved. Still, he sells it after six or seven months at a price that makes it much in demand. He invited us into the spaccio to try some. First he used an apparatus with a taut wire to bisect a drum covered with X's, then he used a regular knife to slice off several pieces, explaining that it wasn't firm enough to be gouged or grated. But, despite its milky-white freshness, it already showed the grace that is peculiarly Parmigiano's. "Some people prefer the *fresco* for eating," said Peppino, "but I like the *stagionato* myself."

As he cleaved and wedged apart a drum aged for eighteen months, I glanced over displays on the wall. Besides a hand-lettered price list, there were framed certificates testifying to cheesemaking excellence, newspaper clippings about the casari and the casello, and several photos showing Mornini father and son with visiting dignitaries and friends. There was even a portrait of Peppino, in dark suit, white shirt, and tie, playing the accordion.

''Here, taste this,'' said the casaro, handing out bite-sized chunks. As we munched, Boschi repeated his Rolls-Royce analogy, though I liked the allusion to the Olympian Jupiter myself. Peppino accepted the praise with a spirited ''perbacco!'' But he admitted that he had made superior Parmigiano in the past, when milk came from native cows and cheese had the stuff to become stravecchio. Casali told him about the attempts to revive Razza Reggiana. ''Let's hope,'' said the casaro. ''Imagine the cheese we'd make up here from those red cows.''

Boschi had ordered ten cheeses to take away; Peppino suggested that they load them immediately. They went into a storeroom, where they weighed the forms one by one and inserted them in a contraption with rotary brushes which Peppino used to give the crusts a final polish. Then, unassisted, he hoisted a drum up onto his shoulder and, stooping under the load, walked unfaltering to the car. Casali and I watched in amazement. Here was a fellow of about seventy with a lame leg and a missing finger, toting a cheese a good two-thirds of his weight.

Ugo seemed amused by our reactions. ''With Peppino it's not a question of strength anymore, just routine,'' he explained.

"He doesn't think about how heavy they are. He just lifts them, the way he's been lifting them forever." Nor, apparently, did he think about suffering from physical conditions that some might lament through life as handicaps. The casaro carefully deposited the cheese in the rear of Boschi's station wagon and rambled inside for the next one. Back and forth he went, that dauntless little big man with the heavy drum on his shoulder, limping spryly and laughing at the fates.

Parmigiano, the consummate hard cheese, is used primarily for grating in recipes compiled over centuries from all Italian regions and beyond. The small bowl of grated cheese on tables of Italian restaurants is almost as familiar a fixture as the salt shaker and pepper grinder. Parmigiano is formally defined as a *formaggio di rifinitura,* in reference to the finishing touches it adds to pasta, soup, risotto, and polenta. Grated or ground it also figures in gratins, batters for deep-fried foods, and a wide array of sauces, including béchamel and Mornay, attesting to its stature in France.

Parmigiano is indispensable with hand-rolled *pasta fresca* of Emilia, such as *tagliatelle alla bolognese, tortellini alla modenese,* Parma's versions of *tortelli,* and Reggio's *cappelletti in brodo.* It is as essential as saffron in *risotto alla milanese,* as familiar as mozzarella on *pizza Margherita,* as basic as basil in *pesto alla genovese.* Shaved into flakes ( with mushrooms or truffles ) it adds verve to various versions of *carpaccio.* It is also the prime flavoring ingredient in the series of southern dishes known as *parmigiana di . . .* ( *melanzana, zucchine,* etc. ).

Its great advantage over most other cooking cheeses is that it can be distributed evenly and when it melts doesn't lump or become stringy. Even the thick, hard rind is edible. It should be saved after grating, scraped to remove any impurities acquired over time, and melted into soups or baked dishes.

But Parmigiano, because of its legendary versatility, is used too often and all too often abused. Indiscriminate diners pile it onto almost any pasta with little regard for the other ingredients. It doesn't usually go well with hot or spicy sauces based on tomatoes or peppers. Cooks are wary of its compatibility with most wild mushrooms. It is extremely difficult to match with fish (granting exceptions for anchovies or sardines).

Its closest admirers prefer Parmigiano as a table cheese, when it is firm but gently yielding to the bite. Small chunks are often served as appetizers, accompanied by a dry white wine, especially a brut sparkler made by the Champagne method. It regularly serves as the cheese course in Emilia, but it can also make a nourishing main course with a side dish of salad—and not only for infants, the elderly, or weight watchers. Or it can be dessert, since it goes nicely with fruit, especially pears, but also apples and grapes. Emilians habitually serve Lambrusco with Parmigiano, though it can stand up to bigger wines, such as Chianti Classico or Barolo, and it provides unique sensations when served with the bone-dry, tasty Marsala Vergine.

Propaganda that boasts of Parmigiano as one of the healthiest of foods seems to ring true. The cheese contains most of the elements of fresh whole milk but with more concentrated proteins, calcium and other essential minerals, and vitamins. Not only that, it is more easily digestible than milk and a quicker source of energy. Classified as semifat (with a moderate 32 percent butterfat), it apparently has the lowest cholesterol content in the international field of major cheeses.

Whether intended for eating fresh or grating, Parmigiano Reggiano should be bought in chunks, preferably wedged directly from the drum, where it stays fresh longer. If packaged, pieces should have enough of the rind attached to show at least a portion of the official brand. The ideal storage place is a cool, moderately dry cellar, where it should be kept in cheesecloth or inside a hard plastic container with vent holes. It may be stored for a short time in cheese paper or foil in the lower part of the refrigerator. It's important to avoid excessive dryness (which causes hardening and loss of flavor) or damp (which encourages mold). Even authentic Parmigiano Reggiano may be sold packaged in tiny cubes or grated form, like the widespread imitations, but no cheese lover should accept such insults to good taste.

Within the Parmigiano Reggiano production zone lie Parma, Reggio, and Modena, prosperous little cities with vibrant lifestyles and a wealth of historical attractions. The consortium (headquarters Via J. F. Kennedy 18, Reggio nell'Emilia) will arrange visits to cheese dairies. These include some ancient caselli that are jewels of rural architecture, constructed in hexagonal or octagonal form to resemble small temples or church baptistries, with arches in which tiles have been assembled artistically to leave openings for ventilation. From time to time casari demonstrate how Parmigiano was made in the old days, in huge copper caldrons heated by the flames of wood fires.

Among restaurants and trattorie in the Parma and Reggio

areas, these are especially recommended for dishes with Parmigiano: Trattoria del Lago near Campegine, Angiol d'Or and Marzia e Bruno at Parma, Picci al Cristallo at Reggio, Da Arnaldo at Rubiera, Trattoria Turci at Grassano di San Polo d'Enza, Alla Luna Piena at Traversetolo.

# Vino
## Lord of the vines

To many Italians, making wine outside the auspices of the *denominazione di origine* laws is a way of flaunting their individuality, so one might imagine that a confirmed nonconformist like Edoardo Valentini of the Abruzzi would be among the first to defy the norms. But no, Valentini conscientiously classifies his wines under the DOCs of Montepulciano d'Abruzzo and Trebbiano d'Abruzzo, appellations that carry little weight beyond the mountainous region across the peninsula from Rome on the Adriatic Sea.

Convention, however, would seem to end there, for his approach, which he describes as ''making wine in the vineyard,'' mocks most modern methods of oenology. And yet, after decades in which he has followed his solitary course while others have been riding the waves of Italy's wine revolution, Valentini seems to be sailing with the currents. These days vanguard oenologists profess to the ''natural methods'' that put the emphasis back on the vines and the intrinsic quality of grapes so that wines need little manipulation in the cellar. But applying fundamentals is not as simple as it sounds, for vineyards that had been renovated with trendy varieties, treated for years with fertilizers and sprays, and pushed to the limits of production can't be converted back to a primary state from one vintage to the next. Nor were high-tech cellars designed to make wine in what Edoardo Valentini would consider nature's way.

He has a decided advantage over the growing ranks of back-to-the-basics wine producers in Italy in that never having gone far forward he has no need to turn around. It should be noted, though, that he doesn't consider himself a producer but rather a *vignaiolo,* a grape grower who serves as a guide and custodian for his wines, a medium between nature's supply and man's demand. He describes his ''supporting role'' as one of minimal intervention, of making minor adjustments at opportune moments to help the wine express the true character of each vintage.

Other grape growers in Italy who avoid artifices might describe their wine as *biologico* or *organico* or similar, terms that Valentini dismisses as superfluous. But what sets his wines apart from those of most other naturalists is class, the virtues of aroma, flavor, and texture considered extraordinary not only by devotees of the rare and different but even by some critics whose tastes run toward the stereotyped. Valentini's red Montepulciano d'Abruzzo from top vintages may have an occasional rival in size and structure in its youth, though no other acquires such depth and elegance over time. His Trebbiano d'Abruzzo, more than just the best wine of the name, is considered one of Italy's most distinguished whites. As it ages, it stands so patently above the crowd that admirers and competitors alike are convinced that he uses mysterious methods to make it.

Valentini laughs at such conjecture while denying that he has anything to hide. Yet he avoids discussing his techniques because he dislikes being misunderstood. Instead he offers such cryptic observations as ''The concepts I follow were known to the ancient Romans'' or ''No rules of winemaking are as important as common sense and intuition.'' He reads compulsively about viticulture and oenology and records every nuance of each vintage in handwritten ledgers. But he prefers to keep the details to himself. Once when an interviewer asked about his methods, he replied: ''If you had lived in Caravaggio's day and had a chance to meet him, would you have wasted his time trying to get him to describe how he mixed his colors?''

I first met Edoardo Valentini in 1978 at the *palazzo* that doubles as his home and cellars at the heights of Loreto Aprutino, a pretty hill town with views onto the Gran Sasso and Maiella, the highest peaks in the Apennines. That encounter began on a tense note when, after reluctantly accepting my telephoned request for a visit, he received me at the mansion's door with a suspicious look and the reminder that he did not pay ''journalists'' for writing about his wines. Reassured of my intentions, he showed me around, apologizing for the clutter created by bottles stacked along stately corridors and staircases and by journals and books piled on antique tables and chairs. That meeting was short because, he said, as a man of the soil he had a busy day ahead in the vineyards. But even though his replies were terse and he glared at the camera when I took his photograph, we struck off what has since become a friendship.

Over the years Edoardo has come to represent a rare constant in Italy's radically evolved society of wine. He had the means to become a gentleman farmer, but instead he has remained a true man of the soil, a rugged individualist whose noble bearing has a friendly touch of rusticity about it, since he manages to combine, with no apparent contradictions, the wisdom of a scholar and the tastes of an aesthete with the wit, cunning, and grit of an old-style *contadino*.

He took a degree in jurisprudence as a youth. But instead of joining his father's law firm in the port city of Pescara, he decided to take charge of the family estate at Loreto Aprutino. There he produces fine extra vergine olive oil and fruit, but his primary concerns are his vines and his wines. He and his field workers tend his 178 acres of vineyards with infinite care. He selects the best grapes from good vintages for his own wines and sells off the rest.

Production is slight: thirty to forty thousand bottles in good years, a fraction of the vineyards' potential. Half to two-thirds is Trebbiano and the rest Montepulciano, which is sold in an aged version as *vecchio* and also comes in a cherry-pink type known as Cerasuolo. Although he makes no effort to publicize them, rarely traveling far from home, his wines have developed a cult following in Italy and abroad, forcing him to ration his meager supplies. Yet, despite demand, he refuses to sell his wines until he considers them ready to drink, no matter how long that might be. Thus in 1993 he was selling Trebbiano from 1988 and 1990 and

Montepulciano from 1987 and 1988. The only wine he sells relatively young is Cerasuolo, after a year in bottle.

Edoardo puts all his wines in personally designed bottles of heavy, dark brown glass that blocks out ultraviolet rays. "Light is the enemy of wine," he explained, "especially white wine for aging." Through the years all his wines have carried the same label design based on a sixteenth-century bookplate illustration, though lettering is done in different-colored ink (green for Trebbiano, red for Montepulciano, and blue for Cerasuolo). His labels used to state each bottle's number from each vintage. But he stopped when he noted that even large commercial wineries were numbering their wines. "That was a quiet form of protest," he said, adding with a grin that "since then a rumor's been going around that I stopped numbering because I've increased production to hundreds of thousands of bottles and don't want to admit it."

The fact is that he could produce that much but doesn't, because quantity would compromise quality. If Edoardo has a secret, it's selection. His three main vineyards—known as Castelluccio, Camposacro, and Colle Cavaliere—all qualify as *crus*. But he refuses to join the nationwide trend to single-vineyard bottlings, insisting that he gets more consistent results by selective picking and blending. He makes only as much wine each year as he judges to be at top standard. He apparently alone in the Abruzzi passed up the subpar 1989 vintage, formally renouncing DOC for the wines he made only to fill his casks and keep them from drying out.

His unsolicited success has made him the envy of the Abruzzi's winemakers, though modern-minded *enotecnici,* who seem to resent the fact that his "country wines" rank well above their more sophisticated bottlings in prestige and price, sometimes criticize rather than praise. Edoardo has been called many things—poet, philosopher, sorcerer, crank—but he continues to make wine with an aloof disregard for trends or formalities and such obstinate devotion to his land that a local journal once described him as the "lord of the vines."

At sixty, with the features of his weather-creased face hemmed by a full head of wavy, graying brown hair and a full beard in a wiry pepper and salt, he seems perhaps mellower in manner than before. Yet his views, accentuated by a perpetually ironic sense of humor, are still expressed with more frankness than conventional wine people might be prepared to accept. But then Edoardo Valentini doesn't spend much time around conventional wine people.

Nor, for that matter, do I anymore after being subjected to a surfeit of regimented tours of Italian wineries whose vineyards and cellars have little to differentiate them from those of Bordeaux or California or Australia and whose wines seem intended to generate similar analogies. My visits to Edoardo at intervals over the years have been like journeys into wine's idyllic past. But reaching his domain is no routine matter since the Abruzzi is separated from my home in Tuscany by more than 200 miles of the rugged central Apennines, through which nothing resembling a direct route can be found.

On my latest visit on a fine day in early May, I crossed the mountains to Ancona and took the Adriatic autostrada to Pescara Nord. Driving southwest along the Tavo River I found that the bridge on the old route to Loreto Aprutino had been washed out by floods a month earlier. So I took a detour through the villages of Santa Lucia and Collecorvino past patches of vineyards and olive groves alternating with grainfields in the sharply sloping clay soil. It was late morning when I reached Loreto and followed the curving cobblestone streets up to the corner of Via del Baio to park in a shady spot beneath the town castle, next to the Valentini palazzo.

Edoardo welcomed me warmly at the door and led me down the entrance hall, which for the first time in my memory was free of stacks of bottles. He had recently acquired cellars for storage in adjacent buildings, he explained, meaning that now he could age all wines as long as he liked and never again consent to sell a bottle before its time. "That's progress," he said.

"It certainly is," came the cheerful voice of his wife, Adriana, who overheard us from the kitchen, where she was preparing lunch. "Now we have some breathing room," she said. "But that's not the only news. Did he tell you that we installed central heating?"

Edoardo seemed a bit abashed by this bow to modernity. "Well, I admit it's a relief not to have to go around relighting wood fires all winter," he explained. "I guess it's a sign of age." We walked through the kitchen into the living room with its intricate mix of different eras in art and furnishings and settled into leather armchairs to talk.

Anything new on the wine front? I asked, hoping to set him off. Edoardo grinned and stroked his beard, then peered at me with professorial severity over the top of his horn-rimmed glasses. "How many times have I told you that with me there's never anything new, just meditated alterations?" Then his tone turned to disgust. "But elsewhere in the region there are all sorts of novelties. They're making Chardonnay and Cabernet and Pinot and lots of wines with bubbles. So, rather than aim for distinctive wines from our native Montepulciano and Trebbiano d'Abruzzo, the tendency seems to be to destroy what little tradition we had."

He rose impatiently from his chair and strode to the window to peer across a wooded gorge toward his extensive lands. "These days everybody talks about quality, but few growers are willing to make the sacrifices in the vineyards needed to realize it," he said. "In their haste to plant everything but native varieties, they forget that vines take decades to adapt to local conditions. Look at it this way. If you took a family of chimpanzees out of Africa and put them in a woods in the Abruzzi, they wouldn't thrive and might not survive. They'd need several generations to acclimatize, to adjust to the habitat. Well, it's the same with vines."

In an age of genetic vine engineering and computerized oenology, there is something reassuring about Edoardo's otherworldly approach to wine. Through trial and error he devised his own form of vine training, a low canopy controlled to keep grape yields at levels to achieve a balance in sugar, acids, and other elements. He crushes grapes using the old roller system and ferments and matures all the wines—even the white and Cerasuolo—in well-seasoned casks, mainly of oak but also of other woods, crowded together in rows in his ancient vaulted cellars.

He relies on traditional racking and settling to clarify the wines, all of which remain just under a year in casks of different dimensions. He reminded me that in almost forty years of experience he has never used a filter, a heating or cooling device, or containers in plastic or stainless steel. His only concessions to contemporary convenience are an electric pump to transfer wine from barrel to barrel and a semiautomatic filling and corking apparatus to save time during bottling, which he carries out directly from the casks.

He abides by his vines and wines from the beginning of each cycle to the end, he explained, because he is dealing with matter that is enzymatically alive and undergoing constant change. ''A long fermentation at natural temperatures is essential,'' he said. ''Any wine obtained in a short time will have a short life. During fermentation and aging a gradual molecular breakdown takes place in the presence of oxygen. Very little, mind you, but wine needs a constant source of oxygen breathed through natural materials: the wood of barrels, the cork that serves as the lung of the bottle. To stay vital, wines must be stored at natural temperatures that change gradually enough to sustain life.''

He looked concerned. ''Now to me these are fundamentals of winemaking. Yet many producers today rely on synthetic materials such as stainless steel and on operations that create artificial conditions: centrifuging and rapid cooling and heating and storage under nitrogen. I suppose such expedients serve a purpose for strictly commercial wines. But I can't imagine who would want to drink them. Most such wines are, clinically speaking, dead.''

In expressing his views, Edoardo often shifts from the practical to the abstract, as in his ensuing theme on the Socratic method. He explained that Socrates' way of repeated questioning of humans to elicit truths could also be applied to wines. ''Each vintage has its own realities that are revealed to those who remain in constant touch with the grapes and the wine. But it takes years of experience to be able to evaluate these truths.''

As Edoardo stood by the window, gesturing passionately as he spoke, I could have imagined him exchanging his loose-fitting cotton and corduroy clothes for a tunic and joining the wine-loving Socrates and Plato in the shadow of the Parthenon to compare vintage notes. How pleased he would have been to visit ancient Rome and review vine-training methods with Columella or hoist goblets of Falernian with Virgil or Horace. But before I could conjure up more historical images he had returned to his chair and shifted to a biological tack.

''Wine is conceived in the vineyard and gestated in the cellar,'' he stated. ''To me, using grapes grown by somebody else to make wine would be *contra natura,* like artificial insemination.'' He likened the cask to the uterus, where wines through fermentation and settling evolve from embryos to newborns. ''What's fascinating is that each cask is different and its character is conveyed to the wine, contributing certain nuances to its personality. Stainless-steel tanks are marvelously convenient devices, they say, but to me putting wine in one would be like consigning it to a burial vault.''

Toward noon we were joined by his son, Francesco Paolo, a lanky youth whose gentle way of speaking contrasted with Edoardo's dynamism. He had been working for several years with his father after taking a degree in psychology—''an infinitely more useful credential for a winemaker,'' Edoardo assured me, than the usual technical institute diploma of *enotecnico.* Francesco readily joined the conversation, picking up on cues and injecting ideas of his own so deftly that at one point Edoardo confided to me proudly that when he goes the estate will pass into abler hands.

Adriana called us to the kitchen, where she was putting the finishing touches on lunch with the infectious gusto of a cook who loves to eat. We gathered around a large wooden table in the spacious room with beamed ceilings and a raised hearth decorated with hand-painted tiles, a specialty of Loreto that gives interiors vivacious color and warmth. She had made *maccheroni alla chitarra,* the noodles traditionally cut with a guitarlike device into quadrangular strands, served with a sauce based on their own olive oil with eggplants, black olives, tomatoes, and *diavolilli,* the chili peppers that lace the Abruzzi's *cucina* with eye-watering piquancy. Then came roast goose of the free-range variety along with oven-browned potatoes and a salad of field greens, followed by *crostata,* a tart made with Adriana's own bitter cherry marmalade.

With these delicacies we tasted various vintages of wines that have kept their inimitable character intact while others have been revolutionized beyond recognition. All three showed the completeness, the harmony of components, that comes from proper aging in barrel and bottle, but beyond their inherent elegance they expressed authentic tastes of the earth, a spontaneous goodness that made them a sheer joy to drink.

Edoardo confirmed his preference for the red Montepulciano, though he wasn't convinced that any of the recent vintages were near their prime. "Harmony is achieved when you reach a balance between the contrasting aromas and flavors in a wine," he said. "But that takes time. I keep telling my customers to be patient, but they don't want to believe that wine needs thorough aging to express its best. Yes, even white wine. People today want to have it all right now.''

Montepulciano could rank among the nation's worthiest native vines, but even Italians tend to associate it incorrectly with the town of the name in Tuscany rather than the Abruzzi, where it probably originated and certainly prevails. Its wines vary from medium-light and fruity to thick and dark, though those of Valentini and a few others mature with uncommon grace, developing a soft yet peppery quality that recalls a well-aged Hermitage from France's Rhône. Cerasuolo is a bracing match with pungently flavored local dishes, but being pink it is usually dismissed by serious wine drinkers.

The latter have even less time for the usually trivial Trebbiano. Italy's most diffused and productive white vine (or family of vines, rather, since the name applies to various varieties and clones) has gained distinction indirectly in southwestern France, where under the names Ugni Blanc or St-Emilion it makes the base wines to be distilled into Cognac. But in Italy, despite its popularity, its wines have been largely discredited by experts. The outstanding exception to the rule is Valentini's Trebbiano d'Abruzzo.

I first tasted that wine from the 1962 vintage in 1968. It came in a heavy brown bottle with a label depicting a character in medieval country garb standing in a vineyard with a mountain in the background. When poured, it showed a deep green-gold color, a sign of age unusual in an Italian white wine, though that worried me less than the sediment visible at the base of the bottle. To my surprise it was delicious, fresh in scent and rich in texture, with flavors of ripe but vital fruit that lingered on the tongue.

For lack of ready references I described it as Burgundian in style, but vintages over a span of nearly thirty years have confirmed that it has too distinctive a personality to be compared with any other wine from any variety, least of all Trebbiano.

Edoardo seems to possess a unique clone of Trebbiano d'Abruzzo, a vine of mysterious origin whose authenticity is often debated. Some relate it to the Bombino Bianco of Apulia or the vine known as Campolese once popular in the region. The Trebbiano family dates to pre-Roman times, possibly originating with the Etruscans, though some strains seem to be related to vines known as Greco, brought to Italy by the Greeks. There is even some speculation that the true Trebbiano d'Abruzzo, whatever that might be, is not a Trebbiano at all.

Since the spread of phylloxera, the vine louse that destroyed most of Europe's vineyards around the turn of the century, varieties in Italy often have been chosen more for productivity than class. So many respectable vines had been lost or forgotten. These days most Trebbiano planted in the Abruzzi is of the notoriously prolific Toscano or Romagnolo subvarieties. Nor is it a well-kept secret that table grapes are sometimes included for good measure. Most vines are trained over high canopies in the system known as *tendone*. Irrigation from water in the Apennines has helped give the region the highest rate of yields among Italy's twenty. So much of what qualifies as Trebbiano d'Abruzzo is light, thin, sometimes refreshingly *frizzante,* but devoid of style, and in general destined to fall apart within a year or two of the harvest.

Given that sort of company, I asked Edoardo, what's the advantage of DOC? Doesn't the name Trebbiano and its lackluster reputation detract from your wine's market value?

"There's no way of knowing," he said. "But that's not the point. Mine is a true Trebbiano of this place, Loreto Aprutino, and I'm proud to call it by its name." Why DOC? "Because I figure that you can make a statement more effectively within a regime than from outside it. If you produce the best wine of the appellation, you challenge the others to try to match you. But if you remain outside with a fancy *vino da tavola* you only compete with yourself."

The competition has failed to develop, however, even though the Abruzzi has considerable potential for quality on sunny slopes of calcareous clays and a climate cooled by the play of breezes between the Apennines and the Adriatic. If anything the Valentini Trebbiano stands out more than ever from the field, like a priceless antique in a room full of plastic furniture.

Edoardo recalled meeting with other producers when the DOC was being formulated more than twenty years ago. "I tried to talk them into planting the true Trebbiano, even offering cuttings of mine. But they laughed. They told me I must be crazy to stick with old vines when I could get tremendous yields from the other Trebbiani. Well, I told them what I thought of them, and ever since then I've gone my own way."

While Valentini's aged Trebbiano has soared in prestige and value, the others have remained in the rank and file of the Abruzzi's invariably youthful whites. "Yes, but wouldn't you know that some of those same growers who refused them in the past came to me recently to ask for cuttings," said Edoardo. "Well, I showed them to the door and told them: 'If you come by night and steal them you might get away with it, but if you come by day, I'll shoot you!' "

The lord of the vines laughed, knowing that even if they stole some cuttings they could never spirit away the wisdom, or the wizardry, behind perhaps the only wine called Trebbiano that has ever been described as great.

Edoardo Valentini does not sell his wines directly to the public, though he might welcome visitors to Loreto Aprutino for knowledgeable discussions about viticulture and oenology in Italian. His wines can be found in the Abruzzi at the Enoteca Templi Romani at Chieti, as well as at the Enoteca Internazionale Bugari at San Benedetto del Tronto in the Marches and in Rome at the Enoteca Trimani, among other select shops. The wines should be considered ready to drink when sold, though the Montepulciano vecchio and Trebbiano will keep for years in cool cellars.

Visitors to the Abruzzi can taste the Valentini wines at the following restaurants, which are also noted for good cooking: Da Duilio, Guerino, and La Vongola at Pescara, Beccaceci at Giulianova, Il Corsaro at Porto di Vasto, Aquila at Avezzano, La Grotta di Aligi at L'Aquila, and L'Angolino di Filippo at Marina di San Vito. Also recommended are Ribo at Guglionesi and Lo Squalo Blu at Termoli in adjacent Molise.

# Culatello
## The fugitive king of the foggy bottoms

*A*s man evolved from scavenger and hunter to herdsman and livestock breeder, he progressed beyond the rudimentary cooking of meat to invent ways to preserve and refine it. In Italy this quest culminated in *salume,* salt-cured meat in the form of hams, sausages, salami, bacon, and less familiar delicacies. Sources may be beef, horse, donkey, goose, turkey, boar, or even chamois, but to the vast majority of *salumieri* the prodigy is the pig. Distinguished salume is made throughout Italy, as in much of Europe, yet for overall quality, diversity, and peaks of excellence perhaps no place on earth can rival Emilia, where the curing and aging of pork is a venerable master craft.

Provincial specialties highlight the array. Emilia-Romagna's capital of Bologna, eulogized as ''the fat,'' weighs in with *mortadella,* the pork loaf also sometimes called *bologna* or baloney.

Modena proffers the pig's trotter sausage *zampone*, eaten nation-wide with luck-bearing lentils at the New Year. Piacenza's *coppa piacentina* is the air-dried neck roll, elsewhere called *capocollo*. Emilians all make the lean and mildly seasoned *salame gentile* that is indeed as genteel as minced meat can be, and *cotechino*, a sausage whose stuffing includes bits of *cotenna*, pigskin tenderized by long simmering.

But the royal realm of salume is Parma, and not only because its name is annexed to the *prosciutto* that reigns as Italy's most widely admired meat product. Prosciutto di Parma, protected by a *denominazione di origine controllata* (DOC) and identified by a trademark with the word PARMA in a crown, is made at the rate of nearly 8 million hams a year. Its production zone, which extends from plains around Parma into hills to the south, is centered at Langhirano, a town on the edge of the Apennines with a unique microclimate noted as ideal for aging *prosciutto crudo*, raw ham. After the initial salt curing, the whole mandolin-shaped leg with the bone is aged for ten to twelve months in *prosciuttifici*, spacious buildings whose multiple shutters may be opened when the weather is fine to let in the gentle air.

Prosciutto di Parma, in delectable rose-petal-pink slices, proves that elegance in aged salume can be achieved on an epic scale. But local arbiters regard prosciutto (from *prosciugare*, to dry), as a sort of prodigal prince that ranks only second in status in Parma's monarchy. To them, the king is *culatello*, from the fleshiest part of the pig's posterior, the buttocks.

Culatello is produced by methods markedly diverse from those used to make prosciutto and is aged in a peculiar kind of environment, the foggy lowlands near the Po River in an area known as the Bassa Parmense, or locally as the Bassa. The "king of salume" is a creature of the fog and the damp, which reach unequaled intensity in the Bassa, an area of flat farmland reclaimed long ago from marshes along the course of Italy's mightiest river.

Culatello is a filet of ham, separated from the bone, which means that making one sacrifices an entire prosciutto. The authentic, traditional type, when found, can cost up to three times as much by weight, so a finished culatello weighing a little over 6½ pounds might be worth as much as an aged prosciutto at the average of about 20 pounds. Put another way, around Parma the two culatelli, fresh or aged, are worth more than all the remaining cuts of the hog put together.

But these days culatello devotees whisper about its splendors rather than shout. For not only is the traditional type scarce but, if trends continue, its already covert commercial sources seem destined to disappear. Remaining producers use locally raised hogs to make a precious few culatelli each winter, mainly for home consumption or as a payment or appreciation to the family doctor, lawyer, or priest. But butchering, curing, and aging are carried out in private.

After salt curing, the meat is sewn into membrane sheaths and trussed tight with strings laced artistically into nets that leave them in the shape of pears after aging for eight months to a year or more in fog-vaporized lofts and moldy *cantine*. There and only there, as centuries of sage workmanship can attest, does culatello achieve tender perfection.

Despite culatello's prestige among gastronomes, the matchless flavors of this rarefied slice of culinary culture aren't savored by

officialdom. The ancestral aging places have been dutifully condemned as unsuitable for foodmaking by the Unità Sanitarie Locali, communal health authorities. Equally severe are antifraud
squads whose controls of food processing have meant that real
culatello must be made and sold on the sly. Suppression of the
craft has been decreed, if indirectly, from on high: by the Italian
government and the European Community, whose policies,
swayed by big business, require meat products of all types,
whether raw, cured, canned, or frozen, to be treated in premises
of operating-room sterility.

Advocates have pointed out that culatello, *quello vero*, of
course, won't mature properly in the required spick-and-span laboratories lined with tiles to seal off the damp. But so far their
pleas have fallen on deaf ears. Hence the king of salumi, or salume
of kings, holds court furtively in the Bassa, a fugitive from what
only fastidious technocrats might consider justice.

There is, however, another kind of ''culatello'' increasingly
available on the open market. It may be made in the Bassa, or
more likely elsewhere, at authorized *salumifici* where some steps
in the curing follow tradition but where aging in air-conditioned
cells does not. Ersatz culatello may be found on menus or in
shops or supermarkets, sometimes handily sliced and packaged,
at little more than half the going rate for the genuine. Some examples might be tasty, but, as they say, the real thing is the
''caviar of the Bassa,'' the other stuff is fish eggs.

The kingdom of culatello lies northwest of Parma in a quadrangular area that fronts for about 12 miles on the Po and extends
southward between the Taro and Ongina streams for about 6
miles, or to where the land begins to rise toward prosciutto coun-

try. Within the area many localities boast a tradition, though none prouder than Zibello, a tranquil town nestled against the levee that protects this lonesome netherland from the Po's flood-waters.

The enterprising townspeople have registered Culatello di Zibello as a trademark while leading a bid for DOC in a zone to cover parts of five other communities of the Bassa—Busseto, Polesine Parmense, Roccabianca, Soragna, and San Secondo—as well as nearby Colorno. Zibello's Mayor Gaetano Mistura explained that the appellation would apply only to culatello made following local traditions, though he confessed that it might be considered a ''ghost product,'' since most is homemade and not for sale. Others predicted that if a DOC is granted, commercial interests will pressure authorities into including industrial cula-tello.

Some citizens of other towns have objected so violently to limiting the name to Zibello that the conflict has been depicted in the press as *la guerra del culatello*. But proposals for a broad appellation of Culatello della Bassa Parmense (or simply della Bassa) have not been well received by partisans who seem to feel that each town rates a DOC of its own. Opposition forces are led by the Arcisodalizio per la Ricerca del Culatello Supremo, a fraternal order based in San Secondo, whose members at an annual tasting designate salume's king of kings.

Salt-cured prosciutto from the Parma area was known in an-cient Roman times, but it is unclear just when or where in the Bassa the first culatello was secreted away from a ham. Historians have dismissed assertions that the Marchesi Pallavicino of Busseto and Conti Rossi of Zibello feasted on it as early as 1322. Still, culatello may have had noble origins, since by tradition the lord of the manor kept the hams and the peasants made do with the rest. Country people fared well, though, thanks to ingenious methods of preservation, for then as now no part of the generous pig was wasted. The first known written mention of culatello came in a listing of the types of salt pork sold in the Duchy of Parma in 1735, after the Farnese family dynasty ended and control of the small but influential state was being fought over by Bourbons and Hapsburgs. Nor has its fate been documented often since. While prosciutto di Parma was acquiring world fame, culatello, or locally *culatel'*, remained the secret glory of the Bassa.

Incidents such as the culatello war are not always taken tongue in cheek in a place where eating, like opera, has been a serious pursuit since the days when Giuseppe Verdi, born near Busseto in 1813, frequented its *trattorie*. Verdi is the idol of the Bassa. Restaurants display photos and paintings of the maestro with plaques and signed menus, exhibits resembling the shrines that elsewhere might commemorate a visit by the Pope or a vision of the Madonna. A host explained: "This isn't Venice or the Amalfi Coast or the Dolomites, understand. Verdiana and gastronomia are what we have to offer."

The Bassa's southern extreme is flanked by the Autostrada del Sole, a stretch of tollway dreaded by motorists in winter for the frequency and density of fogs. But it was just such conditions on a December day more than twenty years ago that led to my discovery of culatello. After plodding through the mist from Bologna past Parma and realizing that I'd never make Milano for lunch, I pulled off the autostrada at Fidenza and, following a star in the Guide Michelin, made my way along narrow lanes through

the murky flatlands to a place called Samboseto. When a tour of
the deserted main street of that farm hamlet turned up no trace
of an eatery, I stopped at what seemed to be the only place open,
a small salumeria whose shelves brimmed with hams, salami,
cheeses, and other choice foodstuffs, to inquire about the ristorante Da Cantarelli.

The man behind the counter grinned. "It isn't exactly a
ristorante," he said, "but it's here." Giuseppe Cantarelli opened
the door to an antechamber that had the homey cheer of a country
osteria, with wood-paneled walls adorned by local artists' paintings and a corner stove that threw off enough heat to steam up
the windows. But the dining room also had touches of palatial
refinement in the linen, porcelain, silver, and crystal arranged on
a dozen or so tables.

Cantarelli stocked the best Champagnes, but he chose a fizzy
bianco from the distant hills as more appropriate with the antipasto, a platter laden with circular slices of meat as subtle as rose-
tinted parchment. Prosciutto, of course. "No, culatello," he
corrected, and with enviable aplomb patted his hind side, "from
here." In those days you weren't supposed to say culo in polite
company, but I hardly needed to double-check the derivation. It
was, as he promised, even mellower than prosciutto, softer in
texture and more sumptuous in flavor.

His wife, Mirella, served her tortelli con le erbette, envelopes
filled with ricotta and greens worthy of all the superlatives I'd
heard about Emilian pasta, and padellata, pork ribs stewed with
beans, a dish of humble origins elevated to haute cuisine. With
that Cantarelli poured a Scorzanera, an unheralded red that tow-
ered over any other I knew from the flatlands. Chunks of Par-

migiano from a local *casello* and a lavish array of freshly baked pastries rounded out a meal that would have been unforgettable even without those revelationary portions of rump.

Da Cantarelli earned a second Michelin star soon after, though to my taste, acquired on frequent visits in the years that followed, that ma-and-pa diner back of the grocery remained immeasurable by orthodox gauges, inimitable, *hors classe*. But things that seem too good to be true have a way of ending. In 1982, when Mirella Cantarelli became ill, her husband, knowing that hired cooks could never match her talents, summoned his customary dignity and closed.

In the late 1970s, when Da Cantarelli was at its peak, the food guides had made Parma the most decorated province of Italy. But since then most of the stars have vanished. Verdi still draws opera buffs to Busseto, but the closest most tourists come to the Bassa these days is the Autostrada del Sole, as they speed by toward Mediterranean beaches, Alpine ski runs, or cities of art. For, after all, what besides gourmet dining might attract visitors to this backwater of sparsely populated villages and lonely farms with all the scenic endowments of eastern Kansas and weather that chills through to the bone in January and brings on sauna-like sweats in July?

Well, to those who live there, and some who don't, the Bassa has its pluses. They say that the drab surroundings inspire human spirit, elucidated by Verdi's genius or on a more familiar scale by the spicy banter heard around the street markets, bars, and trattorie, or the piercing comments that issue from the opera galleries. The land is unrelentingly flat, but in springtime it comes alive with nature's colors, odors, and sounds. A late-summer sunset viewed across its lonesome stretches can evoke the magic of the desert. Then there's the *nebbia,* the fog, which isn't a fleeting maritime sort of mist in the Po bottoms but an entity that seems as tangible as a curtain, as thick as cotton wool—or so the natives put it with a justifiable measure of pride.

Yet even local drivers find it a challenge to navigate through, which is why they'll advise you not to risk a visit in the cold months. But my quest left me with little choice, for the dead of winter is the season when the nebbia works its wonders on cu-latello.

The trail led to Giuseppe Boschi, a restaurateur from the adjacent province of Piacenza, a young man who knows the ins and outs of Parma's salumi as few others do. Boschi warned that it wouldn't be easy to witness the rituals of a glorious local tradition that is now regarded as an unlawful activity, like the manufacture of dangerous drugs. He suggested that first we go and see how prosciutto is produced nowadays and then watch the making of industrial culatello. ''That way you'll appreciate how special the real thing is.''

We drove through low-hanging clouds at the base of pro-sciutto country, past the factories and warehouses of Collecchio and Felino, names renowned for salume, and up the Parma River Valley to Langhirano, sanctuary of the craft, where the sky was fairly clear.

I had hoped to visit a small artisanal producer, but Boschi said that as far as he knew there was none left, that the making of prosciutto had become entirely industrialized. For his own dealings, he buys partly matured prosciutto and does the final aging in his own cellars, thereby losing the right to call it Parma.

He selects from Galloni, a respected firm owned by a family whose members describe their methods as artisanal even though they make 150,000 to 160,000 hams a year. Other companies reportedly turn out about five times that amount.

Galloni workers wearing standard white cloaks perform with an efficiency that seems more in keeping with time-clock-punching technicians than devoted artisans. The prosciuttificio has the traditional tall, shuttered windows along the outer walls to be opened when the weather is mild but not too damp or too dry. Langhirano, at 870 feet above sea level, has a storied climate for aging. Mediterranean breezes crossing the Apennines from Liguria and Tuscany account for the rarefied air that, according to legend, caresses the hams and makes them tender and sweet. But aging chambers also have full temperature and humidity controls. At Galloni they say that the windows are opened often, but much Parma ham is processed under almost entirely artificial conditions in places with less favorable microclimates.

Under DOC rules, Prosciutto di Parma must come from hogs of a year old born, raised, and butchered in Emilia-Romagna or the neighboring Po Valley regions of Lombardy, the Veneto, and Piedmont. Preferred are large gelded males specially bred and fed on formulas to develop ample flesh but less fat than in the past. Particularly prized are those whose diet includes whey from cheesemaking, because the meat is firmer and holds form better during aging, which reduces hams of the normal 22 to 31 pounds to about two-thirds of their original weight. The minimum permitted weight is 15.4 pounds, with an exception for rare boned hams of 12 pounds. Aging of at least ten months is required for small prosciutti (under 20 pounds) and twelve months for the larger.

Thousands of freshly butchered hams arrive at Galloni each winter day. The meat is refrigerated and covered with rock salt massaged into the surface by machines—a process repeated with measured care during the few weeks of *salagione*. The hams are left in cold cells for two months for the *riposo* in which they slowly lose moisture. Then comes the *toelettatura*, in which they are washed in warm water and brushed clean and dried for several days in large, airy rooms. The hams are trimmed of excess fat and shaped into final form for the *prestagionatura*, the first aging of three or four months as they hang on racks set in rows in vast halls. Most of the meat is covered by a layer of skin and fat, but where the flesh is exposed at the top of the bone a *stuccatura* is applied, a protective coating of *sugna* or suet mixed with salt and flour to prevent excessive drying during the *stagionatura*, the final aging of four months or more.

Prosciutto di Parma is described as *dolce* to distinguish it from the saltier, more sharply flavored, and often chewier hams made in other parts of Italy. This sweetness is due to moderate salting, but also to controlled development of yeasts and proteins that ripen flavor and soften texture during a fermentation that takes place during the late stages of aging. Salt isn't a preservative per se but a purifying agent, since it causes the meat to expel the liquid in which harmful microbes could develop. During the final aging the color changes from a dull gray-brown to the mature roseate hue as the meat gains its inimitable flavor, aroma, and texture. These biochemical processes also purify the meat, leaving it free of any trace of pork maladies.

The smoking of hams and sausages serves a similar purpose in many parts of Europe, but in Emilia, where tastes in salumi are decidedly *al naturale,* the practice has never caught on. Nor has heavy seasoning with spices, herbs, or peppers. Parma ham, whose only additive is salt, is a delicious, easily digestible source of calories and proteins, with beneficial elements also in the fat so dreaded by modern consumers that producers have gone to lengths to reduce the content.

The prosciutto crudo of San Daniele in Friuli can rival its succulent peaks, but Parma leads the field in scope and overall quality. During aging each ham is inspected by the consortium's experts, who poke a *gugia,* a long needle made of horse bone, into various points of the meat and sniff to decide if it meets standards. If it does, the Parma ducal crown is branded with hot irons onto the skin. In 1992, production of DOC Prosciutto di Parma reached about 7.8 million hams, though another 5.6 million were aged in the province and sold under private brands. Parma dominates Italy's market, while exporting nearly a million hams a year, mainly within Europe. The U.S. market has grown since an import ban was lifted after it was decided that Prosciutto di Parma was free of pork maladies. The ban had been imposed twenty years earlier after an outbreak in Sardinia of African swine virus, a disease that never reached the mainland.

As we drove back toward the plains, Boschi reminisced over the superiority of salume in his not so distant youth. He said that today's leaner prosciutto lacks the depth of flavor of the old and that it doesn't age as well. After a year and a half or two years, he said, a traditional prosciutto with a healthy layer of fat would develop a deeper red color and white flecks, protein deposits, that indicate the prime of tenderness, aroma, and flavor. He complained that Emilian salume of all types has become too standardized, which is why he has specialist butchers make salame, coppa piacentina, and *spalla* (the prosciutto-like shoulder) to his own taste for aging.

The fog was thickening as we crossed the Bassa in midafternoon, driving past Busseto to an isolated locality called Spigarolo, home of LA.SA.TIP. (for Lavorazione Salumi Tipici). Boschi explained that the firm made about a thousand culatelli a year in the industrial way in the spotless conditions that meet modern requirements for meat processing. He said the owners, the Dassena family, were experts at dressing salumi. "Here's where you'll see the latest techniques," he said as we entered. "Later you'll see the traditions."

Massimo Dassena, a bespectacled bear of a man with blond hair and ruddy complexion, would not have looked out of place in a sausage factory in Bavaria. But he spoke the lingua franca of the Bassa, almost nonstop, while cutting and binding meat with the dexterity of a surgeon. His wife and mother and a young apprentice worked with him around a massive table where they were dividing up the last of the hams that had arrived in that morning's delivery.

First the apprentice trimmed the skin off the ham, taking most of the fat with it. Then he pushed it over to Dassena, who, with a large knife, deftly separated the interior of the upper thigh from the bone to become the culatello. It looked easy, but Boschi said that it takes acute precision to separate the prime cut from the rest. Dassena observed that it was a fine culatello, pointing to the intricate marbling of milky-white fat in the pale pink meat.

He passed the chunk to the apprentice, who wore a leather glove on his left hand so that he could pull the cord to maximum tightness around the piece as he rolled it into a cylinder.

Meanwhile, Dassena cut the exterior portion of the ham from the bone to become the *fiocchetto.* This tasty but less prized portion is also known as *vice culatello* or *sotto culatello* (*sout culatel'* in dialect), because it is dressed and bound in a like manner but aged for less time. Then he cut away the shin, or *zampetto,* saying that it could either be sold whole for cooking or trimmed and used for sausage. Remaining bits from the thigh and tail were passed to the women, who minced the meat to make a local specialty, *cappello del prete,* so called because it is stuffed into a triangular envelope that resembles an old-time priest's hat.

Dassena took each tied culatello and with a knife about the size of a straight razor sculpted away some of the meat at the upper part so that it took the form of a dome. He also removed most of the exterior fat, to Boschi's dismay. ''Everybody likes things slim and trim these days, even culatello,'' said the salumiere, patting his paunch with a satisfied grin.

When the remaining culatelli were ready, they did the *salatura,* rolling each in rock salt laced with coarsely ground black pepper, garlic powder, and a hint of freshly grated nutmeg, then vigorously massaging this *concia,* or seasoning, into the meat. Others use different ingredients and, as Dassena admitted, often a bit of *salnitro* (saltpeter or potassium nitrate), a preservative permitted by law. Boschi frowned. The culatelli then go into a refrigerated cell for three days, where they are regularly turned and massaged, before getting another light salting. The intake is carefully controlled, because even a pinch too much salt will ruin a culatello's mellow flavor.

A final rinse with white wine precedes the *insaccatura* and *legatura*, literally bagging and binding. Since culatello is left with none of the protective skin and surface fat of prosciutto, it is sealed in a membrane sheath sewn snugly around it with cord. Dassena then spanked the surface with a paddle studded with needles, which pierce it to release any air bubbles and allow moisture to escape during drying. The envelope is normally the pig's bladder, or *vescica,* turned inside out, soaked in vinegar, and washed in water to remove any odor.

The legatura, which holds the sheath in place, became a work of art in Dassena's hands. First he tied the cylinder lengthwise in eight sections. Then, starting from the dome, he wound the cord downward in a spiral, lacing it in place with rapid crossweaves aided by a metal hooking device, until he had made eighteen circuits to form a tight web around the bulging form. During ten months or more of aging, a culatello of about 13 to 15 pounds will shrink to just over half the original weight. As the cord loosens around it, it comes to resemble a large pear in a sagging net, a mark of identity as distinctive as the straw-based flask once was for Chianti.

Dassena does the aging in rooms regulated for high relative humidity and moderately cool temperature, raised somewhat for the initial drying when the culatelli lose moisture slowly enough so that liquid doesn't crust on the surface. The final aging takes place in constant cool. A culatello from LA.SA.TIP. is worth less than a traditional type to local cognoscenti, but since risks of spoilage are slight and markets are assured, the family has a safe and steady income.

It was just after four but getting dark when we left Spigarolo, heading north cautiously through a fog that had reached the curtain stage. Boschi said that at our next stop, a village near the Po, if we were lucky we'd see the real thing. He admitted, though, that he hadn't phoned to say we were coming for fear that the man would invent an excuse for not being home. On the way he talked about the inherent inferiority of industrial culatello but said that any salumificio of size had little choice but to work that way. "Too bad, because if Massimo followed tradition, with those hands he'd make culatelli like Stradivari made violins."

We reached a place where a couple of streetlights glowed as dim beacons from above, though any buildings around seemed devoid of illumination. After crossing a narrow bridge over an irrigation canal, we stopped in front of what appeared to be a large farmhouse. "Wait here," said Boschi, disappearing in the murk. He returned a couple of minutes later. "It's okay, he's home. His name is Nino—never mind the rest. I told him you're a friend from America who adores culatello. He doesn't know you're a writer, so leave your notebook here."

Nino's cordial greeting couldn't hide a certain suspicion in the dark eyes that peered at me from under the brim of a felt hat of the type Humphrey Bogart used to wear in the movies, a style that more or less matched the wool jacket that hung loosely over his heavy turtleneck sweater. The man, past sixty, looked thin, almost frail, but he had the thick, heavily veined hands of a chronic worker. Boschi said that he raised his own hogs, a local breed with firm flesh and a wholesome proportion of fat that lends flavor and tenderness to culatello. Nino said that they had been fed for the requisite three hundred days on a diet of *latticello* (whey left over from the making of Parmigiano), *crusca* (bran), and *melica* (feed corn).

His five hogs had been slaughtered in early December by one of the Bassa's *norcini*, the pork butchers who from November to February put in a busy day at each farmhouse, assisted by family and friends. The culatelli are cut immediately, rolled, tied, and salted so that the meat, still warm and moist, readily absorbs the *concia* as it is massaged in. Nino uses only rock salt and cloves of garlic crushed and soaked in white wine, but no pepper or nutmeg. He said he wouldn't dream of adding a preservative like saltpeter. Boschi nodded approval.

The salted culatelli are hung through the day to drain liquids, then washed with white wine and sewn up and bound that evening in the same way that we had seen earlier, if not always so artistically. This rapid preparation at natural temperatures seems to account for the culatello's capacity to age without preservatives, to develop an immunity to potential nemeses that refrigerated meat does not have. Toward evening this annual ceremony, which is sometimes called the *investitura del culatello* (investiture means both dressing and enthronement), becomes a *festa* with free-flowing wine to go with the morsels of fresh pork, roast, fried, and grilled.

We were in Nino's makeshift butchery, which doubles as a storage area for salame, bacon, coppa, and spalla hanging from metal hooks. Along the walls were demijohns of wine and jars of preserves, crates of apples and potatoes and cabbages. The place was neat but hardly spotless. As we climbed the stairs to the drying room, Boschi explained that real culatello will mature properly only in old buildings with wood beams, walls of brick and plaster, and floors of old terra-cotta tiles—all of which help maintain a balanced humidity. But even there ripening is a risky venture, for atmospheric conditions must be just right. Drafts can dry and crack the surface and spoil the meat; excessive humidity can cause unfavorable molds to develop.

Nino asked us to move quickly as he opened the door to the loft and stepped in behind us and closed it to avoid a draft. His ten culatelli hanging from hooks on the beams were a month old and full in form but no longer bulging. He said at that stage they must be embraced by the nebbia, which lends its effects through a window, but only one, because any more apertures would create currents. At the least sign of a breeze, the window is closed. During those rare times when weather is clear or, worse, windy, shutters are locked and floors dampened, but those are emergency measures. The Bassa's winter hallmark is the fog, whose stillness maintains outside temperatures in a range of a few degrees above or below freezing.

Nino explained that during the drying any surface mold must be brushed off so that it can't penetrate the culatello's still-pliable covering. Forms need to be checked daily to be sure no cavities or air bubbles develop. When all goes well, the culatelli blossom—*cominciano a fiurì,* as they put it—like flowers in the mist, where they remain until the first warm days of spring. Then they are taken to a cantina, which elsewhere might refer to an underground cellar but here is invariably a *pian terreno,* since the water level is too close to the surface to permit digging.

Nino led us downstairs and outside across a courtyard, beaming a flashlight through the haze onto a barn built in brick with arches around the hayloft. He opened a heavy door and shined the light inside onto the ponderous wooden beams, thick brick walls, and packed-earth floor of an empty room that seemed as dank and cold as a medieval dungeon. He explained that a window on the north wall is opened at night in the summer to let in cooling air and then shuttered tight to close out the heat of the day. The earthen floor allows humidity to rise from the Bassa's underground lagoon. In this atmosphere the culatelli and fiocchetti mature slowly as the protective crust hardens and becomes coated with powdery mold.

Boschi noted that culatello had vintage years, like wine, and that the best are when there is plenty of fog. He added that the environmental factors of the Bassa's curing and aging rooms can't be artificially duplicated. Nino, nodding assent, said that something in the atmosphere influences the culatello's development almost the way the ''mother'' conditions vinegar. ''But there are so many variables. Each culatello has a life of its own.'' Nino tipped back his hat and scratched his bald head. ''If I fixed this place up with tiles and such the way they require, I'd not only be obliged to spend a lot of money, but I wouldn't be able to make culatello.''

The moment seemed right to ask a question that had come to mind when Boschi mentioned Stradivari, who lived and worked just across the river in Cremona, in Lombardy. Why can genuine culatello be made only in the Bassa and not in apparently similar areas north of the Po? ''Oh, conditions aren't the same at all over there,'' said Nino, as if he were talking about a foreign country. "They've tried, of course, but the culatello doesn't mature," said Boschi. Somewhere I'd read—in a piece no doubt written by an Emilian—that it wasn't just a question of climate but a matter of culture. On Lombardy's side of the river they eat rice and snails and frogs. On Emilia's side they eat pasta and pork.

Back in the house Nino cut open a salame and offered slices around, after apologizing that he had no culatello left from last year. I asked if he had sold it all, an absentminded lapse that brought a grimace from Boschi. "Oh, no," said the *contadino*, eyeing me with renewed suspicion. "I share it among family and friends. You know, as barter or gifts." Boschi winked and said we had to go.

Nino saw us to the car. "It's been a good winter so far," he observed. "Certainly no shortage of fog." Indeed. We spent the better part of an hour negotiating the few kilometers to Busseto along the back roads of the Bassa through layers of what the natives would describe as cotton wool.

It had been a long and instructive day, but when Boschi left for home after dinner and I walked under the arcades of Verdi's fogbound Busseto before settling into a hotel for the night, I realized that I hadn't quite got a definitive grasp on culatello. I recalled hearing that Giuseppe Cantarelli still ran his salumeria and figured that before leaving it might be enlightening to hear what the man who had put culatello on the map years ago would say about it now. The next morning after breakfast I phoned and was invited to come right over.

A *tramontana* had whipped down from the Alps overnight, clearing away the fog and the euphoria among culatello producers but providing at least temporary relief to drivers in a rush. I had no reason to hurry, but I sped across the plain to Samboseto and with an unexpected surge of anxiety entered the store. My doubts were unfounded, though, for there they were: the salami and hams and cheeses and jars and boxes and bottles just the way I remembered them.

Peppino Cantarelli hadn't changed much either, unless his close-cropped hair had become a shade grayer and his pale blue eyes showed a glaze of melancholy that I hadn't noticed before. He greeted me with easy graciousness as if he'd seen me a week earlier. We went into the back room, where the same stove stood in the corner and the same paintings hung on the wall. But the emptiness of the surroundings echoed in Cantarelli's voice as he talked about the Bassa's golden days of gastronomy in a way that left no doubt that they were gone forever.

There was no bitterness in his tone, just resignation as he told of the degradation of local food resources. "The Bassa had it all then," he said, "and I'm not referring to just meat and dairy products. Vegetables and fruit had brilliant flavors. Why, you know we used to find white truffles around the roots of willows and poplars, where farmers used to train their vines. For perfume they conceded nothing to *tartufi d'Alba*. But then they tore out the old vineyards and modernized the farms and now they bring in produce from outside. Yes, even salumi."

He went into the kitchen and, returning with a *moka* pot, poured us each a demitasse of caffè. But surely they don't bring in real culatello, I said, reminding him that I had discovered its splendors in this very room. "Ah, *quello vero,*" said Cantarelli, with a wistful smile. "No, they'll never import that. They'll never replace it either. But you've seen what's happened to the rest. Why, I remember the prosciutto I used to get from an artisan above Langhirano. Pure silk. Now I'm not saying that today's prosciutto isn't good, it's just uniform, no more peaks. But all of our salumi was outstanding once—spalla, coppa, fiocchetto, salame. That's because it came from locally raised pigs and was made under natural conditions. Today I'd say salame is the most reliable of all, because it's the simplest, the least sophisticated.''

And culatello? ''Ah, well, that's another matter,'' he said, recalling that he had always had it made to his specifications for the trattoria. He marveled over the current price—a king's ransom at 80,000 to 100,000 lire a kilogram, compared with 30,000 to 35,000 lire for Prosciutto di Parma. But he seemed reluctant to discuss his dealings. ''Oh, I still acquire the occasional culatello, from contadini, of course, but you have to be careful, because, as you know, they aren't allowed to sell them, and also because each one is different and you can't always tell by looking if they're good or not.''

So, suppose I were to buy a culatello from a contadino, I said, what should I look for? ''Do you know someone?'' he asked, in a way that indicated he wasn't about to reveal his own sources. Nor would I reveal mine, since even if I could find Nino's place again, I could hardly ask him to sell me a culatello. No, I'm afraid I don't know anyone, I said, but just in case I did.

''Well, first, the mold,'' he said. ''If it's white like flour, that means it was aged artificially. Look for *muffa verde*, because the green develops only in natural conditions. Also it should have a fuller pear shape than an industrial type. But you've got to poke it with a gugia and smell. Even among genuine culatelli only four or five out of ten will be first-rate.''

He revealed more secrets. ''The smaller ones are ready around September, but be sure they aren't too small, because that could mean that someone's trying to pass off a fiocchetto as a culatello. Happens all the time around here. The larger ones, which are best, need a year to arrive. They should have subtle streaks of fat with just a hint of yellow in it. People who are afraid of fat can always eat around it.'' He said that a large culatello can age for a year and a half, but no more because it starts to dry out.

Cantarelli laughed when I said that I'd heard somewhere that he used to keep his culatelli hanging inside an old well, and he clicked his tongue in disapproval when I mentioned that some *intenditori* recommend that they be soaked in white wine to moisten them before being cut open. ''That's what I'd call a rescue operation, or last rites,'' he said. ''If a culatello needs resuscitation, it's over the hill.''

Culatello is traditionally served as antipasto. Cantarelli said that it should not be a main course, as some restaurateurs try to make it. ''When guests used to ask for melon or figs to go with it in the summer, I suggested that they have prosciutto instead. When they ground pepper on it or doused it with olive oil, I turned the other way. Culatello needs no frills.'' I asked him to describe the flavor. ''Ah, no.'' He smiled. ''Culatello is something that must be understood and appreciated for its uniqueness. It's indescribable because it's incomparable. Still, like oysters or truffles or caviar, it might not be to everyone's taste.''

When I asked if he saw any hope for a comeback for the

*genuino,* perhaps as Culatello di Zibello DOC, he shook his head sadly. "A DOC for what, for a product that doesn't exist? No, there's little hope that authorities in this country will ever come to their senses." Then, for the first time, his voice crackled with anger. "Can you imagine the French condemning the cellars for aging Roquefort or the caves of Champagne as unsanitary because they're covered with mold? No, of course you can't, because the French respect their culinary traditions, even if they have fewer to defend. We Italians have a fatal flaw. We're obsessed with becoming modern. Someday we'll regret it, but then, unfortunately, it will be too late."

The tardy morning sunshine beaming through the windows reminded me that I had to move on, but Cantarelli had a better idea. "You'll eat a few slices before you go, of course," he said, knowing there was no need to ask. He went out in the back somewhere and soon returned with a plump pear in a saggy net with the proper traces of *muffa verde.* He set it on a cutting board, removed the netting, and wiped the surface with a cloth. Then he cut off the base with a knife and trimmed and tore away the lower portion of the crusted sheath before clamping the form in place in an *affetatrice,* an electric slicer with a large disk blade. As the blade whirled he manipulated the culatello back and forth until he'd sliced enough to fill a platter.

"It's a good one," he promised, sampling a tidbit. Some slice it with a knife so that it's thicker and, as a consequence, redder in color with streaks of white like what has been described as Veronese marble. But Cantarelli liked it sliced paper-thin on the machine, so its color was a roseate red with a suggestion of coral or copper and its flavor seemed even more exquisite. He set out a basket of *coppiette*, rolls with snow-white interiors and tawny crusts, and poured a glass of his zesty bianco from the hills before he sat down to join me. "This is how I like it best, as *merenda*," he said. "Then it's the main item and you can concentrate on it."

As we finished off the platter, I said it seemed a shame that more people couldn't concentrate on such splendid stuff. Cantarelli leaned back in his chair and with a resigned expression predicted that culatello, *quello vero,* wouldn't be around much longer.

Nor, alas, would Giuseppe Cantarelli, who died months later. With the passing of the man who had put culatello on the map, the legend of the king of salume faded deeper into the foggy bottoms of the Bassa.

Culatello is served at the following places in the Bassa Parmense: Trattoria Cotogni at Frescarolo di Busseto and Colombo at Santa Franca di Polesine Parmense (both of which make their own); La Buca at Zibello; Ugo and I Due Foscari (with pleasant hotel) at Busseto. At Roncole Verdi, birthplace of the composer, near Busseto, Guareschi will prepare meals for small groups by reservation. Stendahl Da Bruno at nearby Colorno is noted for culatello and aged prosciutto. Near the zone at Cortina di Alseno (Piacenza), the Albergo-Ristorante Boschi has the finest of Emilian salume selected and aged by Giuseppe Boschi.

exquisite. He set out a basket of *coppiette,* rolls with snow-white interiors and tawny crusts, and poured a glass of his zesty bianco from the hills before he sat down to join me. ''This is how I like it best, as *merenda,''* he said. ''Then it's the main item and you can concentrate on it.''

As we finished off the platter, I said it seemed a shame that more people couldn't concentrate on such splendid stuff. Cantarelli leaned back in his chair and with a resigned expression predicted that culatello, *quello vero,* wouldn't be around much longer.

Nor, alas, would Giuseppe Cantarelli, who died months later. With the passing of the man who had put culatello on the map, the legend of the king of salume faded deeper into the foggy bottoms of the Bassa.

Culatello is served at the following places in the Bassa Parmense: Trattoria Cotogni at Frescarolo di Busseto and Colombo at Santa Franca di Polesine Parmense (both of which make their own); La Buca at Zibello; Ugo and I Due Foscari (with pleasant hotel) at Busseto. At Roncole Verdi, birthplace of the composer, near Busseto, Guareschi will prepare meals for small groups by reservation. Stendahl Da Bruno at nearby Colorno is noted for culatello and aged prosciutto. Near the zone at Cortina di Alseno (Piacenza), the Albergo-Ristorante Boschi has the finest of Emilian salume selected and aged by Giuseppe Boschi.

# Risotto
## The champagne of rice

*R*ice may be the prime nutrient for three-quarters of the planet's people, but in the Italian diet it plays a minor role, far outweighed as a staple by wheat for pasta and bread. So, oddly enough, even if Italy leads Europe in rice production, its per capita consumption rate is among the continent's lowest. Yet where *riso* is prominent—in the watery lowlands of Piedmont, Lombardy, and the Veneto—it has reached its culinary apex in the art of *risotto*.

In most of the world rice is boiled or steamed, but in a traditional risotto it must be braised following diligent procedures. Nowhere is it assembled with greater skill and devotion than in Milan, which, despite the stresses of being Italy's capital of industry and finance, upholds its gastronomic heritage with the golden *risotto alla milanese*. The ritual behind this saffron-laced specialty demonstrates the steps in the crafting of a classical risotto.

A finely chopped onion is glazed in butter and rice is added for the *tostatura,* the preliminary pan roasting that forms a crust to seal in the starch. Then just enough boiling beef stock is added at intervals to keep the rice simmering briskly while being constantly stirred to avoid clotting or sticking as it absorbs flavors and releases starch gradually in an *onda* or wave that binds the dish. Saffron added with a last ladle of broth gilds the rice with color and a certain tang. More butter and grated *grana* cheese are added to the steaming mass before serving, as the *mantecatura* that enhances the creamy texture. Optional ingredients include marrow, wine, chicken broth, meat drippings, or, rarely, a type of salame called *cervellato.* But whatever the recipe, risotto should never be mushy or runny. Each morsel must remain resistant at the core: *al dente,* as in pasta, but with a cushioned effect that rice alone affords.

Perfection can be approached only with rice bred for the unique methods of cooking. Among 120,000 known varieties of rice, Italy grows about fifty. They are grouped in four categories according to size, ranging from the small *comune* or *originario* to *semifino, fino,* and *superfino.* Among the superfino, which is generally best suited to risotto, Arborio is popular, but specialists often prefer Carnaroli from paddies around Vercelli in Piedmont.

Italy's elite rice industry leads the world in techniques, after the transformation from the dismal conditions of manual labor dramatized in the post–World War II film *Bitter Rice* into a highly mechanized field of agriculture. Yet, as Salvatore Russo, who runs a government research center near Vercelli, puts it: ''We boast of our superior rice, but Indians and Chinese and Africans don't eat risotto. What's worse, though, is that neither do most Italians.''

Russo pointed out that per capita rice consumption in Italy has leveled off at less than 10 pounds a year, below the European average and less than a third of the rates of Portugal and Spain. Meanwhile, production has increased steadily, so Italy exports about 60 percent of its crop. Yet supply doesn't meet demand in much of the world: in Latin America, parts of Africa, and most of Asia, where consumption rates range as high as 375 pounds per person.

Russo's analysis provided food for thought, for indeed it is hard to imagine how anything as splendid as risotto could remain restricted in use. But away from the northern heartland, rice rarely has enjoyed much esteem in Italy. From its origins more than seven thousand years ago in Java, *Oryza sativa* made its way across Asia to the Mediterranean, though the ancient Greeks and Romans, who knew rice as a medicine or spice, apparently didn't grow it. In the late Middle Ages, scattered plantings were recorded in southern and central Italy, but most rice was imported from North Africa or Spain or via Venetian trade routes from the east. Major cultivation in the Po flatlands began only in the fifteenth century after the plague and wars had caused famine and rice proved to be more productive than grains grown there at the time.

Rice (often cooked with milk and sugar) may have nourished the hungry and ill, but early dishes didn't inspire gourmets. With time, though, Milanese and Venetians devised appetizing recipes that called for rice in soups or boiled with meat, fish, vegetables, herbs, or spices. The origins of risotto aren't clear, since the term wasn't used regularly in texts before the nineteenth century. The cooking methods may have evolved from the practice of making soup from a *soffritto,* based on lightly fried onions, to which rice and broth were added in limited quantities and braised rather than boiled. Thus risotto could be eaten with a fork instead of a spoon.

Risotto is now served mainly as a first course, an alternative to pasta, though in the past a bowl of rice cooked with vegetables and meat could be a meal in itself. Risotto alla milanese is still often served with *ossobuco* (braised veal shank) in one of Italy's rare examples of a *primo* and *secondo* together.

Pellegrino Artusi, in his influential cookbook *La scienza in cucina e l'arte di mangiar bene,* first published in 1891, gave eleven recipes for risotto, including three versions of the milanese, as well as other classics with frog legs, crayfish, mushrooms, and peas. But the author, who was born in Romagna and lived in Florence, neither strongholds of rice, seemed to have reservations about it. He wrote with one recipe: ''Rice! Now there's a fattening food that the Turks administer to their women to make them like corpulent cushions.''

Today some advocates consider rice a diet food, since even when polished, as it is normally used in Italy, it surpasses all other cereals in its concentration of nutrients. But dietary benefits also depend on the condiments used, and risotto usually calls for butter and cheese. Rice can be as economical as pasta and even more versatile in its uses: in soups, antipasti, salads, stuffings, and pilafs, as a side dish with vegetables, fish, and meat, and even in desserts. Yet campaigns by the Ente Nazionale Risi extolling the virtues of rice seem to have made little impact on sales. In competition with pasta on a national scale, riso has been largely swamped.

The Apennines stand as Italy's mythical barrier between traditional ways of eating. To the south, olive oil, dried pasta, vegetables, and fish are pillars of the "Mediterranean diet." To the north, butter, fresh pasta, rice, polenta, and meat are stalwarts of "northern Italian cuisine." But sweeping generalizations about northern versus southern customs overlook the local peculiarities that make provincial cooking throughout Italy so enticingly variable.

Yet there is something to the notion that the northern legacy includes more substantial dishes that probably date to those winter days when housewives took more time to cook. For risotto as stirred in the traditional way requires patience. Italians in warmer climes rightly or wrongly consider it heavier than pasta. Even today, despite the liberal exchange of foods and recipes around the country, prejudices prevail. Away from the plains of the Po, risotto seems to represent an acquired taste that few Italians, let alone other peoples, have acquired.

Still, risotto may reach levels of authentic glory in other parts of Italy and abroad where cooks follow time-honored methods using the right rices. Variations on the classical risotto theme are practiced in eastern Lombardy and the Veneto, where Vialone Nano, a stout semifino variety noted for its tenacity, is often cooked in liquid without the initial tostatura. Though textures aren't the same, the methods represent valid traditions in dishes such as Mantua's *risotto alla pilota* ( with pork or salame ), Verona's *risoto de tenca* ( with tench ), Padua's *risotto ricco* ( with meat and vegetables), and Venice's *risi e bisi* (with peas). But elsewhere what is all too often presented as risotto on menus is made using ordinary or even instant rice or methods (such as use of pressure cookers) that purists consider deviously expedient.

Rice is grown extensively in the Veneto and Emilia-Romagna, as well as in limited areas of Tuscany, Calabria, and the island of Sardinia. But Italy's realm of rice lies to the west and south of Milan: an everglade of *risaie* extending across the plains along the Ticino and Sesia tributaries of the Po. Cultivation is most intense in Lombardy's Lomellina area near Pavia and in Piedmont around Novara and Vercelli, which is sometimes called Europe's rice capital.

Vercelli lies in a low-profile part of Piedmont, on the banks of the Sesia between the Alps and the Monferrato hills in lowlands marked by soupy winter fogs and sticky summer heat. Its skyline with a chartreuse cathedral dome and a couple of Gothic towers may look inviting from across the plains, but the approach to the center past factories, warehouses, service stations, and apartment blocks testifies that this town of fifty thousand hasn't added much of historical note since the late Middle Ages. Travelers on the nearby Milan-Turin autostrada tend to rush by, perhaps unaware that they're passing the nation's most vaunted rice paddies.

It was just after nine on a cloudy September morning when I arrived at the Istituto Tecnico Agrario G. Ferraris, a glass-fronted edifice on Vercelli's Piazza Vittoria. There my friend Giuseppe Sicheri, an authority on wine, introduced me to the resident rice expert Giovanni Rosso, who not only teaches *risicoltura* but represents the third generation of a family of growers.

Rosso, in a tailored suit, white shirt, and tie, looked almost too dapper to be a teacher or a farmer, though as we toured the countryside in his black Mercedes-Benz he talked about rice with feelings that were undeniably grassroots.

"Riso is a little world of its own," he said with a flush of local pride. "But not much has been written about it, probably because to outsiders it all looks so monotonous. I mean, who would imagine that rice has vintage years, much as wine does, though they're never publicized, or that certain growing areas produce superior quality and could be considered *crus*?"

The grandest of the *crus* lie in the lowlands north of Vercelli in an area known as the Baraggia Vercellese. The Milanese authority Nichi Stefi described the Baraggia as the "Champagne of rice" because it is the most northerly of Italy's growing areas and produces what is indisputably the best-quality superfino for risotto. Rosso pointed out that wine, cheese, olive oil, and some meat products are prominent enough to carry denominations of origin in Italy, but so far no moves had been made to classify rice geographically.

He promised a visit to the Baraggia later. On the way we stopped at the research center to meet Salvatore Russo, who provided a candidly mixed review of how progress in technology had created a surplus that had left the rice industry in crisis. He noted that Italy's average yields are the highest anywhere, thanks to genetic engineering of resistant varieties and abundant use of nitrogen fertilizers. Mechanized harvesting, combined with chemical controls against weeds, insects, and algae, means that each 2½ acres of a risaia now requires forty to fifty man-hours of work a year, compared with seven hundred to eight hundred hours forty years ago. But a steady rise in production had brought a glut that has forced prices down. Italy's luxury rice nonetheless costs more than others on the world market. ''The problem could be solved by persuading Italians to eat more rice,'' said Russo. ''But what do you do, force it down them?''

Beyond the economics, I was concerned about health, for what I'd heard about chemicals up until then might have swayed me to swear off rice forever. Russo explained that treatments are done early in the six-month vegetative cycle, but in any case maturing rice has a natural filter system that removes all traces of extraneous elements. Polished rice, free of its protective shell, is a remarkably pure cereal.

Well, what about *riso integrale*, I asked, the unrefined rice with germ intact known in the trade as *sbramato*? ''If you want my advice, don't eat it unless it's guaranteed to have been grown organically,'' said Russo, adding that its outer membrane is rich in vegetal fats that can go rancid, so it doesn't keep long unless vacuum-packed or coated with a preservative. Rosso said that schools are encouraging organic rice farming, but that could be done only where fresh spring water is available. He noted that even if the integrale has more vitamins and minerals than polished rice, and much more fiber, it requires long cooking, which diminishes nutritional value. He reminded me pointedly that ''it absolutely doesn't work for risotto.''

For centuries, one type of rice prevailed in Italy, known simply as *nostrale* (ours). But in the mid-nineteenth century new varieties from the Far East were introduced and crossbred expressly for the extended cooking of risotto. Russo said that nearly all Italian rice is of the subspecies *japonica*, characterized by a rounded or ovular form, while most grown elsewhere is the slender long-grain type of the *indica* family. Recently *indica* varieties have been grown here in a largely futile attempt to create new markets.

Italian rice is categorized in four groups based not on levels of quality but on length and form of the grain and average cooking time. These range from the smallest comune or originario (twelve to thirteen minutes to cook) up to semifino, fino, and superfino (sixteen to twenty minutes). Superfino, because of its tenacity, is considered best for classical risotto, though among a dozen varieties telling differences can be noted in cooking performance. Yet, as Rosso pointed out, much rice sold in Italy doesn't state the variety, so shoppers are often influenced by low price, an attractive package, or a catchy name. More than 80 percent of production is handled by twenty or so industrial firms, which supply the wholesale trade and supermarkets.

It was nearly noon as Rosso and I drove north across the Sesia into the Baraggia. Sunshine was filtering through clouds, and the harvest, frequently interrupted by early autumn rains, was underway. Huge reaper-threshers called *mietitrebbiatrici* crept through the drained but still muddy fields on caterpillar treads like tanks. Rosso reminded me that even though rice is ''born and raised in water'' it must be dry when picked, so harvesters work only a few hours a day.

The machines do a task that used to involve hand-cutting the stalks with sickles and bundling and hauling the rice to lofts where it was threshed by hand at night. Rosso, now in his late thirties, recalled that his family used to work fifteen to twenty hours a day for two weeks or more at the harvest. Another task was the hand transplanting of rice shoots from seedbeds into concentrated paddies to clear fields for other crops in June. The *trapiantini* worked from dawn to dusk stooped over in water up to their shins, a practice that is now exceedingly rare.

"Considering those ordeals, the *mondine* had it easier," he said, referring to the migrant workers portrayed by Silvana Mangano and company in *Bitter Rice,* the women with straw hats who converged on the area by train and bus 280,000 strong in June to wade through and weed the paddies. Many returned in September to help with the harvest. "It was all exhausting labor, *massacrante,*" as he put it, "the kind of work people just won't do anymore."

Rosso described how the system changed as small farms were consolidated into large and efficient spreads, bringing a couple of decades of prosperity to an area that had been perennially poor. "But growth got ahead of itself and now people are facing hard times again," said the professor in a way that indicated that the crisis had struck close to home.

His tone brightened as he assured me that some of the legendary figures of rice's little world are still around. He mentioned the *acquaioli,* who control water levels in the paddies, which they can flood or drain in a matter of hours using a system dating to 1866, when the epic Canale Cavour was completed through the area. He described the *mediatori,* the shrewd middlemen who buy *risone,* crude rice, from farms and sell it to *riserie,* the mills that clean and polish it. But some roles had disappeared: the *mondine,* made obsolete by herbicides, and the *piloti,* who husked the rice with wooden mortars and pestles, replaced by machines.

Millers are also noted characters, though the breed is rare, since only 150 riserie remain in Italy to process the rice from 7,500 farms. The pride of the Baraggia is the Riseria Re Carlo at Albano Vercellese, an artisanal firm named not for some remote King Charles, as it might seem, but for the founder, Carlo Re, who like many rural people states his family name first. With age, the miller's spirit reportedly had faded, which might explain why he reminded us on arrival that it wasn't a good time to visit. But Rosso had arranged to meet Carlo's son, Piero, a former schoolmate, who seemed happy to see us even if we had cut short his lunch.

Piero Re, tall and husky with a dark complexion and a nose prominent enough to be described as Roman, revealed with a grin that he had just dined on *spaghetti al pomodoro.* "I don't eat all that much rice," he admitted, "maybe because I ate so much when I was young. But my father has risotto or some other rice dish at every meal, and look at him, he's as skinny as a rail." Re Carlo was then crossing the asphalt courtyard between the mill and the family home, no doubt on his way to the kitchen table.

The issue of which rice is best for risotto may be debated among connoisseurs and cooks, but by now the Vercelli area grows all of the superfino varieties that count, while supplying other types for other markets. Posted on the wall was a list of ten types with the price per kilogram hand-lettered. Carnaroli was the most expensive, followed by Baldo, a newly prized superfino, and the fino variety Sant'Andrea, admired locally. Riseria Re Carlo sells superfino and fino in neatly stitched cloth bags of varying colors at 1, 2, or 5 kilograms each.

When asked what made Carnaroli special, Re nodded and

said, "It's not special to me. It's hard to grow and has to be transplanted, and its stalks tend to collapse, so yields are low. That's why it's expensive. Okay, chefs say Carnaroli makes the best risotto, but to cook it right you almost have to be a professional. At home we use Sant'Andrea. It never gives us problems."

The list also included semifino varieties and types named as comune and originario. Re revealed that Rosa Marchetti, a low-priced semifino, is sold mainly to Chinese restaurants in Milan, Turin, and other cities. "Those people tell me it's better than the rice back home, so I guess what they eat in China is what we'd use for chicken feed," said Re. Rosso, grinning at his friend's audacity, reminded him that in the Orient rice is the daily bread.

They provided a study in contrasts: the professor, impeccably dressed, weighing his words with care, and the miller, somewhat disheveled in an ample white T-shirt and loose cotton slacks, expressing thoughts spontaneously. But they exchanged views on rice with a warm respect for each other that dated back to their middle-school days in Vercelli.

Re asserted that rice from the Baraggia holds form and texture decidedly better in risotto than do the same varieties grown elsewhere. Rosso said that a superfino known as Razza 77 was considered superior to Carnaroli by some, but it was such a challenge to grow that it had disappeared. The compact, crystalline Baldo had been developed from a cross that included Razza 77, as had the emerging superfino called Elba. "They provide higher yields with cooking performances similar to that of Carnaroli," he said.

I had assumed that larger yields signaled lesser quality, as with wine grapes and other crops, but Rosso said that wasn't necessarily true. He admitted that yields are generally lower than elsewhere in the Baraggia but that the key to quality is to be found in its firm clay soil, rich in iron and lime, which give the rice tenacity.

The Baraggia is crossed by the Sesia and its tributaries, the Cervo, Rovesenda, and Marchiazza, streams that course down from the Alps to supply water to the Canale Cavour. The canal, built by order of Camillo Benso di Cavour, the Piedmontese who became the first prime minister of a unified Italy, extends some 50 miles between the Dora Baltea River to the southwest and Ticino River flowing out of Lake Maggiore to the northeast.

"This is a pure rice area," said Re, meaning that fields are used only for that crop and not rotated as they sometimes are in the Bassa Vercellese to the south. Noted villages are Albano, Oldenico, Rovasenda, Greggio, Villarboit, San Giacomo, and Arborio. The latter place gave its name to what ranks as the best known superfino rice in Italy and abroad, though much is now grown in the Veneto and Romagna in reclaimed marshland in the Po delta. "It's a second-rate rice," said Re. "It scorches outside before it's cooked inside."

Rosso said that Vercelli's preeminence with rice was due not so much to a favorable climate as to the constant supply of clean water from the canal. Well, then, I asked, was the description "Champagne of rice" accurate? "That's a fitting image," he said, "because the best rice of its kind is grown in the Baraggia. But that's not to say that if other areas had exploited their potential that there wouldn't be a Bordeaux of rice or a Barolo. . . . ''

And what were the other *crus*? They agreed that Lombardy's

Lomellina had special places, though Rosso noted that the Bassa Milanese, south and east of Milan, had been superior because of its pure water sources before urban growth interrupted cultivation there. Re pointed out that Novara province, though adjacent, couldn't match the Baraggia for risotto varieties because of inferior soils. Nor could the Mantua and Verona areas. "Conditions are different there," said Rosso, explaining that that's why they specialize in Vialone Nano. "That's a good rice for soup," said Re, "but not for what we call risotto around here."

Rosso and I were running late for appointments, but before leaving we did a quick tour of the riseria, a mill of fairly recent construction painted an immaculate white inside and out, with plenty of windows for illumination. Rosso already had explained how at harvest time the rice is separated from the stalks and dried in warm-air blowers to lower interior humidity, stabilizing the grain within the husk so that it can be stored in silos for months. This risone is dealt by mediatori to riserie at prices based on the variety and potential yield in polished rice.

Re led us through the mill, explaining key steps in the process. First comes the *sbramatura,* in which the grain is pressed through pairs of rubber rollers rotating at high speed to remove the husk or *lolla.* Then it goes into sets of separators, four vertical racks that shake back and forth furiously as the grain filters downward through slots calibrated to let the desired type pass while trapping and removing the others. This *riso integrale* is covered by a tan membrane, or *pula,* which is removed along with the germ by the abrasive edges of rotating cylinders in what is known as the *raffinatura.* Re said that the pula is sold for use in animal feed and the lolla can be used for fuel. The riseria doesn't sell integrale, said the miller, observing that he prefers to get his fiber eating whole-wheat bread.

The refined rice is passed through another set of separators to remove broken or malformed grains, which cannot exceed 5 percent of the total under law. Then it is polished by more rotating cylinders in three phases of buffing that make it ever whiter. Re sometimes uses a vegetal oil on the final phase to remove any powder and give the rice a protective luster.

Polished rice should come out at 60 percent of the original weight of the risone, though yields can run as low as 40 percent. "We select the best rices, meaning the most costly, and process them periodically in small quantities," said Re. That means they work more in the winter, when people eat more risotto, than in the summer. He said that the crude rice must be checked carefully for quality, since mediatori are rarely trustworthy and the system doesn't permit him to buy risone directly from farmers.

What about vintages? I asked, recalling Rosso's earlier comment. Re admitted that each harvest had its own destiny and that this one (1992) would be mediocre. Cold, damp weather in spring and early summer had inhibited budding, cutting the crop by about 20 percent. Now rain at the harvest had worsened things. "With poor crops you have to be even more selective," said Re, predicting that good Carnaroli would be hard to find.

He noted with displeasure that rice is consumed regularly only in parts of Piedmont. "They eat more in Lombardy, especially in Milan," he said. "Risotto is a culture there." He noted that many small riserie in Italy were feeling the economic pinch, though his operation was doing okay because it involved his wife, brother, and sister, so labor costs were lower. They sell most rice at the riseria or by mail order to regular clients. "But the market's been pretty flat," admitted the miller as we departed. "Even around here rice has lost ground to pasta."

Vercelli doesn't boast as exalted a culinary tradition as do other parts of Piedmont; no city restaurant rates more than a perfunctory nod in the food guides. But I'd learned through the vintners' grapevine that the recently established Osteria Cascina dei Fiori, across the Sesia at Borgo Vercelli, was emerging as an oasis in a gastronomic desert.

Reaching it required a short but bumpy detour off state route 11 down a packed-dirt road through cornfields to a farm converted into an invitingly rustic inn by brothers Massimo and Paolo Milan, the youthful owners, who greeted me cordially even though I was an hour behind schedule. I'd told them by phone about my research into risotto, but before getting down to details, I needed something to assuage a mounting appetite.

Massimo, the husky chef, went to work on the rice while Paolo, the lanky host, served the antipasto: *salame alla douja,* named for the terra-cotta vases in which it is aged under lard, and a delicately seasoned goose-liver mortadella made by Gioacchino Palestro of nearby Mortara. From the ample wine list, prevalently Piedmontese, Paolo suggested Bricco Manzoni, a blend of Nebbiolo and Barbera from Valentino Migliorini at Monforte d'Alba, a red that held up gallantly through the meal. The day's handwritten menu listed three types of risotto, *ai porcini freschi, ai fagiolini all'occhio,* and *con le rane e fior di zucca.* I was spared a tough choice, since a portion of each eventually arrived on a platter.

The challenge was picking a favorite. The fresh porcini, ex-

quisitely firm and fragrant, stood out from the rice. With the
black-eyed beans it struck off a fine-tuned balance. The frog meat
and squash flowers brought together the most exciting tastes and
textures of the trio, though that was the one dish that didn't go
with the wine. Pigeon roasted with a subtly sweet-sour sauce and
served in a nest of *verza,* Savoy cabbage, brought the Bricco Manzoni soaring back in a meal that finished with a sampling of
cheeses (brisk Grana Padano, creamy Fontina, pungent Gorgon-
zola from Novara) and a honey-sweetened apple tart.

When the other guests had gone, Massimo came to talk about
risotto, though I soon realized that it was one thing to hear about
techniques, another to see them. He promised that on my next
visit he'd make a *panissa,* a dish synonymous with risotto in these
parts. My next visit, when might that be, I pondered: How about
tonight? ''*Benissimo,*'' said Massimo, adding to my embarrassment
that he'd have more time because the place would be closed. But
the brothers insisted that I join them for panissa and *lumache*
(snails) from the garden, an offer I couldn't resist. That afternoon
I did a full tour of the Baraggia, the Champagne of the lowlands,
including a stretch on foot along the Canale Cavour to regenerate
an appetite.

When I arrived back at seven, Massimo was assembling the
panissa. He described it as a *piatto povero,* a humble dish, though
with pork, beans, and more it was the most time-consuming of
all his risotti to make. Part of the ritual was over, since he had
prepared the *cotenna,* pigskin boiled in lots of salt water and then
sautéed in a soffritto of onions and fresh pork fat, to which cooked
beans, the *borlotti* variety from the town of Saluggia, were added.

The old-time panissa included more bits of pork, the fatter

the better, as Massimo recalled, since it was originally intended to keep poor rice farmers nourished. But he had modified the recipe to conform to modern tastes by reducing the fats without sacrificing essential flavors. Paolo's wife, Marinella, who helps cook, had prepared a beef stock with onion, carrots, celery, and verza. The accouterments were ready and it was time to start the rice.

Massimo makes panissa and most other risotto in two phases: tostatura and simmering. He used a deep stainless-steel pan for the tostatura, first melting butter with a mild-flavored Ligurian olive oil, then adding a large onion cut into quarters and a bay leaf, then turning up the heat as he poured in rice directly from a cloth bag—no measuring, of course. He prefers Carnaroli from Riseria Re Carlo for all risotto, though he uses Baldo on occasion.

''The rice must be stirred constantly, especially now,'' he said, as he worked it around with a large wooden spoon, occasionally twisting and shaking the vessel. It took about ten minutes for the opaque grains to become what Massimo described as ''hard as pebbles, so that when you flip them against the side of the pot they go ding! ding! That means the starch is sealed in.'' He poured in a simple, acidic white wine from the Veneto to meld the mixture about a minute before he turned off the heat. Then he plopped the mass onto a marble-topped counter, where Marinella picked out the onions and bay leaf and spread the rice out to cool.

Some rice from each tostatura is kept in cold storage as a base for the next couple of meals, a restaurant expedient, since it would otherwise take half an hour or more to make each risotto.

But he said that for home cooking both phases could be done in one pan, preferably a fairly deep, tin-lined copper skillet to provide the most even source of stovetop heat. He set such a vessel atop the range at a point where the rice would simmer briskly and added first the cotenna-bean mixture, then a portion of roasted rice. When that was hot, he poured in a generous dose of red Barbera for the *rosolatura* that gave the rice a vaguely rosy hue.

The broth had been made without salt, so that it remained clear, though Massimo added some bouillon to heighten flavor, even shredding a bit of the cube directly into the rice. Using a strainer to remove solid parts from the stock, he ladled in enough to moisten the rice but not cover it. As he stirred, he explained that the broth, kept at a rolling boil, must be hotter than the simmering rice, which, he said, should go ''blip-blip-blip in rapid sequence, not blub . . . blub . . . blub—then it's cooking too slowly.'' If the grain's exterior cools, it will get mushy, he warned, and the interior may stay hard instead of arriving at the cushiony al dente.

I asked him why some cooks immerse the rice in broth and let it simmer without stirring. ''That's the Venetian way,'' he smiled, saying that he knew it well, since his family had lived near Venice for years. ''It works with a rice like Vialone Nano, but the results aren't the same.'' He elaborated: ''If you boil rice in plain water, any Italian variety, it will have a similarly bland taste. The beauty of rice lies in its texture and its capacity to absorb and retain flavors.'' He said that Carnaroli, cooked by the classical method, is unmatchable unless you can find Razza 77. ''The Venetians have a different concept of rice from ours, as different as, say, the Bolognese and Neapolitans might have about pasta.''

Massimo stirred and ladled for at least a quarter of an hour before he let me sample the rice. It was getting close. Do you do this for every order? I asked. ''I'm afraid so,'' he said, pointing out that Marinella and his own wife, Simona, who was home with the children that evening, share risotto duties. ''That's why we never serve more than twenty-five guests at a meal,'' said Paolo, noting that panissa must be ordered a day ahead of time.

Massimo soon removed the pan from the heat and sliced in morsels of salame della douja, telling us to take our places, because it would be ready in a couple of minutes. With panissa he omits the mantecatura, the lacing with butter and grated grana done before serving most risotto. ''It has all the flavor it needs,'' he announced. Paolo poured the house wine, the same Barbera del Monferrato used in the panissa. We wished each other *buon appetito* and dug in.

Each component of this potpourri—rice, beans, cotenna, salame—provided a counterpoint of texture and taste, yet together they played in perfect harmony. Humble indeed, I dissented, welcoming a second helping, the panissa was nothing less than noble. It found a peer in the Barbera from Amelio Pavese, though Paolo picked a fizzy red Freisa from the same small estate as a wine zesty enough to keep pace with the snails. Removed from their shells, they had been melded into a piquant stew with onion, garlic, tomato, and a bouquet of herbs. Massimo, amid compliments, admitted that he'd snared the creatures himself.

Our meal and conversation rambled on into the night, as the brothers Milan reminisced over their efforts to revive the long-neglected *cucina vercellese* and their hopes to draw the attention of gastronomes to the understated wonders of the little world of rice.

Vercelli and the Baraggia, about an hour's drive on the autostrada from either Milan or Turin, make destinations for a different sort of day trip by risotto devotees. The essential addresses: Riseria Re Carlo, Via Molino 1, 13030 Albano Vercellese, telephone (0161) 73124; Osteria Cascina dei Fiori, Regione Forte, 13012 Borgo Vercelli, telephone (0161) 32827.

# Bistecca alla Fiorentina
## Rare beef in Etruscan places

To Florentines it never used to matter that beef wasn't an integral part of the Mediterranean diet. For well over a century, *bistecca alla fiorentina*, a great slab of a steak grilled over wood coals, ranked as the glory of the Tuscan table. But the recent turning away from red meat for dietary, ethical, and economical reasons has left beef eaters in Italy feeling almost as ostracized as smokers. So intense has been the reversal that many Florentines seem to have forgotten what an authentic bistecca is, or was.

Moved by this rude turn of events, steak lovers in 1991 founded the Accademia della Fiorentina with the aim of restoring the historical image. But, as it turns out, among the academy's ranks of butchers, restaurateurs, gourmets, and scholars, definitions of bistecca differ. Exponents seem more concerned about the size, cut, and cooking of the steak than about the origins of the meat. Today what passes for bistecca alla fiorentina in Florence is much more likely to have come from beef bred abroad than in Tuscany.

Yet no one would deny that the classical fiorentina came from Chianina, statuesque white cattle whose ancestry has been traced back to pre-Roman times when the Etruscans raised them in the Chiana Valley of eastern Tuscany. The term *bistecca* came into use in the eighteenth century from *beefsteak*, via the English, who were already fervent frequenters of Florence. Grilled chops had been known previously as *carbonata* or *braciole*, from *carbone* or *brace*, both of which refer to the coals that the meat was grilled over in the city's *osterie*.

La fiorentina, as it came to be known, was the Italian prototype for bistecca. Florentine butchers, whose cutting methods differ from others, slice and chop the steaks from a triangular rack extending along the loin, or *lombo*, and rib cage, or *costa*. One end renders a *lombata*, a type of T-bone with the filet, the other a *costata*, or rib steak. Either cut may be called bistecca. Curiously, though, that term has come to apply not only to beef but to chops or steaks of *vitello* or *vitella* (milk-fed veal) and even *maiale* (pork).

Chianina steaks come from steers not fully grown: *vitellone*, literally ''big veal,'' rather than adult beef. The meat has a roseate red color with less intensely developed muscle fiber than other breeds. The compact texture is virtually free of the interior fat known as marbling, so Chianina is lower in cholesterol and easier to digest than most beef, but it requires extended hanging to become tender. Some butchers practice an unusually long *frol-*

*latura* of three to four weeks, possible because the loin and ribs
are protected by a layer of subcutaneous fat.

Steaks from Chianina are noted as suave or mellow in flavor
and scent rather than rich or ripe. But a fiorentina must be cooked
just so to convey the singular elegance of beef that requires no
more seasoning than salt and pepper and a drizzle of the cherished
extra vergine olive oil from the Florentine hills. The grilling may
look easy, but a practiced sense of timing is needed to bring the
coals to the perfect point of combustion.

Grillers customarily use the embers of hard oak or olive
branches burned in the hearth, avoiding soft woods or aromatic
charcoal that might give the meat a smoky odor. The coals are
shifted under the grill when they are red-hot but not flaming so
that they sear the steak's exterior, forming the *crosta,* the dark
crust that seals in the juices and reduces the penetration of heat
to the interior. This should remain *al sangue* (red, juicy, and
warm) or *molto al sangue* (virtually raw at the core). The steak,
turned just once, cooks for three to five minutes on a side, depending on thickness. Salt is sprinkled on at the end of the grilling so that it doesn't extract juices. Freshly ground black pepper
and oil are usually added afterward as well.

Florentine hosts, noted for their sarcastic wit and sharp
tongues, may invite guests who order steak well done to eat the
outer portions, though they may bluntly remind those who request special condiments that la fiorentina isn't for them. Tuscans
generally shun the lemon that some Italians squeeze onto steaks.
Butter, whether plain or parsleyed, is a French aberration, as
inappropriate as mustard, horseradish, Worcestershire, or A1

sauce. Herbs, such as fresh rosemary or sage, might be arranged on the edges of the hot serving platter as a decorative touch, though their flavors aren't considered complementary.

In Florence a meal focused on la fiorentina might start with an antipasto or pasta, though a bread soup, such as *ribollita* or *pappa al pomodoro,* would be more substantially Tuscan. With the steak, the requisite side dish is *fagioli,* beans of the *cannellini* or *toscanelli* varieties. In late summer and autumn, freshly shelled beans are stewed slowly in terra-cotta pots in the oven or else simmered over coals in the hearth *al fiasco,* in bulb-shaped Chianti flasks from which the straw has been removed. Tuscans so adore beans, served lukewarm powdered with black pepper and drenched with extra vergine oil, that they have been known as *mangiafagioli.*

Florentines always ate steak with plenty of *pane toscano,* unsalted bread cooked in a wood-fired oven, and drank local Chianti, which used to come in flasks but now rates bottles like the dignified reds of Carmignano, Brunello di Montalcino, and Vino Nobile di Montepulciano. Other rituals once surrounded la fiorentina, but Florentines are no longer so self-righteous about them, since they regularly break the cardinal rule that the steak come from Chianina.

That august native breed is in a tragic state of decline. Cattle were usually reared on small farms in Tuscany, a region with little space for ranches. But since European Common Market policies favor large-scale agriculture, family farms are disappearing and livestock raising has faded. Between 1982 and 1992, Chianina in Italy declined from 250,000 head to 130,000, most still to be found in Tuscany and neighboring Umbria.

Florentine beef purveyors have turned to foreign sources, as-

serting that less costly Charolais, Limousine, and the now prominent Slava are worthy substitutes. To traditionalists the idea of
using imported beef for la fiorentina is as perfidious as using Pinot
Noir or Cabernet Sauvignon for Chianti, whose distinct character
derives from the native Sangiovese grape. The issue is not
whether the steak or the wine is as good, which they might be,
but whether the quality is genuinely Tuscan. Most steak eaters,
however, no longer seem to care.

The Chianina is the largest of all cattle. Bulls have been
known to reach almost 2 tons in weight and stand well over 6
feet in height. They are majestic creatures whose glazed white
coats make them look as if they had been sculpted from Carrara
marble. The long torso tapers away from a massive forward structure marked by a hump on the back and a heavy dewlap draping
at the neck like a scarf, from which protrudes a small but noble
bovine head with coal-black nose and gentle dark eyes beneath
short horns that curve forward like a Viking crown.

The Etruscans used the antique Chianina as work animals,
as recorded in drawings and sculptures. A bronze from the fourth
century B.C. depicted a man known as ''the Sower of Arezzo''
wielding a plow drawn by a yoked team of oxen. A striking
point about that not so primitive work of art is that the figures
and tools portrayed were almost precisely duplicated in real life
until two or three decades ago. Then tractors replaced the beasts
of burden who had toiled up and down slopes pulling plows
and carts at a tireless pace that recounted the tempo of the Tuscan
farm for millennia.

The heart of Etruria, as the Etruscan territory was known,
is the Val di Chiana, a rolling upland on the edge of the Apen-

nines, extending from the main city of Arezzo south to Chiusi in the province of Siena and rimmed by hills on which rise the celebrated towns of Cortona, Montepulciano, and the spa of Chianciano Terme. Farmers through the ages raised the occasional offspring of their work animals as veal. But only in the last century did selective breeding begin, and only in recent times has Chianina been raised primarily for meat.

The quality of beef became known to outsiders via la fiorentina, a steak that more than a few visiting gastronomes agreed had no equal in size, texture, and taste. What is all the more impressive, to cattle breeders at least, is that it comes from vitellone of just fourteen to eighteen months.

Over the last couple of decades, thanks to artificial insemination, Chianina has gained stature abroad: in Argentina where it is usually a purebred, and in other parts of Europe and North America, where it is often crossed with Charolais, Limousine, and Aberdeen Angus. The advantages of crossbreeds is that they inherit the Chianina's vigor and resistance to disease, reproductive capacity, and rapid growth rates that produce beef of reduced fat content.

But Italians for the most part have kept the bloodlines pure, relying on selection or what is called genetic engineering to further increase yields of meat in proportion to fat and bone. In the Chiana Valley, cattle are now invariably raised in stalls and fed on formulas aimed at making the meat more tender and flavorful. Elsewhere they are still sometimes grazed, but experts agree that exercise only makes muscles firmer and meat tougher.

The irony is that at a time when even a Texas cowpoke could wrestle successfully with the name, Chianina has fallen from favor in Tuscany. Giovanna Moretti, a livestock expert in the Val di Chiana, admitted that little is being done to preserve the breed in its place of origin. ''It's true that raising Chianina isn't as profitable as before, but a way must be found to revive production,'' she said. ''It's also a matter of pride. We can't just throw this great patrimony of ours out the window.''

The demise of the Chianina, more than a culinary travesty, has deprived the Tuscan countryside of a picturesque source of animation. Today you can travel the 43 miles from Arezzo to Chiusi without seeing a single bovine. Then again, if you follow the winding roads to the center of the valley, to a village called Pozzo della Chiana, and ask the way to the farm of Sergio Presenti, you might even witness a tandem of great white oxen pulling a plow with a man grasping the handles just like the Sower of Arezzo.

Sergio Presenti, a stocky yeoman with curly gray hair and bright blue eyes, might not resemble an Etruscan. But he looks not at all out of place in a medieval setting, as proved by framed photographs on his dining-room wall from the Palio, the bareback horse race run since 1656 around the perilously curving contours of Siena's Piazza del Campo. Twice each summer Presenti dons a brown peasant's tunic and black tights and leads a double team of his oxen as they pull the wagon bearing the Palio itself—a silk banner depicting the Madonna awarded to the winning horse and his contrada—in a grand procession around the piazza.

''The ceremonies bring in a little extra income,'' he explained, as he showed me through the stalls where he keeps about twenty head of Chianina, raising half for beef and letting the others grow into adults for labor and pageantry. He volunteered to hitch a team to one of his five brightly painted *carri,* carts built almost entirely of wood, right down to the wheel spokes. He led the two largest animals outside, where he attached a ponderous wooden yoke to their shoulders and patiently backed them up to a cart. Then, voicing gentle commands, he paraded them around the courtyard, scattering chickens and geese in their path. "They're slow but sure," he said during the demonstration. "Now you know why I've never owned a tractor."

As the last breeder to train Chianina for work, Presenti is considered an idiosyncratic folk figure in a valley whose *civiltà contadina,* the quaintly rustic country culture that prevailed until the 1960s, is remembered with more amusement than reverence. "Why do I keep doing it?" he grinned at the query. "Because I never learned to do anything else. But I wouldn't want to. I like working with cattle. They're almost like people," he observed, and then added *anzi,* which meant rather better. He promised to invite me back to see him plow fields when the ground was drier than on that November morning.

Presenti, who had sold steers directly to a butcher at nearby Lucignano, was one of the few Chianina devotees I met to express optimism about the future. Another was Lucio Migni of the Anabic association, which certifies Italy's native types of cattle and runs a selective breeding program. Migni is confident that Chianina will regain ground when the message gets across about the nutritional qualities, especially about moderate fat and low cholesterol. Beef from one of the world's oldest breeds of cattle, as he put it, is the best suited to a modern diet.

Some Chianina is sold in central Italy by butchers who vouch for authenticity under the trademark 5R, for *cinque razze,* the native breeds that also include Maremmana, Marchigiana, Romagnola, and Podolica. But most of their shops are located in outlying parts of Tuscany and Umbria. In Florence and environs, few butchers provide Chianina anymore.

An admirable exception is the Antica Macelleria Falorni at Greve, in the Chianti Classico zone south of Florence, where brothers Lorenzo and Stefano Bencistà continue a family tradition dating to 1817. The shop, a landmark on Greve's arcaded central piazza, is noted not only for Chianina and an array of fresh meats and poultry, but also for house specialties such as pâtés, bacon, prosciutto, and various *salume,* including the wild-fennel-flavored *finocchiona* and the small, sharp salame from the wild boar that roam Chianti's wooded hills.

Lorenzo Bencistà, with an ample mustache and dark eyes that crease tight when he smiles, wore the loose white smock of the legendary Tuscan *macellaio.* But he reminded me with undisguised bitterness that the new European meat-processing norms are stifling the versatile skills of his antique craft. The Bencistà brothers, like their Falorni ancestors on their mother's side, had always selected Chianina from local farms and slaughtered and dressed the beef in their small *mattatoio* at the edge of town. But that practice was threatened in 1993, because they lacked the funds to convert their artisanal plant into a high-tech slaughterhouse, as prescribed by the regulations.

Bencistà explained that entirely separate butchering facilities are required for each type of animal: beef, pork, lamb, and poultry. ''Forget about boar and other game—they're excluded.'' Besides the new building and equipment, they would have had to install a complete bathroom for each sector. ''In other words, four baths for three employees,'' he said, ringing his hands in dismay. The estimated conversion cost came to the equivalent of nearly a million dollars.

The brothers pleaded with Italian government ministries to help them find a less costly solution to save a 175-year family tradition. But they got no response, hardly surprising, since bureaucrats have been frightfully busy smoothing the way for international conglomerates to further standardize Europe's food industries. As Bencistà lamented while the fate of their mattatoio hung in the balance: ''Little guys don't carry much weight in the meat business anymore.''

Come what may, they intended to keep selling Chianina in their shop, though in the future they may have to buy it from plants that meet regulations. Bencistà observed that as small-scale butchers they could personally select animals and transport them short distances, making sure that they were calm and rested. ''Big operators can't always take those precautions,'' he said. ''Cattle may be shipped for hundreds of kilometers, so they're agitated and they secrete adrenaline, which affects the taste and texture of the meat.''

But even if they manage to find prime beef, as hoped, Bencistà saw Chianina's decline as irreversible, because most butchers avoid it. He explained that Italians eat less beef than before, but as the gastronomic sybarites of modern Europe they demand the best: steak and hindquarters for roasting and grilling. Butchers are able to buy those cuts of imported beef, but if they deal with locally raised Chianina they have to acquire the whole animal, so they make less profit. ''Smart customers will pay more for a Chianina steak than another, but few people want to know about the lesser parts," he complained. "The trouble is we've got to sell them too."

Bencistà said that Chianina steaks need no preparation beyond a proper frollatura, hanging in refrigerated cells for about three weeks. Unless instructed otherwise, he will cut a fiorentina at the width of *due diti*—two fingers or about 1.5 inches. But some steak lovers—myself included—prefer three fingers, a hefty slab that ranges between 2.5 and 3.3 pounds. Some prefer a four-finger cut, up to 4.4 pounds in weight, though that qualifies as what is called a *gran pezzo,* requiring longer cooking than a bistecca.

The butcher cautioned that shopping for Chianina steak in the Florence area is chancy unless you're well informed. He explained how to tell the difference. Chianina is paler red than most beef, with firm flesh of uniform texture. The steak should have little or no marbling visible in the interior, but it must have a telling strip of *cotenna,* white fat crusted along the edge. He reminded me that Italian cattle cannot be given hormones to hasten growth, so a true Chianina steak will retain shape and color when cut, while imported beef from animals treated with drugs may be flabby and turn dark.

Nearly all the Chianina steaks sold by Antica Macelleria Falorni go to private customers, said Bencistà, adding that the shop no longer supplies restaurants, which make greater profits on imported beef. "That won't stop a restaurateur from telling you it's Chianina," he warned, "but if you check the raw steak, you'll see that he's trying to sell you smoke."

Smoke sellers flourish in contemporary Florence, where relentless tourism has corrupted a once rigid sense of honest value and even plebeian steaks carry princely prices. Not long ago any simple osteria or trattoria or *buca* (if it occupied a basement "hole") could be relied upon for a veritable fiorentina. No longer.

At Buca Lapi, longtime bistecca specialist, they admit that the beef isn't native, as they do at Coco Lezzone, where the cut is so thick that it rates as a gran pezzo. But at Sostanza (also called "Il Troia" or pigpen, in reference to the sloppy service) the owners assured me that they always serve Chianina from "secret suppliers," though the raw steak raised doubts. At least there the meat is grilled faithfully over wood coals, as it is at other reputed "steakhouses" in the Florence area: Bibe on the southwestern edge of the city, La Cave di Maiano near Fiesole, Omero at Arcetri, Antica Trattoria Sanesi at Lastra a Signa, Centanni above Bagno a Ripoli, and Albergo Valdarno at Incisa Valdarno. Elsewhere irreverent cooks often use gas-heated grills.

Chianina steaks have become a rarity even in the Val di Chiana. Around Arezzo a bistecca is usually cut thinner and cooked longer than in Florence. Perhaps that's why Aretini sometimes serve it with chopped anchovies and capers in olive oil, a habit that makes fiorentina purists blanch. At Cortona's Sagra della Bistecca, held each May, steaks are cooked on what is billed as the world's largest grill, but sponsors admit that Chianina is too costly for the fair. A few defenders of Chianina hold out on the southwestern side of the valley in Siena province, where authentic bistecca alla fiorentina is served at Locanda L'Amorosa near Sinalunga, La Chiusa at Montefollonico, and La Grotta at Montepulciano.

Chianina's Etruscan homeland extended into Umbria, where

cattle bred in the province of Perugia are also known as Perugina.
Umbrians took up the cult of la fiorentina as fervently as Tuscans
and if anything have kept a more active faith in Chianina. Steaks
eaten in the region over the last decade or so have come as close
to the apex of beef as any I can recall.

It was at La Bastiglia, a rustic inn on the edge of the handsome hillside town of Spello, that I first saw a bistecca being
grilled over coals blown to a red-hot glow by a fan which pro-
pelled a stream of sparks into the gaping hearth. Working the
grill was Angelo Scolastra, a burly host who beamed like a
Cheshire cat when his steaks were praised. Angelo in his gruff
voice has been known to exclaim with as much enthusiasm as
his guests over the culinary skills of his wife, Sandra, who in
contrast has always remained graciously modest. Umbrian cooking, if similar to Tuscan in its reliance on fresh produce, offers
an even more varied array of seasonal tastes, which Sandra, with
an enviably natural touch, composes into little works of art.

In 1985, Angelo and Sandra and daughter Maria Luisa
moved from La Bastiglia to Villa Roncalli, a palatial restaurant
with rooms and a garden in the nearby town of Foligno. Maria
Luisa suggests menus and selects wines with wisdom and poise
beyond her years, while her father, when the inspiration moves
him, still works the grill. The fireplace is smaller in the villa's
spacious, vaulted dining room and instead of a fan he uses a less
conspicuous ventilator tube to waft the coals, but the steaks invariably uphold past glories.

Angelo buys whole hindquarters of Chianina and keeps them
in a very cold ventilated cell for eighteen days before he separates
the rack of loin and ribs from the rest and leaves them for a few

more days of frollatura. To him the ideal bistecca is a T-bone with filet and entrecôte intact, a three-finger cut, enough for four or five discreet diners or a trio of trenchermen. He prefers to have customers order steak in advance so that he can marinate it for several hours in black pepper and a local extra vergine oil of a lavish jade green. When I reminded him that Florentines generally avoid a marinade, Angelo, with a deprecatory gesture, reminded me that they don't use Chianina either.

A couple of hours before cooking, he built a fire of oak and olive branches to burn down into a bed of coals. I was having lunch on that November day with Domenico Adanti, who owns the Arquata estate at Bevagna, in the hills nearby, and his winemaker, Alvaro Palini, who had brought bottles of Sagrantino di Montefalco and Rosso d'Arquata to drink with the steak.

While Angelo fussed with the fire, Maria Luisa brought a series of Sandra's creations as openers, among them a flan of *gobbi*, artichoke-like cardoons; creamy white polenta with porcini mushrooms; *pasta e ceci*, chick peas puréed in a delectable soup; and envelopes of *tortelloni* filled with ricotta and herbs and topped with flakes of finely scented local truffles.

As we finished the pasta, Angelo announced rather grandly that he was about to cook the steak. Instead of the heavy cast-iron grill typical of Tuscany, he used a lighter, more maneuverable stainless-steel type, explaining that the key to the cooking lies in the coals and the heat intensified by the ventilator. When they're right, he mused, even Tiny, the immense black mongrel who lounges in the corridor, could grill a fiorentina.

Angelo shoveled a layer of embers under the grill and arranged it so that the meat would cook about the width of his fist above them. When the draft had the coals glowing bright and sparks flying merrily toward the fire, he plopped on the steak and smiled knowingly as it reached a rhapsodic sizzle. Using metal pincers, he shifted it around at intervals to be sure it seared evenly before he flipped it over. The cooking time was just under eight minutes, slightly less on the second side. He used his fingers to scatter salt on the surface before shuttling the steak to a platter where the slowly escaping juices mingled with the marinade oil and pepper.

Maria Luisa took over, using a large carving knife to remove the bone and cut the filet and the slightly firmer entrecôte into three pieces each. She arranged them on plates too hot to touch in accordance with the rule that *al sangue* beef must be eaten warm. The cooking was just right: a rare and juicy bright red at the core, melding to a ruddy beige beneath the charred brown crust. In flavor, aroma, and texture it was about as fine as a fiorentina could be, we assured Angelo, and there we were 125 miles from Florence.

Alvaro poured a glass each of Sagrantino and Rosso d'Arquata, both from 1988, so that we could compare. The Sagrantino, named for that unique Umbrian variety, was soaringly rich in flavor, if still youthfully firm. The Rosso, a singular blend of Cabernet, Merlot, and Barbera, had depth and nuance with a mellowness that seemed more in tune with the steak's suave flavors, though either wine could stand beside a fiorentina as proudly as any Chianti Classico, Brunello, or Vino Nobile.

Instead of the usual fagioli, which Umbrians also savor, Angelo had grilled whole porcini mushrooms so that they were brittle outside but as soft as butter within. His mission accomplished, he sat down to join us, though the bistecca ritual wasn't over. I had been given the honor of gouging away at the best part, the meat clinging to the imposing bone. That activity had aroused Tiny, who watched patiently from the doorway, knowing no doubt that he would soon have the privilege of polishing it off in the garden.

Umbria offers many more attractions than food, though visiting gourmets would be well advised to reserve a table, a room, and an authentic bistecca alla fiorentina at Villa Roncalli, Viale Roma 25, 06034 Foligno (Perugia). Telephone: (0742) 67100. Within easy driving distance from Foligno are the city of Perugia, the towns of Assisi, Spello, Bevagna, Spoleto, and Todi, and the black truffle capital of Norcia.

# Aceto Balsamico Tradizionale
## Art, passion, a way of life

*I*n Italy's gastronomic hierarchy only the white truffle of Alba in Piedmont outranks the traditional balsamic vinegar of Modena and Reggio nell'Emilia in value by weight. But the truffle, a gift or, as some might say, a miracle of nature, need merely be dug from the earth and brushed clean before it can be consumed; *aceto balsamico tradizionale* is the product of an elaborate, prolonged, inspired handiwork or, as some might say, a miracle of man.

Unlike conventional vinegars, which are made from wine or fermented fruit juices, aceto balsamico tradizionale derives exclusively from crushed grapes whose unfermented musts are condensed by heating and aging. No flavorings or additives are permitted in the time-honored methods that conduct the dense, sweet musts through a gradual acetification-fermentation process to become vinegar that takes on singular qualities of aroma, flavor, and texture during at least twelve years of aging or often much more in barrels of different sizes and various types of wood. Making it is a labor of skill and devotion, a perpetual rite that also involves elements of mystery and chance in what might be the most complex and extensive production procedure for any comestible.

The reward for such patience is a syrupy liquid of dark amber to ebony color whose suggestion of caramel offset by time-mellowed acidity strike an exotic sweet-sour note to the nose and tongue. *Aceto* means vinegar, but since that term might seem too mundane for a product so divine, the unique *tradizionale* type qualifies under Italian law as a condiment. The people of Emilia often use aceto balsamico on its own as a distinctive flavoring with meat, fish, and vegetable dishes or as the prime ingredient in the sauces that enrich the local cooking. Admirers will sip the finest aged *tradizionale* straight from a small glass or teaspoon, following its ancient role as a cordial, digestive, or elixir.

Aceto balsamico tradizionale has been recognized as a product of controlled name and origin (DOC) in two distinct zones in the provinces of Modena and Reggio nell'Emilia to the west of Bologna. These cover balsamico's historical realm, the Dominii Estensi, the duchy once ruled by the Este family. Refined, wood-aged vinegars were noted there as early as the eleventh century. In the late Middle Ages and Renaissance, fine vinegar was prized as a drink and even reputed to be a remedy against the plague. In the fifteenth century, Lucrezia Borgia, who married an Este at nearby Ferrara, used Modena's vinegar as a tonic for body and soul. A document in the Este archives reveals that in 1556 vinegars were classified in commercial types, ranging from *da agresto* (sour) to *per cucina* (for cooking) to *da tavolo* (for the table) to *per gentiluomini* (for gentlemen).

But only in the eighteenth century, after the Este shifted their dominion from Ferrara to Modena, did the term *balsamico* come to refer to the balmy wood odors of the local vinegars. In the early nineteenth century, Modena's tyrannical Archduke Francesco IV lavished heads of state from Paris to Moscow with his *aceto del duca*. His son Francesco V managed to escape with valuable supplies of vinegar as Este rule ended in disgrace with the Risorgimento.

After that aceto balsamico was rarely sent away. It remained a revered item in homes in the Po Valley farm country around Modena and Reggio and in the hills to the south where the plains yield gently to the Apennines. There the *acetaia*, the loft lined with barrels and crocks that have held dense, dark vinegar for generations, is the most venerated heirloom of many a family, rich and poor, large and small. So esteemed is aged balsamico that many producers keep their token supplies to themselves, giving a little to friends as the most cherished of gifts.

Age is the first but not the only factor behind the elevated worth. Centenarians are rare, of course, but even teenaged balsamico may have been ''educated'' in the barrel by a *madre* (the mother or matrix) whose origins are lost in time. Caches of balsamico in barrels known to have belonged to the Este, Sforza, Valisnieri, and other noble families remain as if eternal, locked away in lofts to be sniffed lovingly through a bunghole from time to time but tasted only occasionally and with due reverence. Proud owners may neglect to mention that barrels have been topped up over the decades with younger vinegar, for otherwise such balsamico would not be liquid but as hard as caramel candy. That hardly affects the legendary status, however. The investment value of such vinegars might be greater than gold, except that they are not usually regarded as investments but as personal treasures, priceless, not for sale.

Yet, until little more than a decade ago, production seemed irreversibly in decline. The market for fine aged balsamico outside Emilia was then confined to fancy food shops and restaurants that offered it as a gastronomic curio. With the advent in the late 1970s of expedient modes of cooking known as *nuova* and *creativa,* Italian chefs seeking new and exciting flavors discovered them in aceto balsamico. In those days bargains were available in even the finest types in commerce—aged thirty to fifty years or sometimes more by Giuseppe Giusti and a few other Modenese merchants. But supplies were limited, and as the word got around and demand grew, prices naturally rose. Substitutes flourished, supplying markets in Italy and abroad with what dedicated producers refer to disparagingly as *aceto industriale.*

The term *balsamico* had been used freely in Italy, as elsewhere, to describe vinegars and sauces that bear a resemblance to the original, sometimes arrived at through methods admirably close to the traditional but often opportunely contrived. The industrial type from Modena, along with surrogates from as far afield as Naples and New Jersey, have given most of the outside world its first taste of the "balsamic vinegar" that has become so fashionable in Italian and other up-market restaurants abroad. Still, certain industrial types can be more enticing than run-of-the-mill vinegars, though some imitations are downright dismal. Traditionalists deplore the travesty, but consumers who have never tasted the genuine article could hardly be expected to appreciate the difference.

In 1987, Aceto Balsamico Tradizionale was granted a dual DOC for the provinces of Modena and Reggio after a long campaign by producers to distinguish it from imitations. Yet what was labeled as "Aceto Balsamico di Modena" had been produced in growing quantity until 1993, when the Italian government banned use of the term *balsamico* and the geographical reference to Modena or Reggio for all but the tradizionale.

This came as a blow to producers who previously had been permitted to blend wine vinegar and caramelized sugar with the basic cooked musts and call it "Aceto Balsamico di Modena." The law required that part of the base be aged at least ten years, but bottlers with stocks of old vinegar could assemble a blend immediately. Sales of relatively cheap "Aceto Balsamico di Modena" had reached an annual rate of about 1.75 million liters (or 7 million 250-milliliter bottles) compared with 1,760 liters of the approved tradizionale in the two provinces (or 17,600 100-milliliter bottles). The industrial vinegar, however tasty, is not to be compared with fine tradizionale. But on markets abroad, where most of both types is sold, the distinction is often not clear and the products are confused.

Despite being overwhelmed by industrial versions, aceto balsamico tradizionale has undergone a slow but steady revival of its own. This phenomenon seems to owe more to feelings of personal pride among producers than to interests in financial gains. Beyond a couple of dozen houses that age balsamico on a scale large enough to sell, an estimated fifteen hundred households in the two provinces boast an *acetaia* with at least one *batteria*, a set of barrels of progressively diminishing size. Even those producers who make the traditional type as a hobby put more into it than the habitual efforts of an ancestral craft. Some consider it their highest form of self fulfillment: art, passion, a way of life.

Vinegar's history has naturally paralleled that of wine; it originated accidentally in western Asia and became subject to more sophisticated treatment as the culture of the vine spread along the Mediterranean. The Romans made vinegar from cooked musts for the sweet-sour effect they adored, as recipes from the texts of Apicius attest. Peoples since have confected their own versions of vinegar, sometimes of commendable class, but there is no denying that Emilians have elevated the craft to its highest levels.

Aceto balsamico tradizionale is so distinct from other vinegars that vain attempts to describe it have come up with soy and Worcestershire sauces—sacrilege akin to likening fine aged wine to sake or beer. Most vinegars come from the common stock of wine turned sour, but true balsamico tradizionale is the fruit of a deliberated endeavor that obliges it to be born and raised a noble.

Renato Bergonzini, professor of history and perspicacious epicure, is the leading spokesman for aceto balsamico in books, speeches, and articles. To him Modena's culinary wealth attests to more than just the bountiful nature of the Po Valley. He theorizes that people who grow up in the plains respond to the lack of charm in the surroundings by developing ''unusually rich internal passions,'' those ''gut feelings'' that explain their competitive spirit, their constant quest for supremacy. ''Deep inside every authentic Modenese churns the emotion that the impossible is within reach," says Bergonzini. "This frivolity, this streak of mania," as he puts it, is the character trait that explains how producers meet the challenge of converting local grapes into vinegar more precious than the finest aged wines.

Indeed, to an outsider the cult of balsamico ranges beyond rational explanation. The leading testimonial to its role in local life is the Consorteria di Aceto Balsamico Naturale of Spilamberto, an association of twelve hundred producers, master tasters, and devotees. The idea of assembling people in caps and gowns to pay homage to vinegar would seem ridiculous anywhere else, but around here they see nothing bizarre at all about participating in a convivial society devoted, in true Emilian fashion, to the delights of the table.

Each June the Consorteria sponsors the Palio di San Giovanni, a competition held at Spilamberto, a town south of Modena, in which producers enter their best balsamico to be judged by *maestri assaggiatori*, tasters who have passed a rigorous course to certify their mastery of vinegar appreciation. Each evening the judges gather at Spilamberto's town hall to examine samples identified only by number. Holding bulbous glass vials up to candle flames to check color and transparency, they rotate the contents to test fluidity before rationing a few drops into a teaspoon for a whiff and taste. Nibbling on breadsticks and sipping water to clear their palates, they compile a score sheet for each sample, awarding points for details of quality and typicality up to a maximum of 400 (250 is considered sufficient for a tradizionale). This ritual is repeated through numerous elimination rounds until the winner out of nearly twelve hundred entries is proclaimed on the feast day of San Giovanni Battista.

Winning the Palio di San Giovanni may be a vinegar maker's highest aspiration. But making an aceto balsamico tradizionale that qualifies as DOC in Modena or Reggio Emilia is itself a major achievement. Each zone's producer consortium, which exercises exclusive right of approval, sets its own standards. Those of the Consorzio tra Produttori dell'Aceto Balsamico Tradizionale di Modena are so rigid that only about a third of the candidates pass the periodic exams, which require unanimous approval from five master tasters who rate each vinegar as simply suitable or unsuitable. Since judges clearly prefer aged types, few vinegars of the minimum twelve years pass, though they may be resubmitted as they mature. Most approved tradizionale is twenty to thirty years old and correspondingly smooth and rich.

All DOC Aceto Balsamico Tradizionale di Modena is bottled at the consortium in containers that hold a single measure of 100 milliliters (3.36 ounces). From 1990 on it has been bottled exclusively in bulbous *bottigliette* designed by artist Giorgetto Giuggiaro—though tradizionale from previous years may still be sold in individual containers. Each bottle carries a seal of guarantee on a strip over the cork and capsule. Producers design their own labels and set their own prices, which in 1993 were running from 120,000 to 135,000 lire retail in Modena. In 1991, only 760 liters were approved, or 7,600 bottles. More than 80 percent of Modena's tradizionale is exported, mainly to Germany, Switzerland, France, the United States, Canada, and Japan. Prices are sometimes lower abroad than they are at home.

Consortium official Marco Costanzini confirmed that production of Aceto Balsamico Tradizionale di Modena is gradually increasing. But it remains a precious drop in a bucket overflowing with the industrial types that had been generating quicker and larger profits for producers before the ban in 1993 left future sales in doubt. Costanzini observed that like Ferrari automobiles (assembled by hand at nearby Maranello), traditional vinegar must remain elite in prestige and price.

Tasters of the Consorzio fra Produttori dell'Aceto Balsamico Tradizionale di Reggio Emilia use the 400-point system to grade in three categories: *Tradizionale, Qualità superiore,* and the highest, *Extra vecchio.* In the consortium's standard 100-milliliter bottle, prices range from about 50,000 lire for tradizionale to 100,000 lire or sometimes more for extra vecchio.

Despite a smaller production base (only sixty producers belong to the consortium, compared with 270 in Modena), Reggio sells more tradizionale: nearly 1,000 liters, or 10,000 bottles, a year of the three types. This has provoked charges of leniency from the Modenese. But Raffaele Piccirilli, a restaurateur who presides over the consortium, defends Reggio's graded system for permitting producers to sell tradizionale at different stages of development, while providing customers a guarantee of quality at corresponding levels of price.

Only connoisseurs will pay the elevated price for the best aged tradizionale, sometimes described as *da bere* (for drinking). Insiders also know the sources of the best regular balsamico, made in the traditional way but not aged long enough to win approval. Being less condensed and somewhat sharper in flavor, it is known as *da condire* (for use in dressings and sauces). It can be excellent value at a fraction of the tradizionale price. Professor Bergonzini argues that such fine vinegar ought to have an official qualification to distinguish it from the blended industrial types. But for now consumers—the majority of them outside Italy—are at the mercy of the market.

Aceto balsamico tradizionale could always be described as sweet-sour, but, as with wines, there are the decidedly sweet and the decidedly sharp and shadings in between. Whatever the type, the tradizionale has a mellifluous quality attainable only through wood aging. Its balmy elegance is owed not to a cool repose in cellars like wine, however, but to a labyrinthine series of maneuvers that only a steadfast craftsman could carry through.

In the end, no two vinegars are ever the same, for a multitude of variables, human and natural, come into play with each batch. There seem to be as many recipes, philosophies, and secrets behind the making of aceto balsamico tradizionale as there are practitioners. Many producers favor well-ripened white Trebbiano grapes from the hills, historically grown on the gentle rises around the town of Castelvetro. But DOC permits the use of four other varieties in the musts: the white Occhio di Gatta and Spergola, and the red Lambrusco and Berzemino, which are also grown on the plains. Although producers insist that grapes are the key to quality, there is no consensus among them about which to use and in what quantities.

Weather affects the ripening of grapes and the rapport between sugar, acidity, and extract that determines the sweetness and density of the musts. Minerals from the soil influence the activity of acetobacters, the bacteria that cause the acetic oxidation that transforms the musts to vinegar while yeasts convert sugar to alcohol during a simultaneous fermentation that continues for years. The law for tradizionale prohibits use of extraneous flavorings or chemical additives. For instance, sulfites, normally used in moderation to preserve wine, are studiously avoided in the musts for balsamico because they would inhibit the essential oxidation.

The initial burnished, harshly sweet flavors of the musts acquire degrees of dryness and sourness as they become vinegar through biochemical processes that are still not fully understood. With time the acetic acids and alcohol diminish as balsamico retains its basic vigor but assumes qualities of mellowness that no other vinegar can match. Skilled producers, whether they rely on ancestral usages, scientific analysis, or savvy intuition, are able to control the progress, smelling and tasting from each barrel frequently and making subtle remedies, while orchestrating the components to attain a desired harmony.

The acetaia is usually located in a well-ventilated loft or attic whose roof is not insulated so that the vinegar feels the impact of the contrasting extremes of climate in Emilia, where summer days can be torrid and winter nights are often freezing. Heat speeds the evolution and cold slows it as the vinegar becomes stabilized and clarified by precipitating solid particles. The diminution in volume over time alone could justify the high price of tradizionale. Cooking in copper caldrons or, these days, in stainless-steel vats reduces the volume of fresh must by 40 to 60 percent. Evaporation during aging accounts for about another 10 percent a year. So 100 liters of fresh must over twelve years render an average of 15 liters of tradizionale.

Every acetaia contains a batteria, a battery of three or more barrels of various types of wood. Oak is preferred in large barrels because its hardness is right for the initial blending, which sets off the acetification-fermentation process that continues through a series of barrels of diminishing size. These *caratelli* or *botticelle,* for the most part built by local coopers, range in capacity from about 100 liters down to 10.

Producers traditionally followed phases of the moon for key operations, such as the *rincalzo,* the annual racking or transfer of about half the contents of each barrel to a smaller one and topping up from the next larger. Barrels are usually filled to about three-quarters of capacity, leaving "breathing" space for air to cause the acetic oxidation. In the past the rectangular bunghole was often left open or loosely covered by a flat stone, but now it is usually protected with cheesecloth.

Opinions vary about how many barrels of which types of wood and in which order will attain the right complexity in aromas and flavors. Chestnut often follows oak, because it darkens color and lends a mellow quality. Cherry, ash, locust, mulberry, and juniper each contribute a certain nuance to the final result. The differences in hard and soft woods and their relative porousness affect the degree of evaporation.

But the role of the various woods is not so much to lend basic flavors and odors when young as to become so auspiciously conditioned over time that they convey character to the vinegar aging in them. The barrels' exteriors are often rubbed with younger vinegar to condition them as they age. This eventually accounts for a blackened sheen typical of old barrels, some of which have been used for half a century or more and are as precious as the vinegar they hold. Some prized old botticelle, if they begin to leak, will have a new barrel constructed around them with painstaking precision so that they can continue to be used.

Appreciation of aceto balsamico tradizionale is a personal matter, though around Modena they tend to like it well aged, with full flavor on the sweet side, and around Reggio they often prefer a younger, more pungent or acidic type. Some Reggiani carry out the last stages of aging in barrels of juniper, which lends a vaguely ginlike bite to their balsamico. Modenese regard that practice as heresy.

In this competitive field, rivalries abound. Some are rooted in the historical differences between the two provinces, as well as between towns and villages within them. The Reggiani lay claim to a longer tradition, since it was at Canossa, a hilltop stronghold in their province, that Count Boniface presented a barrel of prized vinegar to the Holy Roman Emperor Henry III in the eleventh century. But the Modenese, who proved their prowess with balsamico under Este domination, have done more than the Reggiani in modern times to develop the craft and commerce of tradizionale. The Reggiani, who resent the Modenese air of superiority, have not forgiven their neighbors for trying to confine the DOC for tradizionale to Modena province alone. In turn, the Modenese blame the Reggiani for the ''vinegar war,'' the political battles that delayed the law's enactment until 1987, when two separate zones were created. Feuds also persist between families and individuals. Usually grudges are friendly, but they say that some have outlasted vinegars.

Anything as venerable as aceto balsamico would have to have webs of history spun around it, laced with legends, myths, and yarns. It may be, as Professor Bergonzini put it, that in the balmy realm of balsamico a streak of mania propels producers to the heights, but anyone who suspects that eccentricity is a requisite should spend some time tasting and talking vinegar with Sante Bertoni.

With Bergonzini as guide and technical adviser, I went to see Bertoni one fine October morning. We drove away from Modena's familiar flatlands into the overlooked hills to the south, to the village of Montegibbio, site of a nicely restored medieval castle. Nearby lies Bertoni's Azienda Agricola Le Vigne, set amid woods and meadows on peaceful slopes drained by the Secchia River, which marks the border with Reggio province. Bertoni, who bought the farm near his boyhood home in 1973, has gradually revived vineyards and restored buildings, equipping cellars and lofts with vats and barrels in a complex that has been described by Bergonzini and other experts who have seen it as the nonpareil of vinegar works.

Sante Bertoni, an electrical engineer in his mid-fifties, brings a rare dose of modern-minded pragmatism to a craft perennially shrouded by mystique. Though calm and soft-spoken, as Modena's hill people are reputed to be, he is firm in his conviction that the production-aging cycle for aceto balsamico tradizionale can become shorter and more efficient and secure, and result in consistent high quality. Yet he insists that the system he has devised to realize these aims remains entirely within the regime of tradition.

Despite his ambitious commitment, Bertoni makes vinegar only in his spare time, on evenings and weekends. Members of his family—wife, Luisa, sons, Michele and Dario, and daughters, Daniela and Paola—also help with the perennial duties, the exacting operations, manual labor, and just plain busywork that vinegar demands. Earnings from his electrical contracting firm at nearby Sassuolo, where the family lives, have enabled him to invest steadily in a part-time business that only recently began to yield modest returns. Yet, after years of quiet preparation, he is confident that vinegar will soon become moderately profitable.

Bergonzini sees more to the venture than profits. With a zeal that he attributes to his roots in the plains, he proclaimed that Bertoni is destined to lead the new era of aceto balsamico. The professor, who admitted to having been skeptical at first, described Bertoni's techniques as "practical innovations, ingenious shortcuts based on solid logic, yet they seem almost revolutionary in a field where methods had scarcely changed for centuries. He can make first-rate tradizionale in twelve years, while others might take twice that long at greater risk," said Bergonzini. "But don't expect things to change overnight. The old era isn't over yet."

So far public evidence of Bertoni's proficiency is limited, since his tradizionale debuted on the market in 1992. But rivals in the Palio di San Giovanni know about him, since his first entry in 1991 rated an enviable 341 points out of 400, ranking high in a field of considerably older vinegars. Bertoni, though not one to boast, insisted that he has better vinegar maturing in barrels. He promised a tasting, but first he led us on a tour of Le Vigne, the property whose name refers to the vineyards that still render wine, though its appropriate description would be as a vinegar estate.

The fact that Bertoni uses only grapes from his own 5 acres of vines gives him an advantage over most balsamico producers, who buy their grapes or fresh musts. He tends the vines himself, as his trim physique attests, avoiding fertilizers or treatments other than the essential copper sprays to prevent mildew, so that grapes maintain a natural balance of yeasts and other beneficial elements. Since vineyards cover steep slopes at more than 1,000 feet above sea level, grape yields are lower than on the hotter plains, meaning that they have greater acidity as well as heightened aroma and flavor. They are harvested at a peak of ripeness from mid to late October, so that musts are sweet and rich from ample extracts. Though dark-skinned Lambrusco grapes are generally avoided for vinegar on the plains, Bertoni uses them in about equal portions with the small-berried and sweet white Trebbiano di Collina, giving him a distinctive starting blend.

He led us into the cellars, neatly equipped as a small, modern winery. There the freshly picked grapes are soft-crushed in a compact vertical press and the must, separated from skins and stems, is immediately ready for cooking. This *cottura* takes place in open stainless-steel vats heated by gas burners that bring the liquid to temperatures no higher than 175°F for about twenty-four hours. The musts slowly seethe and steam but never boil or burn at the base, as they often did when cooked in copper caldrons over open wood fires. Gentle heating allows yeasts and other microorganisms to survive as the mass is condensed to about half its original volume. The exact degree of reduction depends on the ratio of sugar in the blend, the key measure which Bertoni controls at about 32 percent. He said that some producers prefer it sweeter, but he finds that if the must is too rich, acetification is harder to set off and takes longer. The dense, sweet *mosto cotto* is then placed in glass-lined vats for about two months to precipitate tartrates and mucilage in the cold.

In December or January, the musts are transferred to oak casks of 20-hectoliter (about 530-gallon) capacity, where they are mixed half and half with aging vinegar from previous vintages. To the blend, Bertoni adds about 5 percent of new wine from Trebbiano, which must be completely natural (unsulfured) so that active yeasts stimulate acetic oxidation. A year later, half the contents are transferred to oak casks of 2.5 hectoliters (about 66 gallons) for another twelve months. During this unique two-year process of preliminary cask aging, the musts are already converted to clear vinegar before they enter the batterie. In the normal method, the still-murky cooked musts would be blended directly into the largest barrel of the batteria to begin the process. Bertoni said that his system cuts the acetification time, giving him a running head start, while reducing chances of error and unecessary loss due to evaporation. But the real advantage is that in the batterie his balsamico acquires the attributes of fully mature tradizionale years earlier than others.

As we walked from the cellars upstairs to where the smaller casks and first series of batterie are kept, I was struck by the order of the rooms, with immaculate red tile floors and sheer white plaster walls and ceilings. Screens covered the frames of windows, left ajar to let in the cool morning air. Nowhere were there traces of dust or cobwebs, mold or stains, none of the cracked pottery, battered copper, wizened woods that gave agrestic touches, that aura of antiquity, to most of the dozens of acetaie I had visited before. Bertoni's batterie extended for rows and rows, impeccable ranks of barrels whose warm wood colors seemed almost to glow in the subdued morning light. All of the botticelle had been built by Modena's master cooper Francesco

Renzi, following a centuries-old family tradition. Some had been in use since 1975, when Bertoni started making vinegar at Le Vigne, but most looked almost new, remarkably untarnished, as if they had been spiffed up for the occasion.

Bertoni assured me that his barrels were always kept that way, adding that aceto balsamico is a food product, after all, that requires maximum hygiene. Bergonzini, shuffling blissfully from barrel to barrel for sniffs, joked that his diminutive stature— ''the same height as most ancient Romans''—meant that he barely had to lean to bring his nose close to the bungholes. Bertoni had to bend his taller frame to remove cheesecloth coverings and let us get a fuller whiff. Then he carefully replaced the cloths, dampening their edges with wine so that they would cling to the surface of the barrels.

To stimulate the discussion, I mentioned that Giuseppe Giusti used to leave the bungholes open, or else cover them loosely with *cocchiumi,* flat stones from riverbeds. Giusti had explained that when acid fumes corroded the stones they precipitated minerals into the vinegar, balancing off the acids and improving the flavor. He also maintained that the fruit flies that sometimes gathered on the surface fended off the real nemesis, the dreaded vinegar worm. Bergonzini grinned but Bertoni appeared to frown as I reviewed the methods of the merchant who, until his recent passing, had been regarded as the doyen of aceto balsamico.

I was reminiscing over the time, years earlier, that Bergonzini and I had visited Giusti in his palazzo in the heart of Modena, where on the upper floors he kept an acetaia that looked as if it had scarcely changed since 1605, when his family founded a food shop on the ground floor. "Ah, Giuseppe," said Bergonzini fondly. "Only he could provide that scenario."

You don't mean to tell me, I said, that that acetaia was in some way set up? "No, no," the professor assured me, "it was all tangibly, humanly real, and Giusti believed devoutly in his methods. They worked, for the most part, because he had infinite patience and because he raised those vinegars like children. Giuseppe was the unchallenged master of the old school. But times have changed."

Bertoni, nodding assent, vowed that insects had never played a role in his formulas. He acknowledged, though, that Giusti attached great significance to the use of old barrels to "govern character," a practice that he respects even if his own barrels are for the most part relatively new. That led to the topic of mother. Bertoni explained that what he refers to as *madre* is the combination of aging vinegar left in each barrel and the wood itself, conditioned by perpetual use. Together these matrixes influence aroma and flavor, giving a distinctive style to the younger vinegar as it ages. Bergonzini noted that in the old days madre often referred to the glutinous slime (he likens it to placenta) preserved in each barrel for the same purpose. But Bertoni discards any such matter as a possible source of negative odors and flavors.

Bertoni seemed reluctant to dwell on the contrasts between his contemporary acetaia and a classic dating to the Renaissance. But as we crossed the courtyard from the cellars to the restored brick farmhouse where he keeps barrels for the late stages of aging, he recalled that in his youth his family used the age-old practice of the three-barrel batteria. The concept was simple, he said. The largest barrel was topped up annually with cooked must after a third of its contents was transferred to the middle barrel, from which a like quantity went to the smallest barrel to serve as the family's annual supply of vinegar.

When, years later, Bertoni resumed making vinegar, he took the three-barrel concept as the basis for developing his revolutionary schemes. Yet, though he swears that the principle is the same, the scale has increased dramatically. He has eighty batterie, consisting of 828 barrels, which he uses to make tradizionale to sell, plus a series of twenty-two old botticelle which hold his finest aged vinegars or what might be described as the showpieces.

He began to explain the intricacies of the operation in terms that to my unmechanical mind seemed beyond comprehension. Noticing my plight, he took pen and paper and patiently diagrammed the function of each batteria. As he spoke his feelings for the craft transcended his methodical manner and his words began to flow with such passion that even that vinegar veteran Bergonzini listened with rapt regard. As the patterns became clear to me, I realized that Bertoni conducts his vinegars through that maze of barrels in what might be described as a waltz, since, harking back to the three-barrel concept, the rhythms are in triple time.

His first series of sixty-six batterie of ten barrels each are used for a three-year cycle. The youngest vinegars, from the casks, are introduced into the three largest barrels for what he calls trasformazione. A year later, half of that lot goes to three middle barrels, known as the laboratorio. The next year half of that quantity moves on to the four smallest barrels for maturazione. Capacities range from 75 liters down to 10 in barrels that begin with oak or chestnut and range through a random mix of cherry, mulberry, ash, locust, and (though only in the occasional staves) the aggressively scented juniper.

In a single, conventional batteria the aging vinegar would be transferred down the line to smaller barrels one at a time as the quantity diminishes. But, following Bertoni's steps, the waltz, instead of ending at the end of the first sixty-six batterie, turns into a sort of minuet. At that point, half of the contents of the four smallest barrels of each are transferred to the three largest barrels of another fourteen batterie of twelve barrels each. There the three-year cycle is repeated.

Bertoni explained that when the balsamico reaches the end of the two series of batterie, its average age is more than twelve years, since the final blend includes vinegars started annually over vintages since 1975. Even with the aid of a pocket calculator, I couldn't figure that out. But, as Bergonzini explained, the key is whether the samples drawn by the consortium under guarded conditions qualify as tradizionale in the taste test. Bertoni's first batch came through with flying colors. He doesn't intend to sell all his vinegar as tradizionale, however, even if it could eventually win approval, because the market is still limited. So he had begun drawing off quantities along the line to be bottled and sold as regular ''Aceto Balsamico di Modena,'' though the ban in 1993 would compel him, like other producers, to use another name.

Bertoni, ever conscious of figures, said that each year on average he introduces about 4,000 liters of cooked musts into the system and extracts about 100 liters of balsamico that could qualify as tradizionale. Estimating production expenses—equipment, storage, fuel, electricity, interest on loans, insurance, his family's labor—he figures that a liter of tradizionale costs about 500,000 lire. But that doesn't include the essential extra of "artistic value," which brings the price to 1,000,000 lire a liter or more. He noted that profits weren't enough to support a large family, but that they would make a nice retirement income.

Tasting confirmed that Bertoni's first approved tradizionale showed the concentration, character, and class of some rivals' vinegars of more than twice its age. But, as he had promised, that wasn't his finest. He led us to a corner of the acetaia where barrels in odd shapes and sizes showed the requisite blackened sheen of time. After lifting the lids of several for sniffs, he decided on a miniature botticella that had been recovered from his boy-hood home. He deftly thrust a tiny glass "thief" through the bunghole and withdrew a measure of inky liquid, rationing a couple of drops into each of three teaspoons. "This isn't for sale," he said. "It's for special occasions, gifts, and, of course, the Palio."

Amid the compliments I speculated that he ought to improve his standing in the coming competition. But Bergonzini wasn't so sure, noting that judges whose palates are attuned to the more ornate "old-time" aromas and flavors might not understand or appreciate a balsamico so smooth, balanced, and cleanly defined. "It's a little bit like the changeover from the old type of wine to the new in Italy over the last couple of decades," he said. "At first tasters were skeptical about the progressive styles, though by now they recognize that wine made by modern meth-ods has the same basic character but more class because it's cleaner and better balanced and suited to longer aging. The same is true for balsamico,'' the professor concluded, ''but it will take a while for local opinion to come around.''

The tour over, we descended to the estate's kitchen, where a fire burned in the hearth and an enormous wooden table beckoned us with Emilian hospitality. Bertoni's daughters had set out plates of prosciutto and salame, wedges of Parmigiano, and homemade preserves from fruit and nuts grown on the farm. Bertoni poured light white Trebbiano and vivacious red Lambrusco, honest, palate-refreshing ''biological'' wines that he promised we could drink our fill of and feel no ill effects. There was also *nocino,* a bittersweet liqueur made from an infusion of green walnut husks. Before we left for the valley, our host reached for a vial of *tradizionale* on the table and carefully measured a few drops into our teaspoons. And we bade farewell as the Este dukes might have done, with a magnificent mouthful of vinegar.

Beyond its value as cordial, tonic, or digestive, aceto balsamico tradizionale has manifold uses in the kitchen. Yet, as Renato Bergonzini wrote, in *In cucina con l'Aceto Balsamico,* the best recipes were once jealously guarded family secrets, which, when revealed, become written confessions. He reveals about 150 in the book, ranging through all manner of antipasti, pasta and risotto sauces, soups, seafood, meat, poultry, game, vegetables, and cheese dishes, as well as desserts. Recipes won't be repeated here, but a few serving tips seem in order to convey Emilian vinegar wisdom and emphasize the distinction between fine aged aceto balsamico tradizionale and good regular balsamico not old enough to qualify.

As a rule, regular balsamico is used for salad dressings, as an ingredient in cooked sauces and meat ragouts, or as a flavoring in stews or roast or grilled meats. The best kind may be mixed with olive oil (true extra vergine, of course) in dressings for salads, becoming luxuriant when still slightly moist Parmesan cheese is sliced on top of greens. Emilians often use it in tomato sauces or meat ragouts, where a liberal lacing can heighten flavors remarkably. Bergonzini especially recommends it with rabbit and poultry dishes and breaded veal cutlets. He gives recipes for ice cream and sherbet and even for cocktails and other mixed drinks, where it serves as a luxurious substitute for bitters.

Aceto balsamico tradizionale may stand alone as a condiment or seasoning or lend its splendor to a light sauce or subtle blend with another ingredient that doesn't contrast with it or overwhelm its flavor. Mixed with the finest Tuscan olive oil, it makes an exquisite dressing for thinly sliced raw *porcini* (boletus) mushrooms or, following one of the newer local uses, as an enticing touch with lightly smoked salmon.

Younger tradizionale is sometimes used as a flavoring in mayonnaise or light cream and butter sauces served with vegetables or seafood, preferably poached or steamed sea bass, as well as mollusks and crustaceans. A few drops can add an elevating touch to rare roast beef or lamb. A sprinkling over fresh strawberries or raspberries is a revelation. Perhaps the ultimate in epicurean extravagances is a plate of lightly melted Parmigiano topped with a layer of white truffles and sprinkled with a century-old vinegar, though a fifty-year-old will do in a pinch. Costly, yes, but it is said to be an aphrodisiac.

Nor should aceto balsamico tradizionale be limited to Emilian or Italian food. Well-heeled Japanese, who have become increasingly important customers, reportedly use it as an elaborate substitute for soy sauce with sushi and other dishes.

Storage of aceto balsamico tradizionale in its tiny bottles is ideal in a cool, dry environment, but after the ordeal of hot and cold that it's been through, it will keep well nearly anywhere.

The Modenese have designated a vinegar route through the province. Starting from central Modena (where the Duomo, the Palazzo Ducale, and the Galleria Estense are the main attractions), it heads north through the plains to Soliera, Sorbara, Nonantola, and Rubbiara, then south to San Damaso, San Donnino, Spilamberto, and into the hills to Vignola, Castelvetro, and Montegibbio. It could be extended to take in part of Reggio province, notably in the Scandiano area. Acetaie are located all along the way, but don't expect to be beckoned with signs or tourist trappings.

Among restaurants and trattorie in the zones, these are recommended for dishes with aceto balsamico: Lancellotti at Soliera, Osteria di Rubbiara (near Nonantola), Fini and Borso d'Este at Modena, Al Portone at Scandiano, Picci at Cavriago (near Reggio).

# Caffè Espresso
## The toast of Cefalù

*W*e who rank Italy as the first nation of coffee might seem to be ignoring certain facts. For one, Italians don't grow coffee beans but like other peoples outside the tropics import them raw to be roasted, blended ground, and brewed according to local taste. For another—and this came as a surprise to me after years of jostling through crowded bars to savor precious potions of *caffè espresso*—Italians turn out to be moderate consumers, drinking less than half as much coffee on average as some northern Europeans do. But the real shock came with my discovery that Italian coffee blends rely heavily on cheap types of beans: more on varieties from the common Robusta species than the nobler family of Arabica.

Okay, then, so how on earth could espresso be so great? After pondering that question in light of the above, I chalked up a triumph to fantasy over fact. For what could better explain the supremacy of espresso than that flair Italians have for taking a common commodity and with a fanciful touch or two making it sublime?

They begin with the blending and roasting, which are often trade secrets but in any case must be calibrated so that the beans retain a protective coating of natural oils after being toasted dark and brittle enough to be pulverized. Other coffees are gleaned from coarse grounds of mildly toasted beans whose soluble components are extracted by scalding water through steeping, percolation, or filtering. But espresso derives from freshly ground powder, packed into a metal strainer with minute holes and blasted by pressurized steam that quickly not only conveys solubles into the brew but emulsifies oils, whose volatile components heighten aroma and flavor, while extracting colloids, which enrich body and texture.

That procedure calls for special equipment: replicas of the *macchina a vapore* invented in Naples in 1901 that revolutionized the concept of caffè. No Italian bar could be without an espresso machine, an imposing contraption that hisses and fumes like a dragon as it spews vapor down into strainers with spouts through which dark liquid oozes into *tazzine* that make what the French call a *demitasse* seem roomy.

Espresso refers to both the coffee and the method of making it: by definition on express command. Unless otherwise specified, caffè in a bar means espresso, though that may be distinguished as *ristretto* or *basso* (strong), *lungo* or *alto* (weaker), or *doppio* (a double dose). Devotees have favorite brands and blends and, above all, bars, which, unlike their homonymous counterparts in other countries, are dedicated primarily to the dispensing of caffè to customers who more often than not sip their espresso while standing.

The busier the bar the better, as they say, because that means that the *barista* will be a battle-proven ace who keeps his glittering machine in nonstop action so that there's no accumulation of dregs or oils that can cause stale or rancid tastes. An accomplished barista, who knows just how every habitué likes his caffè, takes pride in serving customers in less than a minute, no matter how barraged he is with orders.

He makes it look easy, but there's more to an exemplary espresso than meets the eye. First comes the choice of a *miscela* or blend of beans roasted at the *torrefazione*. Each of Italy's more than fifteen hundred *torrefattori*, large and small, composes house blends of Arabica or Robusta to meet tastes that vary from one city or region to another. Degrees of toasting also vary, though espresso's *gusto forte* is the result of hotter roasting than for other coffees. In the bar, the beans must be pulverized to precise consistency at frequent intervals, since aromas escape.

With each order, the barista twists the strainer (held by what looks like an ice cream scoop with a plastic handle) off its clamp on the machine and pounds it against the edge of a receptacle to rid the damp dregs from the last batch. With rapid flicks of a lever on an electric grinder he draws powder into the strainer, tamping it flat before clamping the holder back on the machine and switching on the steam. The packed powder must be just porous enough so that water at 194°F under pressure of about 9 atmospheres will propel an even discharge through the spouts.

Extraction is the key to balance among an espresso's myriad components of aroma and flavor. Too short a duration can make it sludgy, potent, and sharp; a few moments too long can leave it thin, flat, and bitter. After fifteen to twenty seconds, as the initial flow becomes a spasmodic dribble and no more than a couple of tablespoons of caffè have been released in the tazzina, the barista snatches it away and places it on a saucer with a spoon, serving it at the bar with an inviting ''*Prego.*''

Espresso strikes first with a pervasive fragrance that some liken to cacao or burnt sugar, as if anything could approximate the exotic spirit of caffè. The next clue to class is the *crema* or *schiuma*, which floats like lather atop the liquid and clings to the sides of the cup. In a blend dominated by Arabica this creamy foam should show a hint of rust in its tawny color. Bubbly, dark foam that vanishes quickly may indicate excessive roasting, stale beans, or an inferior blend. The coffee, served in a preheated tazzina, should be just warm enough to drink without delay. Many take it with sugar, but purists insist that the soul of a true espresso is already *dolce.* One sip is enough to coat the palate with the essence of mocha and revive the faith that this, after all, is what coffee was meant to be.

Still, as those of us who are hooked on it find hard to believe, a dram so intense and apparently skimpy isn't to everyone's lik-ing. In much of the world, coffee is a beverage bland enough to drink with food. But espresso with its gusto forte is more like a liqueur or cordial to be sipped alone after meals or between so that its lingering flavors don't interfere with food or wine. Var-iations on espresso include *caffè corretto,* with a shot of grappa or brandy or rum or even the joltingly bitter Fernet Branca to correct or, some might say, corrupt it. Cooled with ice it's *caffè freddo;* frozen and chopped it's *granita al caffè.* Decaffeinated coffee often goes by the brand name Hag. Roasted beans are the *tre mosche* (three flies) that float atop sambuca. Other liqueurs, led by the classical Caffè Sport Borghetti, have an espresso base.

Italians also mix espresso with milk, which is usually heated by steam jetted through a narrow spigot on the side of the machine so that the *latte* mounts to a dense froth. A dab of milk makes it *caffè macchiato* (stained). With an approximately four-to-one ratio of milk to espresso in a larger cup it becomes *cappuccino* (after the brownish cloaks of Capuchin monks). With even more milk, possibly in a tall glass, it's *caffè latte.* The other extreme is *latte macchiato,* warm milk with a spot of espresso.

A proper *cappuccio,* as it's affectionately known, is itself a handiwork: a medium-hot amalgam of mocha and milky froth in swirls like marble, sometimes with bitter chocolate sprinkled on top. Italians, who drink it in the morning, may be amused or appalled to see foreign visitors order it after lunch or dinner. Cappuccino admirers, who studiously avoid the warmed-over coffee often served with *prima colazione* in Italian hotels, will head to the nearest bar-pasticceria for a stand-up breakfast with a warm *cornetto* or *brioche.*

Whatever the interpretation, caffè has a most appealing taste, since nine out of ten Italians drink it at least occasionally and many consider themselves steady consumers of quality blends. Yet, even though they down more than 9 billion cups of espresso a year, about 160 per capita, intake calculated on imports of raw beans is less than 11 pounds each. Northern Europeans consume much more coffee, led by Finland with nearly 29 pounds a year and the highest quality index among all nations, meaning that it imports mainly Arabica beans.

Italy's relatively limited use is partly explained by small doses, since espresso takes fewer beans per serving than longer coffees do. But I was puzzled to learn that its quality index—as determined by the International Coffee Organization—was lower than that of any northern European country and even that of the United States. For I had assumed that Italians would insist on the best, attuned as they are to the niceties of taste. Instead, more than half of imports come from *Coffea robusta,* which grows mainly in torrid parts of Africa and Indonesia. The more esteemed *Coffea arabica* represents three-quarters of the world's production, though the choicest beans come from the milder climatic zones of South and Central America, the Caribbean, and Ethiopia.

In some countries coffee is sold from single varieties or even estates. But Italians, though they roast beans from different sources separately, nearly always mix them in blends that vary in taste, quality, and price. The most prestigious consist entirely or prevalently of Arabica; the cheapest are invariably Robusta. Yet some blenders, pointing out that coffees in both categories vary in class and character, insist that a good Robusta is preferable to a second-rate Arabica.

Espresso from choice Arabica is noted as fragrant, mellow, and refined. Robusta makes a darker, thicker brew, often noted for astringent, vaguely woody flavors. It also contains more caffeine. Yet espresso, whatever the source, has less caffeine than other coffees. That's because the *tostatura spinta,* or hot roasting, diminishes caffeine and also because less is extracted by the brief steam-pressure process than through boiling or percolation. Many

Italians prefer the more aggressive taste of caffè from Robusta, just as many drink rustic local wines rather than high-bred bottled ones. Torrefattori bank on that, favoring Robusta (at half the average cost of Arabica) in popular bar and home blends.

Most coffee sold in Italy is ground and vacuum-packed to be used in the familiar stovetop *caffettiere* known as *la napoletana* and *la moka*. In both devices scalding water is relayed from one chamber to another through grounds in a strainer. The napoletana is flipped over when water boils so that it seeps down through the grounds. In the moka, boiling water rises through the strainer and a spout to the upper chamber. Both can make good coffee, but the fact that unpressurized water passes through medium-fine grounds (packed powder will block the flow) means that aroma, flavor, and density are limited to levels well below those of true espresso.

Compact home machines can generate ample steam pressure with modified heat so that fine grounds (now sometimes sold in packaged pods) can be used to make espresso worthy of the name. But domestic versions, however lovingly prepared, can't match the best of bars, where the barista's skills with superior equipment in constant use are decisive.

Still, among the tens of thousands of bars in Italy, the quality of caffè varies markedly. All too often in an era of rising costs, proprietors opt for cheap blends or, after accepting financing from a competitive torrefattore, are obliged to use one popular brand. But even with an ideal blend, perfection can be approached only if water is pure. Where it's hard or tastes of chlorine, supplies must be softened or purified or brought in from outside.

Connoisseurs tend to be chauvinistic about caffè, insisting

that, with rare exceptions, espresso is truly espresso only in Italy, although regional rivalries simmer amid the eternal dispute over superiority between north and south. The industry has always been centered in the north, where today the bulk of raw beans comes in through Trieste, the Adriatic city that was long the Austro-Hungarian gateway to the Mediterranean. But the original coffee port was Venice, whose merchants supplied Europe's growing demands after opening trade routes in the early seventeenth century to Arab countries, where coffee is known as *qahwah*.

Wild trees of the genus *Coffea* seem to have been cultivated first at the heights of Kaffa in Abyssinia (now Ethiopia) after shepherds noticed that sheep became frisky when chewing on berries and leaves. Coffee, made initially by steeping whole beans in water to ferment and later by boiling, was diffused through Islam; a café opened at Mecca in the ninth century. Europeans showed little interest in coffee until beans were roasted in the sixteenth century by Turks, whose *kahve* is served with the grounds in a cup after a double boiling. Mohammed himself is said to have been revived by a divine potion of coffee, yet Muslims have banned it from time to time along with the other "ministers of the devil," tobacco, alcohol, and opium.

So, in their turn, have Europeans. For what some celebrated as an elixir of the spirits, others condemned as a drug. The fact is that "Arabian wine" has little food value, though it is reputed to aid digestion by favoring secretion of gastric juices. Its allure, beyond aroma and taste, is the effect of caffeine on the nervous system, making minds alert and stimulating thought, conversation, humor, and passion. Coffee houses became intellectual gathering places in Europe, thus centers of literary and political movements. As such they sometimes posed threats to authority, but scattered attempts to prohibit coffee failed to halt its triumphant rise.

As trade boomed, Arabs strived to maintain a monopoly on production. But in 1690, Dutch sailors stormed ashore at the Red Sea port of Al Mukhä (anglicized as Mocha) in Yemen and, pirate-style, confiscated a plantation of coffee trees. Replanted in Java and Sumatra, they flourished to provide Europe with new sources of mocha. Soon after, the French under Louis XIV brought coffee to the Caribbean, from where it spread through Latin America.

Today Brazil is the largest producer, followed by Colombia and Costa Rica. Coffee, the ''green gold'' of the tropics, ranks as the world's third industry after petroleum and steel in volume of business and employment of people. New York and London are the hubs of the international wheels of commerce on which Italy would appear to be just another spoke.

But numbers could never measure the magnitude of caffè in Italian life, a phenomenon to be witnessed in the daily routine of neighborhood bars or, more romantically, in places where the rituals have been repeated for a century or more. In Venice, where a *bottega del caffè* opened in 1640, Florian and Quadri remain landmarks on St. Mark's Square. Rome has its Caffè Greco and L'Aragno, Naples its Gambrinus, Turin its Fiorio and Torino, Florence its Paszkowski, Palermo its Alba and Caflisch. Milan has been renowned for its coffee bars since a literary review called *Caffè* was founded in 1764 ''to lighten the spirit and revive the soul.''

Still, it must be admitted that during its early ascendancy as a national institution, caffè had little to distinguish it from the coffee of other countries. For it wasn't until the turn of this century that a Neapolitan by the name of Bezzerra was credited with inventing the espresso machine. Bezzerra, tired of waiting for coffee to seep through the napoletana, devised an apparatus with a boiler from which hot vapor could be forced through the grounds under pressure. His apparatus was risky to use, but the first espresso was promising enough to inspire imitations.

Achille Gaggia, a Milanese, created devices that could work up 9 to 10 atmospheres of pressure at controlled temperatures, first using pistons, then hydraulic pumps, innovations that made his the leading name in espresso machines to this day. The early *macchine a vapore* were often dome-shaped and chromium- or brass-plated, resembling baroque-style fountains, with elaborate faucets, knobs, dials, and ornaments. These were gradually replaced by rectangular cases in stainless steel and plastic as more sophisticated mechanisms were developed. The firm of Faema, in 1961, introduced a transfer method to heat pressurized cold water rapidly, making bulky boilers obsolete and heralding the efficient and adaptable systems used today.

Grinding of the roasted beans, once performed by hand turning a crank atop a wooden box, is now done rapidly by machines that make a powder of precise consistency. Some noted Italian caffès have maintained their own torrefazione, or an artisanal source nearby, though industrial firms control most of the market. By now, every Italian village, north and south, whatever else it might lack in amenities, boasts a bar with an espresso machine.

It seems fitting that espresso was pioneered in Naples, for the city is still considered Italy's mecca of caffè. Credit goes in part to its pure water but even more to that spirited knack that Neapolitans have for heightening the sensual pleasures of everyday things. Still, in my experience, the *tazzulella* of caffè served in Naples can be rivaled by that of Palermo and other Sicilian towns, where I don't recall ever sipping less than a dignified espresso.

That is one point on which my friend Marco De Bartoli might agree, though normally he's skeptical about any outside praise of modern Sicily. Marco, who makes the truest and best wines of Marsala, is a stubborn advocate of the remaining gastronomic treasures of an island that has too often squandered its historical assets. With customary irreverence, he attributes the goodness of caffè in Sicily to the fact that it originates elsewhere. "If we Sicilians had been able to grow coffee," he conjectures, "we'd have spoiled the market long ago."

Marco seems not so much a cynic as an idealist embittered by the corruption, greed, fear, and inertia that prevent Sicily from asserting its magnanimous nature. He maintains that the region was better off under the Bourbon kings, "when Sicily was proudly Sicilian and not a distant and dreaded adjunct of the mythical united Italy." He admits that by instinct he feels Sicilian rather than Italian. But he's so disgusted by the degradation of his island's mosaic of antique cultures, of its once glorious heritage of food and drink, that he's ashamed to call himself a Sicilian. "If anyone asks," he half jokes in a vernacular with the broad intonations of a drawl, "I tell them I'm a *uomo mediterraneo,* a creature of the sea."

He looks the part of Mediterranean man, with wavy black hair, a long nose that curves nobly like a sheikh's, and dark eyes that reserve a hint of melancholy even when he laughs, as he often does while voicing candid comments about the foibles of his homeland. We'd started out talking about coffee over breakfast at his estate near the port of Marsala in Western Sicily, where I'd arrived the evening before, but Marco as always had been veering off on tangents.

I steered him back on course with the reminder that I'd come all that way to find the source of an unforgettable espresso tasted in Marsala years earlier. Marco said that he had set up a visit to the torrefazione that morning, but it had moved from cramped quarters in the center of town to a new plant outside as business had grown. In case it had grown too big, he'd arranged a visit later to a real artisan shop halfway across the island at Cefalù.

So devoted is Marco to caffè that on trips abroad he takes along his favorite miscela and a miniature but effective espresso gadget with a power transformer so that it can be used in America, where it's most vital. ''Don't misunderstand,'' he said. ''I adore America. But the coffee, Dio mio, it's a national tragedy. Not just the tasteless cafeteria or instant coffee, but even espresso made using machines and miscela from Italy comes out thin, like French express. And then they serve lemon peels with it. . . . '' A sour grimace concluded his critique.

We were at Baglio Samperi, a compound of low-slung buildings with inner courtyards in a Moorish style, set amid vineyards of Marsala a short distance from the sea. There Marco maintains— with no clear demarcation between quarters—a cozy country home with guest rooms and offices, cellars and storehouses lined with barrels and casks and cages of bottles, and a body shop and garage to maintain some sixty vintage automobiles.

He began his collection—half hobby, half business—years ago when he raced sports cars, driving in Sicily's famous but since abandoned Targa Florio. Some cars are stripped-down hulks being remodeled, but a few are exhilaratingly usable. On that cool, damp December day he piloted a Lancia Alfetta GTV 2005, a red 1984 model with a revamped engine, across Marsala's flat hinterland to ZiCaffè S.p.A., whose plant is girded by a high wall. As Marco announced our arrival over an intercom, a heavy metal gate slid open to allow us inside.

The Zi is for Zichittella, the family of torrefattori whose blends came to be appreciated well beyond Marsala since the founding in 1929. Antonio Zichittella, a cordial young man who had forsaken a career as a physician to become the export manager, showed us around, explaining how the new facilities with largely automatic processing had enabled them to expand markets through southern Italy and abroad. But he insisted that the company philosophy hadn't changed, since the beans are still carefully selected and blends are determined by taste.

Before demonstrating the roasting, Zichittella discussed the beans, each of which is actually half of the pit or seed of the cherrylike fruit of evergreen trees that produce year-round in many tropical places. Robusta beans are usually extracted after the berry has dried in the sun so that the brittle skin can be peeled away easily. But the preferred and more costly method for Arabica is washing, in which the berries soak in water and ferment for two or three days before a mechanism removes the skin and pulp, as well as a membrane around the bean.

The raw beans, partly dried at the source for long preservation, are packed in heavy jute bags holding 132 pounds with the variety and place of origin stamped on the sides. They are shipped on order, usually to Trieste, and relayed to Marsala. ZiCaffè buys through brokers in New York and London, who set prices according to quality, though coffee crops are so uneven that they have to rely on intelligence reports and be especially choosy with certain sources of Robusta. He opened bags to show the differences. Arabica beans, mainly from Colombia and Brazil, were quite uniform in pale green-gray color with size and shape similar to halves of small peanuts. Robusta, mainly from equatorial Africa, ranged through shades of green, brown, and gray in beans of irregular size, some no larger than split peas.

The beans are dry-cleaned in blowers and then relayed through chutes to the torrefazione ovens, horizontal drums that revolve slowly while being heated to 428° to 437°F. Roasting takes around ten minutes, as the beans turn to dusky brown from a normal toast or almost black from the heavier *tosta di mora* that results in the stronger flavor of Robusta appreciated in much of the Mezzogiorno. Zichitella said that choice Arabica, used in the prestigious blends, is toasted at milder temperatures to retain aroma, flavor, and acidity.

But whatever the type, the roasting of beans for espresso causes evaporation that reduces the weight by about 20 percent, while a buildup of carbon dioxide causes them to swell in volume by 50 percent or more. The hotter roasting and greater weight loss make the espresso process costlier than the moderate toasting used for coffees in other countries. Zichitella said they use gas as the cleanest and most efficient fuel for heating, noting that wood fires used by a rare few artisan torrefazioni cause smoky odors.

Each type of bean is roasted in individual batches, then transferred to automatic sorters where blends are determined by computers programmed by the family after tasting samples of each. Zicaffè makes several blends, most ground and vacuum-packed for retail sales. But a portion of whole beans is sold in 1-kilogram packages as the Miscela Bar, used mainly in western Sicily. Zichittella assured me that the blend is the same as I tasted in that memorable espresso years earlier. The visit to ZiCaffè provided useful insights into the workings of the coffee industry, but as we left just before noon, I mentioned to Marco that I had something more artisanal in mind. No sooner had we cleared the gate than we were off to Cefalù.

We would take the autostrada to Palermo and beyond, but Marco chose a shortcut through the town of Salemi to pick up the expressway. The road of weather-warped asphalt crossed tapered knolls and shallow, rocky canyons, a route that roused Marco's racing spirit as he assailed its curves and grades with abrupt shifts—down with rapid repercussions and up again with mellow revs of acceleration—improvising fugues on the Alfetta's scale of gears.

As he drove he talked about the fortunes of Marsala, a wine originated by English merchants in the eighteenth century that became the pride of Sicily. But its antique splendors, achieved through long wood aging, are hard to impress on modern palates. Marsala's steady decline was evident in the forlorn rows of vines set amid olive groves and meadows of abandoned farms. Still, Marco remains tenaciously devoted to a wine that takes about half of his time at Baglio Samperi to make and the other half on the road trying to sell.

He stopped in Palermo to drop off an order at Politeama Vini, a wine bar where we had a quick lunch: morsels of fresh fish with salad, peppers, eggplant, fennel, olives, oranges, and tangerines, tastes of Mediterranean sunshine on a wet winter day. On the way out of the city, we visited a caffè-pasticceria for an exemplary espresso after sampling pastries that upheld Sicily's reputation as the treasure island of sweets.

Back on the autostrada, we barreled through rainsqualls heading east past Bagheria, a town once renowned for aristocratic villas and parks, now depicted by Marco as a squalor of reinforced concrete and a hangout for mafia hit men. The specter of Cosa Nostra launched him on a discourse about crime and corruption, so rampant in Sicily that the army had been called in to occupy the island like an enemy territory, which is exactly how some other Italians perceive it. Mediterranean man continued his laments until the turnoff for Cefalù, where his mood seemed to brighten at the sight of the port and its promontory, looming ahead through the shifting clouds like the Rock of Gibraltar.

As he guided the Alfetta through the narrow streets, Marco described Cefalù as an oasis of peace that had prospered from tourism attracted to its fine sand beaches and a cathedral built in gratitude by the Norman King Roger II after he was saved from a shipwreck there. When we reached the Duomo, Marco with a wily maneuver improvised a parking place on the cobblestones in the square beneath the imposing twin towers.

From the Piazza del Duomo it was a damp dash up the Corso Ruggero to the Torrefazione Serio. The narrow shop was lined with wooden shelves laden with packages of cakes, biscuits, candies, marmalades, teas, and bottles of spirits and wines, including Marco's Marsala. But the feature item was, of course, coffee, whole roasted beans in glass-fronted bins with round metal lids and hand-lettered signs stating the varieties of each miscela and the price. Visible in a room at the back was the wood-fueled torrefazione oven in fire-engine red with chrome trimming and various tubes, wheels, dials, levers, and ducts projecting from a cylindrical block with a funnel attached to the upper end of what resembled the prow of a steam locomotive.

Behind the counter an elderly lady dressed in black smiled warmly as she recognized Marco and told us that her son Giuseppe had phoned to say he'd be there soon. While we waited, Anna Serio told of how her husband, Pasquale, had opened the shop thirty-five years ago and had run it until his death the previous year. Now her son, though he worked full-time as a construction engineer, continued the torrefazione in memory of his father.

"You might call it keeping the faith," said Giuseppe Serio, as he came in out of the storm to describe the torrefazione. "Anyway, I do it more for love than money. When you grow up with something as intimate as coffee it becomes part of your soul." He recalled that his father roasted beans twice a week to distribute in the area, but he does them every ten or fifteen days to supply only the shop and the nearby Bar Duomo, run by his brother Giovanni. It takes time away from his regular work, he admitted, "but it's a great satisfaction, an event I look forward to, even in summer when it gets terribly hot in here."

Giuseppe, slim, bald, and bespectacled, had the air of a mild-mannered professor as he discussed the intimacies of caffè. A search through files located a catalogue with descriptions of scores of beans, though he said he relies mainly on eight or ten varieties, divided between Arabica and Robusta. The Arabica comes from Colombia, Costa Rica, Brazil (Santos), Ethiopia (Mocca), Kenya, Haiti, and rarely Peru. Robusta represents Zaire, the Congo, Indonesia (Java), and India (Parchment). He buys the raw beans from importers in Trieste and Naples, ordering only a couple of dozen bags at a time, since there's little space in the shop storeroom.

Early on the morning of the chosen day, he builds a fire in the compact stove beneath the oven, using neatly split olive logs for even, durable heat. It takes about half an hour for the oven to register 200°C (392°F) or slightly more on the thermometer dial. Wood roasting requires frequent interventions, so Giuseppe usually gets help from his wife, Rosa Alba, and sister Lella in doing twelve to fifteen batches of 66 pounds—half a bag—each. The raw beans are poured through the funnel into the drum, which is smaller than industrial ovens and doesn't get as hot. As they spin and roast, an exhaust removes membrane flakes that fall off them so that they don't burn and create odors. I asked Giuseppe if wood smoke affected the aroma, recalling Antonio Zichittella's words. ''I never noticed,'' he confessed, ''but if it does, maybe it's a good thing.''

He explained that during toasting the beans are partly carbonized as they swell and take on a burnished color. Meanwhile, natural sugars caramelize as the more than six hundred substances that account for aroma and flavor are transmitted through the oils. Each batch takes twenty to thirty minutes, depending on the type, though Giuseppe relies on sight and smell to decide when the beans are toasted. Then he opens a side door on the oven so that they cascade into a circular tub with a fine-mesh base. There four revolving paddles with brushes stir the beans while a vacuum underneath sucks away heat and wafts mocha fumes out through a duct to the street, to the delight of passersby.

Giuseppe said that they do a lot of business on those days, even though they sell the previous batches. The newly roasted beans, still dry on the outside, are harsh in flavor. When cool enough to handle, he does his blends and then leaves the beans in jute bags for four or five days, as oils emerge to give them an ebony sheen. He said that aromas and flavors are most intense in the first week, though whole beans can keep for a month or so if sealed in waxed paper, foil, or jars. They must be kept dry, he warned, because they'll rapidly absorb humidity, and that compromises flavor. He recommended buying whole beans and grinding them just before use, noting that ground coffee, even if vacuum-packed, quickly loses aroma.

Yet most of Torrefazione Serio's loyal customers request that the beans be ground there, though coarse enough to use in home coffee makers. The five blends range up in price as the proportion of Arabica increases. Miscela Famiglia and Extra are largely Robusta. Miscela Santiago is prevalently Arabica, which is used exclusively in the most expensive blend. But Miscela Bar, about half and half, is the best-seller.

That's used at the Bar Duomo, where we went with Giuseppe to meet his brother Giovanni and sample the caffè. The rain had eased a bit as we made our way down the street amid a flow of the faithful en route to the six-o'clock vesper service.

They seemed to be mainly older women in dark cloaks with black lace shawls over heads and shoulders, crouching under umbrellas as they hurried across the piazza and up the steps to the Duomo. Giuseppe suggested that I take advantage of the lighting during the service to view the Byzantine mosaics. But first I would meditate over an espresso.

A window display of freshly baked pastries beckoned customers to the corner bar, where Giovanni greeted us from behind the steaming espresso machine. Giuseppe ordered caffè for Marco and me, saying that he personally preferred the pure Arabica. Sicilians are used to the gusto forte of Robusta, he said, noting that "many people drink caffè with the eyes more than the nose and mouth, looking for strong, dark color rather than the refined fragrance and flavor of Arabica." He tried to combine the best of both in the bar blend, he told us, as Giovanni, with a congenial *prego,* served up our tazzine.

Rich crema covered the liquid like a layer of gold leaf. The soaring aroma, clearly Arabica, signaled that sugar would have been an intrusion. The texture was medium dense, just right, the temperature medium hot. I wondered if the gentle toasting of the beans over wood heat accounted for the mellow flavors that lingered on the tongue like those of a gracefully aged wine. "Like Marco's Vecchio Samperi Solera," suggested Giuseppe, as Giovanni beamed contentedly behind the bar. Marco said nothing as he sipped and rolled his eyes upward with a magnanimous Mediterranean smile.

# Index

Montegibbio, balsamic vinegar in, 274–283
Montepulciano d'Abruzzo wine, 182, 184, 185, 188, 192, 195
Moretti, Giovanna, 251
Mornini, Peppino, 161–176
Mornini, Ugo, 164–173, 175–176
*mortadella* (*bologna;* baloney), 197
mozzarella, 127, 147
mushrooms, porcini, 42, 238–239, 259
mycology, 23, 42

Naples, 75
in author's youth, 132–133
coffee in, 295, 296, 297
*see also pizza napoletana*
Neive, truffles in, 33–36
Nino (*culatello* maker), 212–216, 218
Norcia, truffles in, 24, 43
*nuova cucina, la,* 14–15
nutrition, 29–30, 101
bread and, 62, 65
pasta and, 77, 80

oleic acid, 100, 101, 102
*olio di sansa di oliva,* 101, 120
*olio extra vergine di oliva* (extra virgin olive oil), 97–124
complexity of, 101–102
culinary uses of, 123–124
DOC and, 16, 100, 108–109
extraction of, 102–103, 105, 109, 113–114, 117, 122
filtering of, 103
price of, 100, 122
storage of, 103

*olio fiore,* 102, 120
olive oil, 13, 97–124
classifications of, 100–101
extra virgin, *see olio extra vergine di oliva* (extra virgin olive oil)
flavor and aroma of, 102, 103, 107–108, 121, 122
health concerns and, 100, 101
pizza and, 146, 148
olives, olive trees, 109–113, 115–118
harvesting of, 98, 102, 112–113, 117, 118, 122
in historical perspective, 104–105
hoeing of, 111, 112, 116
pruning of, 110–111
Oliveto, olive oil in, 115–122
Ordine dei Cavalieri del Tartufo e dei Vini di Alba, 27
Osino, pasta making in, 78–81, 87–88
Osteria Cascina dei Fiori (Borgo Vercelli), 238–243
*osterie,* 15, 52
Cocollini family, 63, 68
ovens:
bread, 52, 55, 57–59, 61, 64–67
pizza, 64, 65

Padua, rice in, 227–228
*pagnotte* (oval breads), 61, 62, 65, 143
Palestra, Gioachino, 238
Palini, Alvaro, 258, 259
Palio di San Giovanni, 267–268
Pallavicino, Marchesi, 201
*panelli (schiacciate),* 61, 64, 128
*pane toscano* (Tuscan bread), 51–69, 248